The Jew in American Literature

by

SOL LIPTZIN

NEW YORK

BLOCH PUBLISHING COMPANY

ALSO BY SOL LIPTZIN

GENERATION OF DECISION

GERMANY'S STEPCHILDREN

ARTHUR SCHNITZLER

RICHARD BEER-HOFMANN

THE FLOWERING OF YIDDISH LITERATURE

THE WEAVERS IN GERMAN LITERATURE

LYRIC PIONEERS OF MODERN GERMANY

THE ENGLISH LEGEND OF HEINRICH HEINE

HISTORICAL SURVEY OF GERMAN LITERATURE

FROM NOVALIS TO NIETZSCHE

SHELLEY IN GERMANY

ELIAKUM ZUNSER

PERETZ

HEINE

Copyright 1966, by
BLOCH PUBLISHING CO., INC.

Library of Congress Catalog Card Number 66-21078

PRINTED IN THE UNITED STATES OF AMERICA

CONTENTS

INTRODUCTION

Jewishness has become an important theme of American literature in the 1960's. The Jew has become a kind of culture hero among United States intellectuals and artists. The outstanding bestseller during 1965 was Saul Bellow's *Herzog* and during 1966 James A. Michener's *The Source*. The present study supplies the background for an understanding of this upsurge of interest in Jews and Jewishness.

A single volume cannot cover comprehensively the entire vast subject of THE JEW IN AMERICAN LITERATURE. However, the principal layers of the image and self-image of the American Jew, as reflected in belles-lettres, can be outlined and the contributions of American writers, Jews and non-Jews, to a profounder insight into the past and present of the Jewish sector of the American population can be recorded.

In a preliminary study *Generation of Decision: Jewish Rejuvenation in America,* 1958, the author called attention to the impact of the Jew upon the American mind and the repercussions of that impact upon the Jewish character. Since the book is now out of print, some of its observations have been incorporated in the present volume.

As Jews enter upon the last third of the twentieth century, their personalities are being shaped to the largest degree by intense, daily American experiences and to a much lesser degree by ever paling, ever rarer Jewish experiences. The fading of their Jewish consciousness was temporarily arrested

1

by repercussions of the European Jewish catastrophe and by the dramatic rebirth of Israel. However, as these tragic and heroic events recede in time, the meaningfulness of retaining Jewish identity in America is again questioned.

Since the founding of the Jewish state, members of the American Jewish community can freely choose between three alternatives. They can migrate to the land of their Biblical forefathers, bringing to it their valuable American know-how, enriching the nascent Israeli personality with a precious American ingredient. Or, they can assimilate into American life and rid themselves entirely both of the burden of Jewishness and of the blessing of this burden. Or else, they can continue a bicultural existence in Jewish time and American space, improving the quality and intensity of their Jewish living, buttressing themselves with Jewish religious and cultural institutions which would survive the ravages of encircling non-Jewish forces, and striving towards a Golden Age of American Jewishness.

The choice is an individual choice but it is best based on knowledge and not on inertia. The present study seeks to contribute to this knowledge of what it means and what it has meant to be a Jew in America. Since literature is a seismograph of life, a survey of the changing image and role of the Jew in American literature casts light upon past and present attitudes of Jews and towards Jews and may stimulate further thinking on looming possibilities.

The Jew in American Literature

CHAPTER I

THE COLONIAL ERA

Throughout the seventeenth and eighteenth centuries, the Jew was a subject for American literature but he did not figure to any important extent as a creator of American literature. Even as a subject, however, it was more often the Biblical Jew rather than the contemporary one who inspired creative minds.

The influence of the few Jews who came to America's shores and whose numbers probably did not exceed three thousand by the end of the Colonial Era was insignificant in comparison with the impact of the Biblical Jews upon the early American settlements.

For the Puritans who colonized New England the Bible was the supreme authority. It spelled out for them God's will. They were ever mindful of the fact that the idealized founder of the Christian faith had been a Jew and that Christian civilization and Christian ethics stemmed from ancient Israel. They saw themselves as instruments of Providence, as successors of the Hebrews who had once been God's Chosen People but who had forfeited this privilege by refusing to accept the new revelation brought by Jesus. They were prepared to take up the burden once borne by Israel and to organize their new commonwealth according to the covenant entered into at Mt. Sinai and incorporated in the Torah. This sacred text could indeed serve as the fundamental law of the New

5

Jerusalem of the Puritans and it deserved to be studied in its purest form, in the original Hebrew, God's own tongue.

The earliest settlers included scholars with an excellent command of Hebrew, generally acquired at English universities. Among such noted Hebraists were the Puritan leaders John Cotton (1584–1652), Thomas Shepard (1605?–1649), Nathaniel Ward (1578?–1652), John Harvard (1607–1638), Michael Wigglesworth (1631–1705), Richard Mather (1596–1669), Henry Dunster (1609?–1659), the first president of Harvard College, and Charles Chauncy (1592–1672), his successor.

William Bradford, a founder of Plymouth Colony and its governor from 1621 to 1656, studied Hebrew to the end of his days and recorded the prevalent adoration of this tongue in these words: "Though I am grown aged, yet I have had a longing desire to see with my own eyes something of that most ancient language and holy tongue in which the law and oracle of God were written; and in which God and angels spoke to the holy patriarchs of old time; and what names were given to things from creation. And though I cannot attain so much herein, yet I am refreshed to have seen some glimpse hereof (as Moses saw the land of Canaan from afar off). My aim and desire is to see how the words and phrases lie in the holy text and to discern somewhat of the same for my own content." [1]

Cotton Mather, in his *Magnalia Christi Americana*, 1702, reported that his grandfather John Cotton understood Hebrew so well and so readily that he was able to discourse in it.[2] There is no evidence that he actually did discourse in it, although he probably interspersed Hebrew phrases now and then in his learned conversations with Puritan divines, a

[1] William Bradford, *Of Plymouth Plantation*, New York, 1952, p. XXVIII.
[2] David de Sola Pool, "Hebrew Learning Among the Puritans of New England Prior to 1700," *American Jewish Historical Society Publications*, XX (1911), 36.

habit indulged in by religious scholars and clergymen of his day. Ever since the Renaissance, men of classical education and broad culture were wont to display their knowledge of Latin and Greek by frequent quotations in the original. This tendency was expanded to Hebrew by those cultured persons who mastered even the rudiments of the language.

Puritans preferred to choose Hebrew names culled from the Bible for their children and to assign to their towns and villages names reminiscent of ancient Hebrew settlements.

The first significant book printed in a British colony in North America was the *Bay Psalm Book,* issued in 1640 by the Cambridge press, which had been set up the preceding year. This book was a metrical translation of the Psalms rendered directly from the Hebrew text. In contrast to the King James' Version, which aimed not only at accuracy but also at stylistic felicity, the Puritan scholars felt, and expressed their feeling in the Preface penned by Richard Mather, that "God's altar needs not our polishings." Religious truth was paramount and hence the more literal the translation the less would it offend the consciences of those worshippers who wished to "sing in Sion the Lord's songs of prayse according to his own wille." How much more literal and how much less literary than the King James' Version was their rendering, despite the fact that their version was metrical while the latter version was in prose, becomes apparent if the two translations are compared. For example, the very first lines of the opening Psalm in the *Bay Psalm Book* read as follows:

O Blessed man, that in th' advice
  of wicked doeth not walk;
nor stand in sinners way, nor sit
  in chayre of scornful folk,
But in the law of Jehovah,
  is his longing delight:

and in his law doth meditate,
by day and eke by night.

The same passage in the King James' Version reads:

Blessed is the man
That walketh not in the counsel of the ungodly,
Nor standeth in the way of sinners,
Nor sitteth in the seat of the scornful.
But his delight is in the law of the Lord;
And in his law doth he meditate day and night.

As the archetype of all tongues and as the key to the Bible, Hebrew was prescribed for all students of Harvard from the very beginning and was especially emphasized during the incumbency of Harvard's first two presidents, Henry Dunster and Charles Chauncy. This college was founded primarily to perpetuate a learned ministry for the churches of New England. Ability to read the Bible in the ancient tongue was necessary, since graduates in their lifelong career as clergymen would be called upon to elucidate the holy text for their parishioners. As Cotton Mather explained in his *Magnalia*, it was not the opinion of men, but the exact wording of the Scripture which must decide any controversy.[3]

One of the requirements for graduation from Harvard was the ability to translate from Old Testament Hebrew into Latin. Students assembled in the College Hall daily to listen to the reading of a passage in Hebrew. For over a century and a half, until 1817, the Commencement exercises included an oration in Hebrew. However, Hebrew was not too popular among the students, most of whom dreaded examinations in its grammatical structure, especially its irregular verbs.[4]

The difficulty of mastering Hebrew was increased, from the

---

[3] Cotton Mather, *Magnalia Christi Americana*, Hartford, 1920, II, 53.
[4] Isidore S. Meyer, "Hebrew at Harvard (1636–1700)," *American Jewish Historical Society Publications*, XXXV (1939), 159.

students' viewpoint, by the fact that the only textbooks available were in Latin. Not until the eighteenth century did Hebrew-English textbooks come into use. These were prepared and published by Judah Monis in 1735, by Stephen Sewall in 1763, at Harvard, and by Samuel Johnson, 1767, upon his retirement as president of King's College, later renamed Columbia University.

Judah Monis (1683–1764) taught Hebrew at Harvard from 1722 to 1760 and Stephen Sewall (1734–1804) was his successor from 1764 to 1785. Not until 1787, when the Colonial Era had ended and the new Republic had arisen, was the prescribed study of Hebrew made elective in Harvard for all students, although a few students were allowed from 1782 on to substitute French for Hebrew, provided they received special permission.[5] Samuel Johnson (1696–1772), who presided over King's College during its first decade, 1754–1764, required all tutors to have a knowledge of Hebrew but not all students. However, Yale College, founded in 1701, more than half a century before King's College, continued to insist on Hebrew for all its students and included Hebrew words in its official seal. Two of Yale's presidents, Timothy Cutler (1694–1765) and Ezra Stiles (1727–1795), were noted Hebrew scholars in their generations.

Other colleges, which arose during the Colonial Period and which taught Hebrew from the beginning, included Dartmouth—founded in 1769, Princeton—founded in 1746, and Brown—founded in 1764. The signers of the Declaration of Independence included graduates of New England colleges and some of them, who had completed the prescribed curriculum for the degree of Bachelor of Arts, knew not only Latin and Greek, but also some Hebrew.[6]

[5] Abraham I. Katsh, *Hebrew Language, Literature, and Culture in American Institutions of Higher Learning*, New York, 1950, p. 4.
[6] James J. Walsh, *Education of the Founding Fathers of the Republic*, New York, 1935, p. 35.

Love for Hebrew implied a love for the Hebrews of old, patriarchs and prophets, heroic judges and Maccabean warriors, but this love did not extend to contemporary, living Jews. These were not welcome in Puritan New England and when on rare occasions a Jew did find his way to Massachusetts, zealous efforts were made to convert him to Christianity.

Cotton Mather's *Diary* was replete with references to his efforts in this direction. Often he expressed the hope that it might be vouchsafed him during his years on earth to bring a Jew within the Christian fold. A typical expression of this missionary yearning was his prayer of July 18, 1696: "This day, from the dust, where I lay prostrate, before the Lord, I lifted my cries: For the conversion of the Jewish Nation, and for my own having the happiness, at some time or other, to baptize a Jew, that should by my ministry, be brought home unto the Lord." [7]

Three years later Cotton Mather published *The Faith of the Fathers,* dedicating this pamphlet to the Jewish Nation. He implored the Jews to see the error of their ways, not to remain unregenerate, but to accept the only true, complete Jewish religion as developed by Jesus. In his *Diary,* he wrote on April 9, 1699: "This week, I attempted a further service to the name of the Lord. . . . I prefaced the Catechism with an address to the Jewish Nation, telling them in some lively terms, that if they would but return to the faith of the Old Testament, and believe with their own Ancient and blessed Patriarchs, this was all that we desired of them or for them. I gave this book to the Printer and it was immediately published. Its title is *The Faith of the Fathers.*" [8]

[7] Lee M. Friedman, "Cotton Mather and the Jews," *American Jewish Historical Society Publications,* XXVI (1918), 202.

[8] *Ibid.,* p. 203.

After the appearance of this publication, he noted in his *Diary* under May 21, 1699: "I have advice from Heaven— Yea, more than this; That I shall shortly see some Harvest of my Prayers and Pains, and the Jewish Nation also." [9] When this hope was not fulfilled, he published a second tract in 1701, entitled *American Tears upon the Ruins of the Greek Churches*, in which he called attention to the conversion in London of a Jew, Shalome Ben Shalomoh. His own efforts were constantly being frustrated by the stubbornness of the stiff-necked Jews. He was especially concerned with a Jew who was permitted to trade in Massachusetts and who seemed to be a likely object for conversion. Of this Jew, for whom he prayed throughout the night of July 4 to July 5, 1713, he made the following diary-entry: "Vigil-prayer. For the conversion of the poor Jew, who is this Day returned once more unto New England, and who has now for 19 years together been the Subject of our Cares and Hopes and Prayers." [10] For another month he continued to pray for this Jew and then he gave up, or else the Jew failed to show up.

When news reached Cotton Mather of the conversion of three Jewish children in Berlin, who cast off their parents and embraced Christianity despite discouragement from the Protestant minister, he expressed the hope in the pamphlet *Faith Encouraged*, 1718, that the example of these daughters of Isaac Veits, ranging in age from eight to twelve, would be an inspiring model to be followed by others. "If but one Soul of all that Beloved People should be found, and reached and touched, by the Things to be now laid before them, it will be well worth while the Pains of these Expostulations. It may be, the same Spirit, who wrought upon the Babes at Berlin, will fall upon some of that Beloved People, while they have

[9] *Ibid.*, p. 205.
[10] *Ibid.*, p. 207.

these Words before them. We will prophesy over these Dry
Bones, and see what the Spirit of Life will do upon them!" [11]

In this zeal for saving Jews for Christianity, Cotton Mather
was but following in the footsteps of his father Increase
Mather, who as early as 1669 had collected a group of sermons dealing with the conversion of the Israelitish Nation in
a tract entitled *Mystery of Israel's Salvation*. There Increase
Mather tried to prove that all the descendants of the twelve
tribes would yet be saved; he speculated as to when this
would happen; he explained why this must come about; and
he explained that the kind of salvation the tribes of Israel
would partake of would be glorious and wonderful, spiritual
and temporal. In 1709, he reiterated his belief in the inevitability of this development in his *Dissertation Concerning the
Future Conversion of the Jewish Nation*.

If all twelve tribes were to accept Christianity so that the
Messianic age might dawn, then the descendants of the missing ten tribes had to be found and the descendants of the
other two tribes convinced of the truth of the New Testament. A search must, therefore, be made for the ten tribes at
the same time as the teaching of Jesus was brought to the professing Jews. To many Puritans, the evidence was irrefutable
that the North American Indians were the offspring of the
dispersed of Israel. Thomas Cromwell, a rich buccaneer, who
died in Boston in 1646, assured the Governor of Massachusetts Thomas Dudley that he had himself witnessed Indians to the south being circumcized. Others claimed that the
word Hallelujah could be discerned in the chanting of
Canadian Indians. The New England Indians were said to
share with the Israelites the custom of the separation of the
women on certain occasions. John Eliot, who lived among the
Algonquins, claimed that these Indians spoke in parables just
as the Israelites had done in Biblical days; Indians anointed

[11] *Ibid.*, p. 209.

their heads; Indians delighted in celebrating victories by dancing; Indians computed time by nights and months; Indians gave dowries for wives; Indians chanted loud dirges for their dead; Indians disliked swine.[12] Was this not evidence enough of the Israelitish origin of the Indians?

Samuel Sewall (1652–1730), who was Chief Justice of the Massachusetts Bay Colony from 1718 to 1728, befriended the Indians because he believed them to be part of God's anointed people; he had scruples as to whether a declaration of war against them was just or prudent. "He was a commissioner from the corporation for propagating the gospel among them, and with his own substance built them a synagogue and did many other charitable acts." [13]

In a letter of 1686, Sewall wrote: "Dr. Thorowgood writ a treatise about thirty years ago entitled *Jews in America,* showing Americans to be Abraham's Posterity. If so, the day of their Espousals will make all the Christian world glad, and the rich among the people will desire their favor. How advantageous then and seasonable would it be by a holy anticipation to desire favor of God for them; especially seeing 'tis hoped the set time to favor Zion is very near come." [14]

Anne Bradstreet (1612?–1672), the earliest woman poet in America, daughter of one governor of Massachusetts and wife of another, speculated in her poetic epic *The Four Monarchies* as to whether the descendants of the lost Ten Tribes were to be sought among the Indians of the East or the Indians of the West, but of one fact she was certain: "yet know we this, they shall return and Zion see with bliss." [15]

William Penn believed that within his province of Penn-

[12] Cotton Mather, *Magnalia Christi Americana,* Hartford, 1855, I, 560.

[13] Thomas Hutchinson, *History of the Colony and Province of Massachusetts Bay,* Cambridge, Mass., 1936, II, 203.

[14] Samuel Sewall, *Letter-Book,* Massachusetts Historical Society Collection, Boston, 1886, I, 22.

[15] Anne Bradstreet, *Works,* Charleston, S.C., 1867, p. 196.

sylvania were to be found the true descendants of the lost Ten Tribes and he was happy to be adopted by one of the Indian tribes as a brother.

Ezra Stiles, who was engaged in missionary work after graduation from Yale in 1750, hunted for the lost Ten Tribes among the Indians whom he tried to convert. But he also did not neglect the descendants of the other two Jewish tribes, whom he encountered at Newport. He was present at the dedication of the Touro Synagogue in 1763, the oldest surviving synagogue of America. He associated frequently with Rabbi Isaac Karigal, with whom he could converse in Hebrew. He admired the Jewish merchant Aaron Lopez, whom he likened to a Socrates and a Manasseh Ben Israel. It was a source of grief to him that he never found any descendants of the Lost Tribes and that he was never able to persuade this most prominent Jewish merchant of Colonial Rhode Island to accept Christianity. He finally concluded that perhaps it was God's will that Jews remain Jews.[16]

As late as 1788, Jonathan Edwards, in his booklet *Language of the Muhhekaneew Indians*, still tried to trace the origin of the tongues of the American Indians to the ancient Hebrew.

Decades after the Colonial Era had ended and the Eastern Seaboard had been settled, hopes continued to be entertained that in the unexplored parts of America the Ten Tribes might still be found. In 1816, Elias Boudinot published in Trenton, the capital of New Jersey, the booklet *Star in the West, or A Humble Attempt to Discover the Long Lost Ten Tribes of Israel Preparatory to their Return to their Beloved City Jerusalem*. More than a decade later, Mordecai M. Noah published in 1827 his *Discourse on the Evidences of the*

---

[16] Morris Jastrow, "References to Jews in the Diary of Ezra Stiles," *American Jewish Historical Society Publications*, X (1902), 5–36; W. Willner, "Ezra Stiles and the Jews," *Ibid.*, VIII (1900), 119–126.

American Indians Being the Descendants of the Lost Tribes of Israel.

There were probably no more than about two hundred and fifty Jews in all of North America during the seventeenth century. The first group of twenty-three Jews landed in New Amsterdam in September 1654 and in the same decade the first Jews came to Newport, Rhode Island. In the former colony, they had to fight for the right to worship together and for economic survival against a hostile Dutch governor, Peter Stuyvesant, who only reluctantly and after considerable pressure relaxed some unbearable restrictions. In the latter colony, on the other hand, they were assured of complete religious equality by the founder Roger Williams from the first moment of their arrival within its borders.

Roger Williams held that it was wrong to molest any person, Jew or Gentile, for professing any religious doctrine dictated by conscience or to persecute anyone for practicing such beliefs. He believed in the separation of Church and State. In 1655, he illustrated his approach towards religious liberty by means of a vivid parable of a ship at sea: "It hath fallen out sometimes, that both papists and protestants, Jews and Turks, may be embarked upon one ship; upon which supposal I affirm, that all the liberty of conscience, that I ever pleaded for, turns upon these two hinges—that none of the papists, Jews, or Turks, be forced to come to the ship's prayers or worship, nor be compelled from their own particular prayers or worship." [17]

Roger Williams did not assume that other religions were equally as good as his own brand of Christianity but he did insist upon the equal rights of all persons to practice whatever beliefs their conscience dictated to them. He held that God did not require uniformity of religion to be enforced by

[17] M. H. Morris, "Roger Williams and the Jews," *American Jewish Archives,* III, 2 (Jan. 1951), 24–27.

any civil state. Indeed, such uniformity would be a denial of the principles of Christianity and of the civil order which should be based on the separation of Church and State.

During the Colonial period there were at least five settlements in North America with a significant Jewish population: Newport, New Amsterdam, renamed New York after its conquest by the English, Savannah, Charleston, and Philadelphia. The Jewish settlers came largely from Sephardic backgrounds and spoke Spanish and Portuguese in their homes and English in their trades and commercial undertakings. But there were also some Jews from German-speaking countries who had found their way to the New World. A few even stemmed from Polish and Eastern European provinces. The Jewish communities contributed to the material and cultural growth of the seaboard towns and were, on the whole, well received by their neighbors and business associates.

The Swedish botanist Peter Kalm (1716–1779), who was sent to America in 1748 by the Swedish Academy of Sciences and who spent three years there, reported that by then he found Jews enjoying all the privileges common to other inhabitants. He attended a service in a New York synagogue and he saw Jews dwelling in fine houses and carrying on important ventures in business and commerce.[18]

Despite the presence of Jews in an ever increasing number of colonies and despite their growing affluence and economic importance, their impress upon the soul of America during Colonial days was not significant, especially when compared with the impact of Biblical Jews. Repeatedly, it was the ancient Israelites who were held up as models for individual and group behavior. Especially was this true during the years of dissatisfaction with the rule of King George III. Preachers often inspired the colonists to resist the oppression of the mother country by stressing that the Americans were as much

[18] Peter Kalm, *Travels Into North America*, London, 1772, I, 191.

a unique and chosen people, instruments of divine will, as the Jews had been in ancient days. Throughout the Revolutionary struggle, the Bible was invoked as the ideal political textbook, since it embodied the basic law given by God to the Jewish people at the time when this people was under his particular care and protection.

When the Continental Congress on July 4, 1776, adopted the Declaration of Independence, it also approved a resolution appointing Benjamin Franklin, John Adams, and Thomas Jefferson as a committee to prepare a suitable seal for the newly proclaimed United States of America. There was general agreement that Biblical symbolism was most appropriate. Franklin suggested that the seal ought to show Moses lifting up his wand and dividing the Red Sea while Pharaoh was being overwhelmed by its waters. Jefferson proposed that it show the children of Israel in the wilderness led by a cloud by day and a pillar of fire by night. The Great Seal which was finally adopted shows a pyramid representing the thirteen colonies, topped by the all-seeing eye of Jehovah, who is surrounded by a cloud of glory, a symbol of the protecting Divine Presence.

During the years of debating the new governmental structure to be erected by the victorious colonies, the ancient Hebrew commonwealth continued to serve as a model. Typical of the sermons delivered shortly before the ratification of the American Constitution was the one preached by Samuel Langdon on June 5, 1788, at Concord, New Hampshire and later published under the title *The Republic of the Israelites an Example to the American States.*

Langdon told his distinguished audience that the Israelites of old should be considered as a pattern to the world in all ages and that from them Americans might learn what, on the one hand, would exalt the national character and what, on the other hand, would bring about national ruin. When the

Israelites first came out of Egyptian bondage, they too were a multitude without any other order except what they had kept up, very feebly, under the ancient patriarchal authority. They had no proper national or military establishment when Moses led them across the Red Sea. Nevertheless, within three months, they were forged by him into a united political organism. Able representatives were chosen out of all the tribes as captains and as rulers of thousands, hundreds, fifties, and tens. The Israelites accepted these representatives as military officers and as judges in controversial matters. Soon thereafter there arose a synhedrion or senate of seventy men to assist the chief commander Moses with his heavy burden of governing. "And as to the choice of the Senate, doubtless the people were consulted, who appear to have had a voice in all public affairs from time to time, the whole congregation being called together on all important occasions; the government therefore was a proper republic." [19]

Besides this general government, each tribe had its autonomous government which might serve as a model for each state of the American union. Each tribe had its elders and a prince, according to a patriarchal order with which Moses and the central government of the Israelite Republic did not interfere. Each tribe had the right to meet and to arrive at whatever decisions were necessary for the promotion of the common interest of the tribe. Each tribe was headed by a president and a senate, but all members of the tribe were consulted on crucial matters. Moreover, after the Israelites came out of the wilderness and settled in Canaan, they selected as judges in every walled city elders who were most distinguished for wisdom and integrity and they let these judges decide controversial matters within the cities. From these decisions of the local judges, an appeal could be made to

[19] Samuel Langdon, *The Republic of the Israelites an Example to the American States*, Exeter, 1788, p. 9.

higher courts having jurisdiction over the entire tribe. In very great and difficult cases, a final appeal could also be made to the chief magistrate and the supreme senate of the republic. The Israelites also had in their Torah a complete Code of Laws founded upon principles of reason, justice, and social virtue. Hence, in a very short time the Israelites progressed from abject slavery, ignorance, and mob status to a well-regulated national establishment superior to that of any other nation. Had the Israelites adhered to their constitution, the Torah, they would not have gotten into trouble. In the course of time, however, they neglected their government, they corrupted their religion, they grew dissolute in their morals, and thus brought about their catastrophic end.

The American union of thirteen states was comparable to the Israelite union of twelve tribes. The American constitution was also founded on rational, equitable, and liberal principles. "The God of heaven hath not indeed visibly displayed the glory of his majesty and power before our eyes, as he came down in the sight of Israel on the burning mount; nor has he written with his own finger the laws of our civil polity: but the signal interpositions of divine providence, in saving us from the vengeance of a powerful irritated nation, from which we were unavoidably separated by their inadmissible claim of absolute parliamentary power over us; in giving us a Washington to be captain-general of our armies; in carrying us through the various distressing scenes of war and desolation, and making us twice triumphant over numerous armies, surrounded and captivated in the midst of their career; and finally giving us peace, with a large territory, and acknowledged independence; all these laid together fall little short of real miracles and an heavenly charter of liberty for these United States. And when we reflect, how wonderfully the order of these states was preserved when government was dissolved or supported only by feeble props;

with how much sobriety, wisdom, and unanimity they formed and received the diversified yet similar constitutions in the different states; with what prudence, fidelity, patience, and success the Congress have managed the general government, under the great disadvantages of a very imperfect and impotent confederation; we cannot but acknowledge that God hath graciously patronized our cause, and taken us under his special care, as he did his ancient covenant people." [20]

Langdon ended his sermon with an appeal for the ratification of the American Constitution, which had already been ratified by eight states and which needed the assent of New Hampshire as the ninth state in order to be carried into effect. On June 21, 1788, this ratification then took place.

Under the adopted constitution, the separation of church and state, first proclaimed by Roger Williams of Rhode Island, became a cardinal principle of American democracy and whatever restrictions Jews still suffered from in individual states were abolished in the course of time. Jews enjoyed the good will of their neighbors. Jews continued to be judged in the light of their Biblical past rather than because of any group achievement on the American scene. They were merchants engaged in a variety of large and small enterprises and only very few could be classed as intellectuals. Certainly there were no creative literary figures among them throughout the Colonial and Revolutionary Eras. Even as subjects for literature they were unnoticed before the nineteenth century. Their most prominent revolutionary patriot, Haym Salomon, did not make his appearance in fiction before 1858, when John Richter Jones included him as the pawnbroker Solomon Isaacki in the novel *The Quaker Soldier; or The British in Philadelphia.*

Two chapters were devoted to this character, who was

[20] *Ibid.,* pp. 31–32.

utterly unlike the horrible Jewish stereotypes that still stalked through English fiction. He was described as follows: "The face and forehead were grand, full of intellect and benevolence with a slight seasoning of something like cunning, though not enough to impair the general effect; you could not but wonder what these features were doing on the shoulders of a pawnbroker. . . . In support of the cause of the Revolution none was more ready to sacrifice what men hold more precious; few were more meritorious." [21]

It was in the shop of this pawnbroker that the American patriots met and plotted against the British and it was he who at the close of the narrative led the American rebels to the rescue of the heroine who had been abducted by the British.

Not until the early nineteenth century, when Mordecai M. Noah wrote his first play *The Fortress of Sorrento* in 1808 did American Jewry become articulate and produce works of literary value.

[21] Edward D. Coleman, "Jewish Prototypes in American and English *Romans* and *Drames a Clef," American Jewish Historical Society Publications,* XXXV (1939), 242.

CHAPTER II

THE YOUNG REPUBLIC

The first American Jews to make an impact upon the American scene through their literary creativity were Mordecai Manuel Noah, Samuel B. H. Judah, Jonas B. Phillips and Isaac Harby.

Noah was born in Philadelphia in 1785 but the greater part of his life was associated with New York, where he died in 1851. He was publicist and dramatist, realistic politician and Utopian visionary. He is today best remembered for his Ararat-project, his effort to establish a Jewish state on Grand Island in the Niagara River, between the United States and Canada. He lives in Jewish history as a pioneer of Zionism, a precursor of Moses Hess and Theodor Herzl. During his lifetime, however, it was his non-Jewish activities which established his reputation and influence. He was diplomat, sheriff, judge, surveyor of New York's harbor, major of the state militia, and a leader of Tammany, the Democratic organization that long dominated New York politics. He was editor of the newspaper *The National Advocate* from 1816 on and founder of the *New York Enquirer* in 1826. Under the later name *Courier and Enquirer,* the latter organ helped to mold American public opinion throughout many years. Afterwards, Noah edited the newspaper *New York Sun* as well as the literary magazine *Times and Weekly Messenger.*

A contemporary of Noah, George P. Morris, wrote of him in 1829 that "he was the great literary and political lion in the city of New York, that he told the best story, rounded the best sentence, and wrote the best plays of all his contemporaries, that he was the life and spirit of all circles, that his wit was everywhere repeated, and that as editor, critic and author he was looked up to as an oracle." [1]

In American literature, Noah's contribution was chiefly in the medium of drama. His first play, written as early as 1808, was entitled *The Fortress of Sorrento.* Its romantic subject-matter is reminiscent of the libretto to Beethoven's *Fidelio,* the story of a faithful wife who puts on male attire in order to rescue her husband from the prison to which he has been unjustly consigned by enemies. This play was never performed. Noah, who wished to acquire a library of dramas, gave the manuscript to the New York publisher David Longworth in exchange for a copy of every play the latter had published.

Noah's first acted play was *Paul and Alexis; or The Orphans of the Rhine,* written in 1812. Soon thereafter he was sent abroad as an American diplomatic representative. He was consul in Tunis in 1813, when the American government was having difficulties with the pirates of the Barbary Coast, as the southwestern Mediterranean region was then called. He recorded his observations of scenes and people abroad in his book, published in 1819 and entitled *Travels in England, France, Spain, and the Barbary States in the Years 1813–1814, and 1815.*

On returning to New York, Noah again sought to win theatrical laurels with an historical drama, *She Would Be a Soldier; or The Plains of Chippewa,* 1819. Its subject was the War of 1812. A second historical drama was completed two years later and was based on events of the Revolutionary War. Entitled *Marion; or The Hero of Lake George,* it had as background the Battle of Saratoga and the surrender of

[1] Leon Huhner, *Essays and Addresses,* New York, 1959, p. 29.

General Burgoyne. Here too a wife disguises herself as a man in order to save her husband from prison.

Aware of the rising interest in the Greeks, who were then struggling for liberation from Turkish rule and whose heroic resistance was inspiring Byron's and Shelley's lyrics of Hellenic glory, Noah in 1822 penned his drama *The Grecian Captive or The Fall of Athens,* in which he anticipated a Greek victory that had not yet taken place. At performances of the play, the hero appeared on an elephant and the heroine on a camel. Every member of the audience, upon entering the theater, got a copy of the text as a souvenir.

Two years earlier, another play by Noah dealing with recent historic events, *The Siege of Tripoli,* was successfully staged in New York, but came to a sudden end after the third performance when the theater burned down just after the audience had left. It dealt with the troubles experienced by American citizens captured and held for ransom by the pirates of the southern Mediterranean. This theme had been dramatized as early as 1794 by Susanna Haswell Rowson. Her *Slaves in Algiers: or A Struggle for Freedom* was the first American play containing a Jewish character, even though British plays with Jewish villains had been presented to American audiences ever since 1752 when *The Merchant of Venice* was staged at Williamsburg, Virginia, a performance which George Washington, then a British major and living nearby, might have witnessed. Mrs. Rowson's drama held up the Jew to contempt and ridicule. She portrayed the Jew as a scoundrel who even forswore his own faith and embraced Mohammedanism when it offered him advantages. He described himself as a forger and a crook, as one who cheated the Gentiles because Moses so commanded. This little Israelite miser was prepared to accept money from everyone and to betray everyone, but in the end he himself was black-

mailed into helping captive Americans to escape, so that
virtue might be vindicated and the curtain come down upon
a happy conclusion. This play was performed at Philadelphia, Boston, New York, and Hartford. It satisfied theatergoers' predilections for Jews as stage-villains. It spawned
James Ellison's drama on the same subject *The American
Captive; or Siege of Tripoli*. In this play of 1812, which also
preceded Noah's, the miserly Jew Ishmael too was put into a
situation where he had to help free an American captive
whom he had earlier intended to betray. He smuggled the
American out of the country of Moslems by disguising him as
a fellow Jew.

Noah's *Siege of Tripoli* deviated from the two earlier
plays on this theme by dispensing with Jewish characters. Despite his intense Jewishness, he did not include a single Jewish figure, hero or villain, or a single Jewish subject in any of
his plays. The most plausible explanation seems to be that
he did not want to present bad Jews and that his audiences
did not want to see good Jews on the stage, except Biblical
ones, despite the fact that these theatergoers might have
pleasant daily contacts with Jews in normal business relationships and communal activities. Audiences had so long been
fed on Shylock—the flinthearted Jew of Venice, on Barabbas
—the monstrous Jew of Malta, and on other villainous Jews
by lesser dramatists than the talented Elizabethans. They
were not ready to accept Jewish characters that ran counter
to the established tradition of the wicked and miserly stage-
Jew. In Germany, it required the genius of Gotthold
Ephraim Lessing to dent this tradition with his *Nathan the
Wise,* 1779. In England, Richard Cumberland, seeking to
atone for his early defamation of this much maligned group,
had made a similar attempt with his play *The Jew,* 1794, but
was not equally successful. Noah, who had himself suffered

from unjustified anti-Jewishness during his brief diplomatic career, could not expose his own people to derision without stultifying himself. He, therefore, refrained altogether from portraying Jews in his plays or from touching on Jewish themes in any of his dramatic plots.

This attitude was also adopted by another Jewish playwright of his generation, Jonas B. Phillips (1805–1869). A descendant of a Colonial family of Jewish merchants prominent in Charleston and Philadelphia, he began as an author of melodramas and ended as a respected lawyer and assistant district attorney for the county of New York. His most popular play was *The Evil Eye*, staged on and off from 1831 to 1899. Only one of his dramatic works, however, was of literary value, the tragedy *Camillus*. Inspired by Shakespeare's *Coriolanus* and first produced in Philadelphia in 1833, it centered about an exiled Roman tribune who returned to save his country from the Gauls.

The reluctance of Jews to use the stage as a medium for the discussion of Jewish subjects or for the depiction of Jewish characters can also be seen in the case of Isaac Harby (1788–1828). A pioneer of the Reform Movement in Judaism in his native Charleston, Harby had established in early years a fine reputation as essayist, literary critic, and dramatist. His earliest work, written at seventeen, was *Alexander Severus*, a comedy in five acts. His first staged play was *The Gordian Knot, or Causes and Effects*, written when he was only nineteen. It was a romantic melodrama of vengeance and had a happy ending. A later drama, *Alberti*, performed in Charleston in 1819, also stressed the theme of vengeance. It was based on Vittorio Alfieri's *Conspiracy of the Pazzi*. The scene was Florence of the Renaissance. "The play is easily one of the best of its kind from the point of view of expression. The blank verse is flexible and interesting, and the construction is more unified than in *The Gordian Knot*. . . . He is one of the writers of the time whose work has the touch of inspiration." [2]

President James Monroe attended the second performance of this play and the gala audience helped to spread Harby's fame.

As dramatic critic of the *New York Evening Post,* Harby displayed originality and great courage. His comments on a performance of *The Merchant of Venice* showed him to be no slavish admirer even of the greatest of dramatists. He took issue with Shakespeare's depiction of Shylock. He felt that Shakespeare had sinned against all plausibility when, in a city notorious for its oppression and degradation of Jews, he had Shylock approach the court, knife in hand, and demand the pound of flesh. Harby regretted that Shakespeare "suffered his mighty mind to be swayed by the passions and false taste of an age he was destined to instruct and immortalize." [3]

Upon Harby's death, Penina Moise printed a moving elegy in *The Mercury,* on December 27, 1828, in which she hailed him as the light of her youth, the person from whom her spirit caught its proudest aspiration to high thought and who fired with ambitious hopes her own soul. She praised his wit, his vivacity, his buoyant brilliancy.

Only a single playwright of Jewish origin, Samuel B. H. Judah, wrote on a Jewish theme but he did so anonymously and without any affection for the group from which he stemmed. Born in 1799 in New York City, he dropped out of public sight toward the end of his life so that even the year of his death, which is assumed to be 1876, is not absolutely certain. Like Phillips and Harby, he too began with melodramas. Such were *The Mountain Torrent,* 1820, and *Rose of Arragon,* 1822. He then completed within four days, ac-

[2] A. H. Quinn, *A History of the American Drama From the Beginning to the Civil War,* New York, 1943, p. 192.

[3] L. C. Moise, *Biography of Isaac Harby,* Charleston, S.C., 1931, p. 17.

cording to his boast, an historical drama of the Revolutionary War. Entitled *A Tale of Lexington,* it was received with unbounded applause, according to his assertion, when it was performed in New York on Independence Day, 1822. His career as a playwright ended in his early twenties, however, because of his scandalous poetic satire *Gotham and the Gothamites,* 1823, which caricatured prominent citizens of New York, including his co-religionist and fellow-dramatist Mordecai M. Noah, and which landed him in prison for libelous defamation of character. Upon his release, strangely enough, he became a lawyer, was admitted to the bar in 1825 despite his past record, became financially successful and thereafter published his literary products anonymously or under the pseudonym Terentius Phologombos. One of these products was on a Jewish theme, a Biblical play entitled *The Maid of Midian.* It was a tragedy "founded on the massacre of the Midian captives by order of Moses," and was never performed, probably because of the author's sacrilegious approach.

Judah was also credited with being the creater of an anonymous ballad, *The Battles of Joshua,* in which Joshua was depicted as enslaving the Gibeonites and behaving cruelly toward the conquered peoples of Canaan.

In contrast to Jewish writers, most of whom suffered from inhibitions and sought to avoid being too conspicuously Jewish, American writers of non-Jewish origins were more at ease in commenting on Jewish scenes and situations. Ralph Waldo Emerson, Orestes A. Brownson, Lydia Maria Child, Henry Wadsworth Longfellow and Nathanial Hawthorne were typical of such writers in pre-Civil War New England.

Emerson, who kept a journal since his late twenties, in which he noted his thoughts and impressions, recorded in 1833 that, while at Rome, he was invited to go to the baptism of a Jew but turned down the invitation since he did not want to witness what seemed to him to be a weary farce. " 'Tis said they buy the Jews at 150 scudos the head, to be sprinkled." [4]

On the same European trip in 1833, he came to Ferrara and passed through the Jewish Quarter where two thousand eight hundred Jews were "shut every night, as in Rome, like dogs." [5]

The mistreatment of Jews abroad grated upon his soul that had been nurtured on the Bible and he was saddened by the sights of Jewish misery in the Italian ghettos. Stripped of all supernatural authority, the Bible was still for him the most original literary masterpiece in all the world. "This old collection of the ejaculations of love and dread, of the supreme desires and contritions of men, proceeding out of the region of the grand and eternal, by whatsoever different mouths spoken, and through a wide extent of times and countries, seems the alphabet of the nations, and all posterior literature either the chronicle of facts under very inferior Ideas, or, when it rises to sentiment, the combinations, analogies or degradations of this. . . . People imagine that the place which the Bible holds in the world, it owes to miracles. It owes it simply to the fact that it came out of a profounder depth of thought than any other book, and the effect must be precisely proportionate." [6]

Emerson's Boston compatriot Orestes A. Brownson was equally enthusiastic in his tribute to Biblical ideals and Biblical personalities. In the *Boston Quarterly Review* of July 1842, he defended Moses against the St. Simonian disciple Pierre Leroux, who saw the Jewish lawgiver merely as a precursor of St. Simon. While agreeing that there might be some St. Simonism in the code of Moses, Brownson found

[4] R. W. Emerson, *Journals (1833–1835)*, New York, 1910, p. 88.
[5] *Ibid.*, p. 127.
[6] *Ibid.*, pp. 334–335.

that the liberator from Egyptian bondage was eminently a Jew, Oriental in the boldness of his genius, in the richness of his imagination, in the warmth of his temper—an Oriental under the Hebrew type. And what was this Hebrew type? It was a unique psychic configuration. It had no prototypes and no analogies in any of the existing nations of our globe. "It is distinct, peculiar, remarkable for its serene beauty, its chastity, simplicity, freedom from the extravagant, the grotesque, the superstitious, the marvelous. It is distinguished from that of all the other nations of antiquity by its good sense, its sobriety, its reserve, no less than by its force and energy. Yet was the Jew a poet. He struck the harp with freedom, boldness and delicacy, and drew from it tones which had been caught only from the seraphim, and which were not heard without the heart's rising anew to its Father and its God. To the Jew, then, let us leave ungrudgingly the honor of having originated, through Providence, his own literature, and by that, of having become the chosen of God to instruct the nations in the deepest principles of philosophy, of jurisprudence, and theology; and at the same time to charm them by the divinest music, and kindle their aspirations for God by the sublimest poetry." [7]

Equally glowing tributes to Jews are to be found in the orations of non-Jewish Americans. They did not feel the need to speak in subdued and muted tones about Jewish achievements. They could battle for Jewish rights without any subjective qualms. Typical of such orations was the speech delivered by the Baltimore representative John S. Tyson to the Maryland legislature when he called upon this body in 1829 to remove the last disabilities under which the Jews of that state were still suffering. "Who made them Jews? The same Being who made you a Christian. They had as little control over the Power who made them sons of Abraham, as you have

[7] O. A. Brownson, *Works*, Detroit, 1883, p. 134.

over that, which cast your lot among a Christian people. Born
as you are in a Christian community, taught no other faith,
or taught other only as an object of execration, is it wonderful that you profess the Christian religion? Born as the Jews
are, descendants of a line of ancestry traceable to the first
periods of the world's existence—all professing the same faith,
a faith communicated by God himself in the midst of thunder and lightning upon Mt. Sinai—educated in this faith
from their earliest infancy, and wedded to it by the cementing power of persecution, is it wonderful that they should
continue to profess it? The wonder would be if they were to
burst the mighty mound of circumstances and come over to
the camp of Christian comity. Sir! if they had been born as
you were, they would have been Christians—if you had been
born as they were, you would have been a Jew. When therefore you censure the Hebrews for not being Christians, you
arraign the mighty Being who holds in his hands the reins of
destiny, and who for purposes inscrutable to us, has cast their
lot in the midst of necessities which compel them to be
Jews." [8]

Efforts to convert Jews to Christianity were motivated not
by hostility towards them but rather by kind sentiments, the
desire to save the souls of good and honest human beings who
had not yet found their way to salvation through Jesus.
When missionaries of the American Society for Meliorating
the Condition of the Jews founded a periodical *Israel's Advocate* in 1823 to propagate the gospel among the children of
Abraham, they were not too successful and their periodical
did not survive beyond the following year. It provoked a Jew,
S. H. Jackson, to counter such Christian propaganda with a
periodical which proudly bore the title *The Jew* and which
included on its first page the statement that its purpose was to
defend Judaism against all adversaries, particularly against

[8] *The Israelite,* July 13, 1855, p. 7.

the attacks of *Israel's Advocate*. In the issue of November 1824, Jackson reprinted the wise and restrained answer of Moses Mendelssohn to the invitation of Deacon Lavater of Zürich either to accept Christianity or to refute its tenets. In this answer the Jewish philosopher refrained from attacking Christianity but insisted on his being permitted to remain a Jew.

When *Israel's Advocate* ceased publication soon thereafter, Jackson's periodical also went out of existence a few months later.

Jewish defense organs were not necessary during decades when attacks upon Jews did not appear in American organs of opinion. Nor was the work of missionaries needed in the free democratic atmosphere of the early Republic to loosen the ties of Jews to Jewishness. These ties were normally extremely tenuous. Assimilation to the majority population, which was non-Jewish, offered no difficulties. When the call of passion impelled a Jewish young man to a non-Jewish mate, there seemed to be no rational objection on his part to his espousing the faith of the latter, especially since young Jews who grew up on the ever expanding frontier, where fortune beckoned, were in most cases without Jewish education or positive Jewish experiences.

Jewish frontiersmen were generally peddlers, the ancestors of the large department store owners of later decades. These peddlers were replacing the Yankee peddlers of an earlier era. In American novels, they were depicted most sympathetically, in contrast to the unfavorable stereotypes of old clothes dealers that then stalked through British fiction. For example, the Jewish peddler depicted in Otto Ruppius' novel of 1857, entitled *The Peddler*, and based on the author's actual contacts with German-Jewish hawkers of the frontier communities, represented a far nobler type than the clever and villainous Jew Gabriel von Gelt, in George Lippard's novel of 1845, *The Quaker City,* which followed British and European models and had no relation to American Jewish reality.

The latter novel, which bore the sub-title *The Monks of Monk-Hall,* purported to reveal the Mysteries of Philadelphia in the sensational manner of Eugene Sue's *Mysteries of Paris,* 1844, which had become a best seller. Lippard's novel immediately attracted wide popularity. It sold 40,000 copies within a year. In unveiling the secret life of Philadelphia society, it depicted crimes, murders, and ghastly atrocities. The Jewish character involved in these horrors was introduced as follows: "A short, thickset, little man, dressed in a suit of glossy black cloth, advanced from the open door. His face, which from its remarkable length, gave you the idea of a horse's head, affixed to the remnant of a human body, seemed to lie upon his heart, while his shoulders arose on either side as high as his ears, and his back protruding in a shapeless hump, was visible above the outline of his head. . . . The diminutive stature of the strange visitor, the hump on his back, and the manner in which his face seemed to rest on his chest, all gave additional effect to the expression of his face and eyes. '*Jew*,' was written on his face as clearly and distinctly as though he had fallen asleep at the building of the Temple at Jerusalem in the days of Solomon, the rake and moralist; and after a nap of three thousand years had waked up in the Quaker City, in a state of perfect and hebraic preservation." [9]

When this Jew reappeared later in the novel, attention was again directed to the unnatural length of his face and the absurd disproportion of his small and humpbacked body, which looked more like a shapeless lump dressed in a man's attire than the frame of a human being.[10]

[9] George Lippard, *The Quaker City,* Philadelphia, 1845, p. 149.
[10] *Ibid.,* p. 192.

What a contrast between the Lippard caricature of a Jew, a stereotype that harked back to the Middle Ages and that was just then being resurrected in England by Charles Dickens as Fagin in *Oliver Twist,* and the noble, philanthropic peddler in the novel by Otto Ruppius, a writer who was able to observe many Jewish representatives of this calling during his twelve years in America!

Ruppius, who was born in 1819, had been forced to flee from Germany after participating in the Revolution of 1848. Two years after his arrival in America, he settled as a music teacher in Louisville. This was in 1851, the very same year in which the cultured, music loving parents of Louis D. Brandeis also arrived in this Kentucky community. Here Ruppius came to know educated Jews who did not disdain to carry a pack on their backs on weekdays in honest efforts to make a living but who knew the values of a holier existence which the Sabbath afforded them and who acted towards their neighbors in exemplary fashion.

When a conflagration destroyed his home in 1853, Ruppius moved on to Milwaukee, where he edited a German periodical. Six years later, he again moved on to another American center which had a considerable German-Jewish population, St. Louis.

It was while in Milwaukee, where Jewish peddlers like the Gimbels were later to emerge from peddling to department store empires, that Ruppius wrote his novel, in which he incorporated his experiences with Jewish peddlers who were honest, benevolent, good-natured human beings.

The novel, which deals with the struggle for existence of a young German immigrant, is to a large extent autobiographic. Like Ruppius, the hero is a young intellectual, a lawyer named Helmstedt, who has to leave Germany because of his political radicalism. Swindlers who prey upon unsuspecting newcomers soon reduce his finances to zero. An old

Jewish peddler appears as a savior in the hour of greatest need. With a practical knowledge of American life, the Jew is able to direct young Helmstedt on the correct path and to obtain for him a position as bookkeeper on a farm in Alabama. Once more, the honest but inexperienced young man is about to face ruin, when he is unjustly suspected of murdering his rival for the hand of the farmer's daughter. But again the peddler comes upon the scene and saves him by bringing proof of innocence. Helmstedt then marries the girl and the Jewish peddler, on dying, rewards the non-Jew whom he has taken under his protection by making him the executor of his large estate and the guardian of his nephew.

Helmstedt, at the beginning of the narrative, had started with the assumption that a Jew never did anything without expecting a profit but his experience taught him that this assumption was unwarranted and the residue of prejudice. Thereafter he would shed prejudices.

From records and diaries of pre-Civil War peddlers, we are often able to reconstruct the experiences of young Jewish lads who were wrested from their normal environment abroad and forced suddenly to shift for themselves in a land whose language they hardly comprehended and whose ways seemed most peculiar to them. And yet, within a few years, these lads somehow found their way to fortune and to an end of their wandering. The stories of such peddlers as Adam Gimbel, Lazarus Straus, and Meyer Guggenheim have often been told. Less sensational but more typical was the rise of other less well known peddlers. Such a one was Abraham Kohn, who arrived in 1842 from Bavaria and whose diary of immigrant years was discovered a century later.

On landing in New York, this lad of twenty-three was given a bundle with various articles and told to go out into the country and peddle. His first reaction was one of lamentation: "This, then, is the vaunted luck of the immigrants from

Bavaria! O misguided fools, led astray by avarice and cupidity! You have left your friends and acquaintances, your relatives and your parents, your home and your fatherland, your language and your customs, your faith and your religion— only to sell your wares in the wild places of America, in isolated farmhouses and tiny hamlets. . . . Only rarely do you succeed, and then only in the smallest way. Is this a fate worth the losses you have suffered, the dangers you have met on land and sea? Is this an equal exchange for the parents and kinsmen you have given up? Is this the celebrated freedom of America's soil? . . . O, that I had never seen this land, but had remained in Germany, apprenticed to a humble country craftsman! Though oppressed by taxes and discriminated against as a Jew, I should still be happier than in the great capital of America, free from royal taxes and every man's religions equal. . . . There is woe—threefold woe—in this fortune which appears so glamorous to those in Europe. Dreaming of such a fortune leads a man to depart from his home. But when he awakens from his dreams, he finds himself in the cold and icy night, treading his lonely way in America." [11]

Nevertheless, within less than two years we find this lamenting peddler as the proprietor of a store in Chicago. His English improved from year to year. By 1860, he was elected city clerk of Chicago and worked for the election of Abraham Lincoln as President.

The friendly attitude of the Chicago community towards its Jewish residents enabled these to prosper and to become easily integrated into the American cultural life. This attitude was eloquently expressed in an article in the *Chicago Tribune* of 1855 entitled "An Hour With the Children of Israel," and reprinted in the Anglo-Jewish periodical *The*

[11] A. V. Goodman, "A Jewish Peddler's Diary 1842–1843," *American Jewish Archives,* June 1951, pp. 96–98.

Asmonean on August 24th of the same year. The article, abounding in praise for the Jews of Chicago, concluded with these words: "The Israelites in this city are numerous, and they are nearly all wealthy and much respected by all who know them. There are no better citizens than they are. They are never guilty of debauchery, crime or misdemeanor; they are never seen in our police courts; they never become paupers, and never are found to be engaged in political conspiracies or mixed up in the schemes of political demogogues. They are models of industry, sobriety and thrift, and put to shame the conduct of many who affect to despise and look down upon them."

This sympathetic, even idealizing approach was typical not only of the arising midwestern frontier communities whither the German-Jewish immigrants were finding their way but it also prevailed throughout communities from the Atlantic to the Pacific.

In the very same year as the *Chicago Tribune* voiced its eulogy, the *San Francisco Sun* published an editorial on the second day of Rosh Hashanah, September 14, 1855, in which Jews were vigorously defended against accusations of bad conduct. Whatever faults might be laid at their door stemmed, in the editor's opinion, from their historic position as victims of relentless persecution. They bore the scars of centuries of oppression, when every rude soldier was at liberty to spit at them and every low scoundrel to smite them. If Jews resented such insults, infuriated mobs might tear them to pieces. "It was reserved for the broad shield of the American Constitution to reinstate the Jew in his religious and political rights. Here he may not only enjoy his property unmolested, but becomes an equal among his peers. There is no excess of blind enthusiasm to demolish his synagogue; no partial law to reject him from honorable place; no grinding taxation to consume his estates; no stigma upon his calling or his name, which render him a mark for contumely or an object of contempt. Like every other man, he is a gentleman by a gentleman's title deeds, and none but bigots and fanatics would seek to judge him by any other standard."

The editorial continued by extolling the patriotism of the Jews: "The American Jew is only less proud of his country than of his religion. To say that he is a mere dweller upon the soil, because it affords him the means of support, is to libel the most noble traits of his character. The graves of his ancestors are around him. His heaven is as near to him on the golden shores of the Pacific, as upon the sacred Mount of Olives or within the classic walls of Jerusalem. His God is omnipotent, omnipresent and omniscient. He has knelt before that Awful Presence alike on the deserts of Arabia and the frozen zones of Siberia; and why should he here—where the law recognizes his religion and his political privileges, withhold an affection to which he is impelled by every consideration of prosperity to himself, and future happiness to his children? His respect for our laws is shown in the fact that he seldom violates them. His wealth has gone towards building up and enriching our cities. He cultivates the arts, and goes heart and soul with our active citizens in every useful enterprise. He quarrels but little; heads a mob—never. You will find him in our Courts of Justice, on the Bench, at the Bar, in the Jury box, but seldom ever arraigned for a heinous criminal offence. This is the American Jew. Let his good qualities be imitated—his bad ones should be forgotten." [12]

The concluding paragraphs of this editorial were reprinted in the *Easton Express* on the front page of the first issue of this Pennsylvania newspaper, the issue of November 5, 1855. Similar sentiments were voiced by the Boston Abolitionist, Lydia Maria Child, who in pre-Civil War years edited the New York weekly, *National Anti-Slavery Standard,* and who

[12] *American Jewish Historical Society Publications,* XLV (1956), 270.

never forgot that her own Unitarian faith was rooted in Jewish monotheism. Whether reporting on a Jewish synagogue service or on a meeting of a Jewish society, she could not refrain from affixing a romantic halo about the Jews she met.

A picturesque exoticism and a mystic aroma also hovered about the Jews depicted by her friend John Greenleaf Whittier and by Henry Wadsworth Longfellow. Even a practical political leader like Daniel Webster, who undoubtedly had some contact with Jews, nevertheless associated them not with their contemporary callings, interests, virtues and vices but rather with historic traits that allegedly stemmed from their chosenness at Sinai. In a letter to Mordecai M. Noah on November 9, 1849, he wrote: "I feel, and have ever felt respect and sympathy for all that remains of that extraordinary people who preserved through the darkness and idolatry of so many centuries, the knowledge of one supreme spiritual Being. . . . The Hebrew Scriptures I regard as the fountain from which we draw all we know of the world around us, and of our own character and destiny as intelligent, moral, and responsible beings." [13]

The New Englanders continued to see Jews in the light of Biblical prophecy and Talmudic lore. Their poets did not show keen insight into American Jewish reality but did glorify the Jewish past and did revivify half-forgotten legends. They continued the tradition of philo-semitism which had been brought to America's shores by their Colonial forebears.

[13] Daniel Webster, *Private Correspondence*, Boston, 1857, II, 347.

CHAPTER III

THE NEW ENGLAND POETS

Although Jewish poets were beginning to appear on the American scene ever since the early nineteenth century, publishing their verse primarily in Anglo-Jewish periodicals, not even the most talented among them, such as Adah Isaacs Mencken or Penina Moise, could vie with the New England masters of verse Henry Wadsworth Longfellow, John Greenleaf Whittier, or Oliver Wendell Holmes. It was these non-Jewish bards who enriched American literature with memorable poems of Jewish content.

Longfellow knew some Hebrew but never really mastered the language and was dependent upon translated material for his sources. He met Jews during his years abroad, from 1826 on, but there is no evidence that he associated with them to any extent. Thus, travelling by coach in Southern Germany in 1835, he felt sure that one of his fellow-passengers must have been a Jew because the latter had "the customary hooked nose and half-moon of his tribe; though he could hardly be less than sixty years old he travelled day and night, so as to avoid paying for a lodging." [1] But not until 1848 did Longfellow make the acquaintance of a Jewish intellectual, the revolutionary refugee Emanuel Vitalis Scherb, who knew Hebrew and who aroused the poet's interest in the Talmud.

[1] John J. Appel, "Longfellow's Presentation of the Spanish Jews," *American Jewish Historical Society Publications*, XLV (1955), 22.

Longfellow wrote his first poem on a Jewish theme, in 1852, after he visited the city of Newport, which contained the oldest American synagogue and which had once been a thriving center of Jewish shipping and commerce. There he found not a single living Jew, because most offspring of the Colonial Jews had already been completely integrated into Christian families and into the Christian faith and the last professing Jew had left the town three decades earlier. The only Jews in Newport were the dead ones in the cemetery, reposing under weatherbeaten tombstones. In his diary, Longfellow included the following entry on July 9, 1852: "Went this morning into the Jewish burying-ground with a polite old gentleman who keeps the key. There are few graves. Nearly all are low tombstones of marble, with Hebrew inscriptions and a few words added in English or Portuguese. At the foot of each, the letters A.A.D.G. It is a shady nook at the corner of two dusty frequented streets, with an iron fence and a granite gateway, erected at the expense of Mr. Touro of New Orleans. Over one of the graves grows a weeping willow—a grandchild of the willow over Napoleon's grave in St. Helena." [2]

These silent Hebrews in their graves close to the teeming streets of the seaport town reminded Longfellow of their past activities during former generations when they had erected the magnificent, deserted synagogue and had worshipped God there in the ancient Hebrew. His poem, entitled *The Jewish Cemetery at Newport,* lamented that the portals of the synagogue were closed, that no Psalms of David broke the silence within the venerable walls, and that no rabbi was there to read the ancient Decalogue in the grand dialect of the prophets. The Jews had come to Newport to escape Christian hate and merciless persecution. Abroad they had dwelt in narrow streets and obscure lanes, amidst mirk and

[2] *American Jewish Historical Society Publications,* X (1902), 170.

mire. Theirs had been a life of anguish, mocked and jeered
and spurned by Christian feet.

> Pride and humiliation hand in hand
> Walked with them through the world where 'er
>   they went;
> Trampled and beaten were they as the sand,
> And yet unshaken as the continent.

Yet, these very Jews who in the Old World had withstood
the attacks of all the bleak centuries gave up their separateness in the New World and dissolved in its free atmosphere.
Only in the cemetery did they survive as dead relics of a
glorious past. As a distinct group, Jews were beyond hope of
resurrection:

> But ah! what once has been shall be no more!
> The groaning earth in travail and in pain
> Brings forth its races, but does not restore,
> And the dead nations never rise again.

In earlier drafts of the poem, Longfellow had included three
stanzas about the constant harassment of the Jews and about
their finding surcease from oppression only in the grave. He
also had a different closing stanza which is omitted in the
published version:

> Ah, long they wandered over land and wave,
> The world around them but a waste of sand;
> And only from the hillock of the grave,
> With dying eyes beheld the Promised Land.

Longfellow was sad that these picturesque figures of a
hoary past were fading from the American scene but he never
doubted that their historic fate was sealed and that they
would disappear completely in the American ethnic amalgam. He had come to know such an exotic Jew in Isaac

Edrehi, a son of the learned mystic and cabbalist Moses Edrehi of Morocco. The elderly Edrehi had travelled far and wide and, in addition to Hebrew books, had published in London in 1836 *An Historical Account of the Ten Tribes.* This weird book, full of esoteric references, was a collection of curious matters relating to Jews in various parts of the world but especially the Jews supposedly settled beyond the mythical Sambatyon River. The younger Edrehi had lived with his father in Morocco, Jerusalem, Amsterdam and London, before emigrating to America. Here he sought to gain subscribers to reprint his father's book and probably met Longfellow in Boston before 1858, while soliciting subscriptions. Edrehi ended as a physician in Philadelphia. Of his descendants, J. Montrose Edrehi was in the nineteen-sixties a prominent lawyer in Pensacola, Florida.

The Jew, described by Longfellow in the *Prelude* to *Tales of a Wayside Inn,* was probably a synthetic poetic figure based not only on the poet's recollection of the living younger Edrehi but also on the portrait of the older Edrehi which looked out from the frontispiece of the strange volume published in Boston. The Spanish Jew was described as follows:

> A Spanish Jew from Alicant
> With aspect grand and grave was there;
> Vender of silks and fabrics rare,
> And attar of rose from the Levant.
> Like an old Patriarch he appeared,
> Abraham or Isaac, or at least
> Some later Prophet or High-Priest;
> With lustrous eyes, and olive skin,
> And, wildly tossed from cheeks and chin,
> The tumbling cataract of his beard.
> His garments breathed a spicy scent
> Of cinnamon and sandal blent,

Like the soft aromatic gales
That meet the mariner, who sails
Through the Moluccas, and the seas
That wash the shores of Celebes.
All stories that recorded are
By Pierre Alphonse he knew by heart,
And it was rumored he could say
The Parables of Sandabar,
And all the Fables of Pilpay,
Or if not all, the greater part!
Well versed was he in Hebrew books,
Talmud and Targum and the lore
Of Kabala; and evermore
There was a mystery in his looks;
His eyes seemed gazing far away,
As if in vision or in trance
He heard the solemn sackbut play,
And saw the Jewish maidens dance.[3]

Longfellow had this Spanish Jew relate four tales. Two of these, "Kambalu" and "Scanderberg" were of non-Jewish content. The other two, "Azrael" and "The Legend of Rabbi Ben Levi" centered about the Angel of Death.

The theme of "Azrael" is that no person, high or low, can escape death. The effort to do so only facilitates its coming. This is illustrated in the case of a Rajah of Hindostan who, while visiting King Solomon, saw there a white figure in the twilight air. When King Solomon explained that this was a figure he knew well, that it was the Death-Angel called Azrael, the Rajah implored his host:

"Save me from Azrael, save me from death!
O king, that hast dominion o'er the wind,
Bid it arise and bear me hence to Ind."

[3] H. W. Longfellow, *Complete Poetical Works*, Boston, 1893, p. 206.

The king pleased his guest and gave the appropriate command to the wind, which thereupon seized the Rajah and transported him to his native land.

> Then said the Angel smiling: "If this man
> Be Rajah Runjeet-Sing of Hindostan
> Thou hast done well in listening to his prayer;
> I was upon my way to seek him there."

The legend of Rabbi Ben Levi was told to Longfellow by his friend Emmanuel Vitalis Scherb. It narrates how the old, saintly Rabbi obtained the Death-Angel's sword by a ruse and leaped with it into Paradise. Compelled to return it upon God's command, he did so but only on condition that no human eye should ever again look on it in the final hour of severance from life.

Another Talmudic legend which Longfellow printed in the *Atlantic Monthly* in April 1858, was that of "Sandalphon," the Angel of Prayer. According to a story attributed to Isaac M. Wise, the leader of American Reform Judaism, Longfellow learned of this legend during a visit which this rabbi made to his home. As they walked beneath the elms, the poet was so impressed by the marvellous tale of this Angel of Glory that it haunted him and held him entranced until he reduced it to verse.[4] In reality, Longfellow knew this story from John Peter Stehelin's *The Traditions of the Jews,* which was published in London in 1732. He owned a copy of this volume and underlined five passages, all of them referring to Sandalphon. He may either have discussed the legend further with Rabbi Wise after reading it or else Rabbi Wise may have called his attention to this published version. In either case, Stehelin must be accepted as Longfellow's principal source. Another source was Heinrich Corrodi's *Kritische Geschichte des Chiliasmus,* where the legend also appeared

---

[4] *American Jewish Historical Society Publications,* 1902, X, 170.

and was read to the poet by Scherb on November 2, 1857.

Longfellow's interest in Jewish material also led him to attempt a five act verse drama *Judas Maccabaeus*. In 1850, he thought of writing a poem on this subject but not until more than two decades later, in December 1871, did he give this thought fruition by dramatizing the collision between Judaism and Hellenism. His source was Josephus and, considering the fact that he worked on this drama less than a dozen days, not much more than a smooth versification of his source could be expected of this bard who was more gifted in lyric and narrative verse than in drama.

Of Longfellow's New England contemporaries, none was more steeped in Biblical lore than John Greenleaf Whittier. He constantly utilized Biblical imagery and Biblical vocabulary. But he also made repeated use of post-Biblical Jewish subjects in his poetry.

Although Whittier was a fervent Quaker, he nevertheless felt that no religious sect should claim exclusive right to truths which God was dispensing to all mankind like rain and sunshine. God was manifesting himself to all races and peoples, the lowly as well as the haughty. No matter how strange any creed or ritual might seem, there must be emanating from it some hints of divine law. No one religious scroll encompassed the entire fulness of God's truth. This truth was to be found in Vedic verses, in classics of Cathay sages, in Koran and Talmud, no less than in the Old and New Testaments. Hence, for more than half-a-century, Whittier also sought inspiration in post-Biblical themes.

In 1829, he retold in "Judith at the Tent of Holofernes," the heroic story of Israel's lone and peerless maiden of Bethulia whom stern patriotic duty led to avenge her people's wrong upon Assyria's champion.

In 1837, in a poem entitled "Palestine," Whittier sang of his ardent longing for the blessed land of Judea, which he could traverse only in imagination. Its historic hills and dales live

within him. He looks out from the goat-crags of Mount
Tabor to catch the gleam of Galilee's dark waters.

> Hark, a sound in the valley! where, swollen and
>   strong,
> Thy river, O Kishon, is sweeping along;
> Where the Canaanite strove with Jehovah in vain,
> And thy torrent grew dark with the blood of the
>   slain.

> There down from the mountains stern Zebulon came,
> And Naphthali's stag, with his eyeballs of flame,
> And the chariots of Jabin rolled harmlessly on,
> For the arm of the Lord was Abinoam's son!

> There sleep the still rocks and the caverns which
>   rang
> To the song which the beautiful prophetess sang,
> When the princes of Issachar stood by her side,
> And the shout of a host in its triumph replied. . . .

> And throned on her hills sits Jerusalem yet,
> But with dust on her forehead, and chains on her
>   feet;
> For the crown of her pride to the mocker hath
>   gone,
> And the holy Shechinah is dark where it shone.[5]

After the Biblical poems on "Ezekiel," written in 1844, and
on Samson in the monologue "The Wife of Manoah to Her
Husband," written in 1847, Whittier composed his best
poem on a Jewish theme "The Two Rabbins" in 1868.

One of the Rabbis was the sage Nathan, who walked
blameless through the evil world until at fifty he met a temptation too strong to resist and he sinned miserably. As atonement, he put on sackcloth and ashes and set out for Ecbatana

[5] J. G. Whittier, *Complete Poetical Works*, Boston, 1894, p. 419.

to lay his sin before the wise and righteous Rabbi Ben Isaac. Before the gates of this city Rabbi Nathan encountered another sinner who was setting out to seek consolation from him. It was Rabbi Ben Isaac. Each forgot his own troubles, in the agony and stress of pitying love. Each made the woes of the other his own. Each prayed for the other.

> Peace, for his friend besought, his own became;
> His prayers were answered in another's name;
> And, when at last they rose to embrace,
> Each saw God's pardon in his brother's face!

> Long after, when his headstone gathered moss,
> Traced on the targum-marge of Onkelos
> In Rabbi Nathan's hand these words were read:
> "Hope not the cure of sin till Self is dead;
> Forget it in love's service, and the debt
> Thou canst not pay the angels shall forget;
> Heaven's gate is shut to him who comes alone;
> Save thou a soul, and it shall save thy own! " [6]

In a note of June 1868, Whittier referred to this poem as "a fantasy of mine, which I like better than most things I have written of late." [7]

In 1877, Whittier versified a lovely legend about King Solomon and the Queen of Sheba. Entitled "King Solomon and the Ants," it deals with an incident during the procession of the Jewish monarch and the Ethiopian queen out from Jerusalem. As the wisest of mortals, Solomon knew the languages of all creatures, great and small. While the king's path led across an ant-hill, he overheard the ants complaining that the good and just king was about to crush them heedlessly under his feet. When he told the Queen of Sheba of

[6] *Ibid.*, p. 92.
[7] S. T. Pickard, *Life and Letters of John Greenleaf Whittier*, Boston, 1894, II, 531.

their complaint, her first reaction was that these lowly creatures should be happy to perish beneath the feet of a God-anointed king. But Solomon thought, on the contrary, that the wise and strong should be solicitous of the welfare of the weak. And he turned his horse aside. His retinue followed his example and the ant-hill was unharmed. Then did the Queen grasp the secret of Solomon's worth and wisdom. Then did she realize that his kingdom was happy because he heeded the murmurs of the poor far more than the flattery of the great.

Whittier's last poem on a Jewish theme was "Rabbi Ishmael," written in 1881. His source was a Talmudic passage about the High Priest Ishmael Ben Elisha, who once entered the Holy of Holies to burn incense and there beheld the Lord of Hosts sitting upon a throne. And the Lord asked the priest's blessing. Ishmael replied: "May it please Thee to make Thy compassion prevail over Thine anger; may it be revealed above Thy other attributes; mayest Thou deal with Thy children according to it, and not according to the strict measure of judgment." And it seemed to Rabbi Ishmael that God bowed his head in assent, as though to answer "Amen" to this blessing.

Whittier, who was inspired by this passage, could not as a Christian reconcile himself to the concept of man blessing God, a concept acceptable to the Jewish source, and so he modified it. He has the voice of the Lord ask Ishmael what blessing he desired for man. And the High Priest pleaded with the Almighty to let mercy prevail beyond all judgments, a blessing which the Eternal readily and gladly granted.

Beautiful as is this poem of Whittier, it nevertheless completely reverses the moral implicit in the Talmudic passage, namely that God needed man's blessing even as man needed God's. Though based on a Jewish source, "Rabbi Ishmael" is permeated by Christian sentiment.

Like other New England poets, Oliver Wendell Holmes

too grew up in an environment that stressed Biblical precepts and that was filled with admiration for Biblical Jews. He had, however, no contact with living Jews until he went abroad to study medicine in Paris. His father, the Reverend Abiel Holmes (1763–1837), was an orthodox Calvinist minister who had studied at Yale during the incumbency of Ezra Stiles, its president from 1777 to 1795. The father had written a biography of Stiles in which he stressed the latter's interest in Hebrew and Jewish culture. Young Holmes, in a letter to his parents on November 4, 1834, wrote that in Paris he was meeting all sorts of people and that he found Jew and Gentile differed much less in real life than he had assumed on the basis of his previous reading. The pleasant cooperation of Jew and non-Jew came to his attention a few years later when he learned that the New Orleans Jewish philanthropist Judah Touro and the non-Jewish Boston merchant Amos Lawrence had agreed to share equally the expense of completing the Bunker Hill Monument. When this monument was dedicated by President John Tyler on June 17, 1843, Holmes recited a poem in honor of the two patriotic donors.

> Amos and Judah—venerated names,
> Patriarch and Prophet press their equal claims,
> Like generous coursers running "neck to neck,"
> Each aids the work by giving it a check,
> Christian and Jew, they carry out one plan,
> For though of different faith, each is in heart
>   a Man.[8]

Holmes had no patience with prejudice against Jews. He held that a person's religious thinking and choice of church

[8] Oscar Kraines, "The Holmes Family and the Jews," *Chicago Jewish Forum*, XVII (1958), 30.

and worship should be respected by all men, especially by those who professed deep religious feelings.

In *The Professor at the Breakfast Table*, 1859, he wrote that "the story of sweating gold was only one of the many fables got up to make the Jews odious and afford a pretext for plundering them." He felt that antisemitism would disappear as soon as the Christian world would learn modesty and humility and would stop overestimating itself. Then the Hebrews would partake of the general benefit which would accrue to mankind. He had become aware of unconscious bigotry in his own soul and had fought it. He depicted this struggle within himself in a poem which he composed and recited as early as 1856 under the title "A Hebrew Tale," but which he rewrote in 1874 and published under the new title "At the Pantomime."

In this poem, Holmes described his attendance on a hot August day at a pageant which was crammed with people from roof to floor. The audience included quite a few black-bearded, swarthy Hebrews and dark, orient-eyed, bejewelled women. He felt most uncomfortable in their midst. He imagined that the hook-nosed Jew at his left, with the coal-black hair and the smoke-brown hue, must be a sneaky usurer, a ducat-sweating thief, and a cheat. He saw in him a spawn of the race that slew Christ. He recalled grisly stories of Jews who caught Christian children and crucified them. However, as the show went on, his conscience began to trouble him. He looked at his neighbor at the right, a Jewish boy of olive hue, dark curls, and gentle, loving eyes, and imagined that the Boy of Bethlehem, born to the Virgin Mary, must have looked thus. Then he felt ashamed of his prejudice towards these people whose peerless blood flowed unmingled since time immemorial. In what way were his ancestors, the Norman thieves and Danish pirates, any better than the He-

brews whose frame the Lord of Glory deigned to wear? How
could one scorn these kinsmen of Jesus?

> I see that radiant image rise,
> The flowing hair, the pitying eyes,
> The faintly crimsoned cheek that shows
> The blush of Sharon's opening rose,—
> Thy hands would clasp his hallowed feet
> Whose brethren soil thy Christian seat,
> Thy lips would press his garment's hem
> That curl in wrathful scorn for them!
>
> A sudden mist, a watery screen,
> Dropped like a veil before the scene;
> The shadow floated from my soul,
> And to my lips a whisper stole,—
> "Thy prophets caught the Spirit's flame,
> From thee the Son of Mary came,
> With thee the Father deigned to dwell,—
> Peace be upon thee, Israel!" [9]

While the best poems about Jews were being written by
the New England poets, nevertheless, these poems were
basically Christian in sentiment and not Jewish. They were
the literary products of sensitive outsiders who looked in
upon the Jewish scene, admired the Jewish past, tolerated the
Jewish present, and were indifferent to a Jewish future. Not
until the twentieth century were native Jewish poets to arise
who were steeped in Jewish traditions and who were able, by
peering into their own hearts, to give intimate and adequate
expression to Jewish sentiment and to aspirations of the Jewish soul. A modest beginning was made in the nineteenth
century, however, by three women poets of limited talent but
deep love for Jewishness: Adah Isaacs Menken, Penina
Moise, and Emma Lazarus.

[9] O. W. Holmes, *Complete Poetical Works*, Boston, 1895, p. 189.

Chapter IV

THE NINETEENTH CENTURY
JEWISH LYRIC

The first American lyricist of Jewish origin whose fame reached out to a wide audience was Adah Isaacs Menken. However, it was less her poetic talent than her personality which fascinated her contemporaries and which has held the interest of biographers until the present. One of her biographers. E. C. Mayne, in his volume of 1909 *Enchanters of Men,* included her among the outstanding sirens of all times. Another, Nat Fleischer, entitled his life story of her, published in 1941, *The Reckless Lady.* A third, Allen Lesser called her *La Belle Menken* in his study of 1938 and *The Enchanting Rebel* in his more extensive biography of 1947. Swinburne wrote of her "Lo, this is she that was the world's delight," and immortalized her in his own verses under the name of Dolores, the Lady of Pain.

Many are the stories she told of her origin and early years, imaginative stories with here and there a grain of truth, and these confused her first biographers. It seems probable that she was born on June 15, 1835, in the village of Milneburg, a suburb of New Orleans, and it is certain that she died in Paris on August 10, 1868. But who her parents were long remained a mystery and the long list of her lovers, ranging from monarchs and princes to famed authors on two continents, once had publicity value but is based on only slender factual evidence.

Some biographers maintained that she was the daughter of a Scot, James McCord, and a lady of French descent, and that she was baptized as Adois Dolores McCord. In reality, she was born to a young Jewish couple and was given the name of Adah Bertha. When she was two years old, her father, whose family name was Theobold, died and her mother remarried.

The story that her stepfather was a Dr. Josiah Campbell, chief surgeon of the United States Army at Baton Rouge, is fiction. There is no evidence that such a person even existed. The man her widowed mother married was named Josephs. He was probably a lawyer. He died when Adah was fourteen. Her mother saw to it that she was given a good education in the classics and foreign languages. She also knew some Hebrew and must have been raised in Jewish traditions because she clung to her faith until her dying day and never throughout her theatrical career gave performances on Yom Kippur, the Day of Atonement. Tales of her early loves, a girlhood marriage, capture by Indians, a miraculous rescue by United States militia, are also hardly credible, although she herself was probably responsible for their dissemination.

Adah was twenty-one when she met a Jewish musician Alexander Isaac Menken, son of a Cincinnati drygoods merchant, and married him. Thereafter she preferred to be known as Adah Isaacs Menken, adding an *s* to her husband's middle name before adopting it as her own middle name. At first the couple lived with her family in New Orleans and then with his family in Cincinnati. In the latter city, Isaac M. Wise had founded *The Israelite* and it was in this weekly that her first poems appeared from September 25, 1857, to April 22, 1859. They were mainly of Jewish content, full of longing for her people's return to its pristine glory. In her opinion, it was not the destiny of the Jews to pine eternally in exile, scorned by many and pitied by a few. A homecoming to their own historic land was in store for them in the Messianic age,

which could not be long delayed. The Messiah must come
and effect their restoration.

> Awake! ye souls of Israel's land,
>   Your drowsy slumbers break;
> Rise! heart with heart—Rise! hand in hand!
>   All idle strife foresake! [1]

When her husband lost his wealth in the panic of 1857,
Adah, who had been trained in dancing, singing, and acting,
and who had had some experience with an amateur dramatic
group in New Orleans, supported herself and him by going
on the professional stage. Her success and his failure embit-
tered their marriage relationship. He took to drinking. Finally, he forced her to leave by giving her a rabbinical
divorce. She assumed that this religious divorce was legally
binding, even though they had also been married by a Justice
of the Peace in Texas. When she came to New York in 1859,
she fell in love with the handsome Irish heavyweight boxing
champion John Carmel Heenan and married him before he
left for England to fight for the world championship. Soon
thereafter, the story spread that she was still legally the wife
of Menken and a scandal broke out in the press. Heenan then
deserted her and even denied that he had ever been married
to her, although she was then expecting his child. The distracted actress reached the depths of despair when her baby
died and soon thereafter her mother. In the closing days of
1860, poor, homeless, and without a friend, she contemplated
suicide and composed lyrics of deepest gloom. By the middle
of the following year, however, she recovered sufficiently to
return to the stage, a fearless person, devoid of illusions and
matured in the crucible of pain.

She celebrated her greatest triumphs in the role of
Mazeppa, in a play adapted from Lord Byron's poem by

[1] Allen Lesser, *Weave a Wreath of Laurel*, New York, 1938, p. 31.

Henry Milner. Her daredevil stunt of being driven onto a steep ramp on the stage, strapped to a fiery steed and dressed in flesh-colored tights, was the sensation of the theatrical year 1861. Community after community went wild with enthusiasm.

In the midst of the Civil War, she, who was born a Southerner, never concealed her sympathy with the Confederate cause. As a result, she was arrested as a spy at the end of a Baltimore performance. Nevertheless, the following year she was said to have been the luncheon guest of President Lincoln, who invited her and her third husband, the satirical columnist Robert H. Newell, to the White House, discussed stage topics with her, and had her act out before him the sleepwalking scene from *Macbeth*.

During her stay in San Francisco, where she was adored as a goddess of the stage, she came to know Mark Twain, Bret Harte, Artemus Ward, and Joaquin Miller, but got into difficulties with her husband.

Joaquin Miller, one of her most ardent admirers, recalled the impression she made upon her California circle in these words: "Books, a shelf-load of books, could not hold the half that has been written of this Jewish woman's beauty of form. And beautiful she was in form; but to me her fascination lay in her beauty of mind; her soul and sweet sympathy, her sensibility to all that was beautiful in form, colors, action, life, heart, humanity." [2]

After divorcing Newell, she married a wealthy New Yorker James Barkley but soon separated from this fourth husband by sailing abroad. In Paris and London she enchanted old and young, from the aging Alexandre Dumas and Théophile Gautier to Rossetti, Burne-Jones, and Swinburne.

Swinburne described her enticing beauty in this stanza of "Dolores":

[2] Joaquin Miller, *Adah Isaacs Menken*, Ysleta, 1934, p. 6.

Thou art fair in the fearless old fashion
And thy limbs are as melodies yet,
And move to the music of passion
With lithe and lascivious regret;
What ailed us, O gods, to desert you
For creeds that refuse and restrain?
Come down and redeem us from virtue
Our Lady of Pain.

She replied to Swinburne with verses of her own "To A. C. S.":

We drank the red wine of desire,
My heart at a conqueror's feet,
And there flamed into celestial fire
A love that was bitter as sweet;
Now the idol I worshipped lies broken,
Its shrine is deserted and lone,
And over the desolate token
Time's black weeds have grown!

In 1868, she collapsed during a Paris rehearsal. She was visited during her final illness by many admirers, including the American poets Longfellow and Thomas Buchanan Read. She died about a week before her slender volume of selected lyrics appeared. It was entitled *Infelicia* and was dedicated to Charles Dickens. Its contents revealed a soul in torment, despite apparent worldly success and glory.

Of her Jewish poems, only two were included: "Judith" and "Hear O Israel." Her heroine Judith, who wanted to draw up wild passionate kisses from the bleeding mouth of Holofernes, anticipated Oscar Wilde's heroine Salome, who wanted to kiss the mouth of Iokanaan, even after the head was severed from the body.

"Hear O Israel" showed evidence of Walt Whitman's influence. She had met the poet during her stay in New York and had hailed him as a thinker who was centuries ahead of his contemporaries. She followed his free rhythms in these verses:

> Hear, O Israel! and plead my cause against the ungodly nation!
> 'Midst the terrible conflict of Love and Peace,
> I departed from thee, my people, and spread
>   my tent of many colors in the land of Egypt.
> In their crimson and fine linen I girded my white form.
> Sapphires gleamed their purple light from out the darkness of my hair.
> The silver folds of their temple foot-cloth was spread beneath my sandal'd feet.
> Thus I slumbered through the daylight.
>   Slumbered 'midst the vapor of sin,
>   Slumbered 'midst the battle and din,
>   Wakened 'midst the strangle of breath,
>   Wakened 'midst the struggle of death!

Most critics found the poems without merit, but one reviewer attributed them to Swinburne because of their excellence and Joaquin Miller reflected the extravagent evaluation of Menken, the poetess, by those who had felt the impact of her living personality, when he wrote: "If you care for poetry, grand, sublime, majestic, get this one little book of Adah Isaacs Menken and read it from lid to lid. It is the best that America has yet to offer in the line of sublime thought." [3]

What a contrast between the fiery, storm-tossed, unconventional, short-lived Menken, who whirled unsated through cities and lands, and her quiet, timid, respectable contemporary Penina Moise, the Jewish lyricist who throughout a

---

[3] Joaquin Miller, *Adah Isaacs Menken*, Ysleta, 1934, p. 5.

long life of eighty-three years rarely left her native town of Charleston, South Carolina!

Penina's father, Abram Moise, was born in Alsace but lived in San Domingo until the insurrection of 1791 forced him to flee the West Indian island and sail for Charleston. Here the poetess was born on April 23, 1797.

When she was twelve, her father died and she had to shift for herself. Compelled to leave school, she nevertheless continued to educate herself with the aid of books until she ruined her eyesight. "Blind, poor, and getting her living in her old age by keeping a little school, she yet created a literary salon to which the best minds of Charleston flocked. Her Friday afternoons were centers of intellectual intercourse. . . . Twenty-five years of blindness did not diminish her fondness for life's pleasures. She lived in books." [4]

In addition to her teaching, nursing, religious and charitable work, Penina Moise contributed lyrics to periodicals in Washington, Boston, New York, and New Orleans. She published in 1833 a volume of her poems entitled *Fancy's Sketchbook*. She composed for her Charleston synagogue a volume of hymns and verse renderings of the Psalms. Some of her hymns were sung for many years by American congregations. These hymns breathed submission to the will of God, no matter what fate befell one. They included hymns for Sabbaths, festivals, confirmations, school celebrations, and various special occasions.

Penina Moise's original poems rarely rise above mediocrity even when she is deeply stirred by outrages perpetrated against the Jews, as in her "Lines On the Persecution of the Jews of Damascus." Most moving is her final poem "A Farewell Message to All Friends," in which the old, blind, poor lyricist expressed her gratitude for a life well spent and for

[4] Penina Moise, *Secular and Religious Works*, Charleston, S.C., 1911, p. X.

friendships that made her existence, despite her frailties, a happy one.

Emma Lazarus, the third of the women-poets who pioneered in the Jewish lyric, was by far the most talented and the most influential. Her verses from "The New Colossus," 1883, engraved on the pedestal of the Statue of Liberty at the entrance to New York's harbor, voiced America's invitation to the underprivileged of the Old World to come and share in the freedom and opportunities of the New World:

> Give me your tired, your poor,
> Your huddled masses yearning to breathe free,
> The wretched refuse of your teeming shore;
> Send these, the homeless, tempest-tost to me,
> I lift my lamp beside the golden door!

The poetess was stirred to such verses by her experiences in getting to know at first hand the refugees from the Russian pogroms, in whom she recognized most valuable human material and also kinsmen.

Though descended of Sephardic lineage, she did not share the feeling of superiority toward the Eastern European Jewish immigrants which others of her circle assumed. She had lived as a shy and reticent girl, withdrawn from public affairs and surrounded by good books that stimulated her imagination and filled her with a sweet melancholy not unmixed with happiness, but she had been shocked into dynamic activity by the suffering she witnessed of Jews who had been victimized solely because of their Jewishness. Were not these Russian-Jewish immigrants experiencing a tragic fate comparable to that of her proud Sephardic ancestors who were expelled from their Iberian homes and forced to seek refuge in ever new and only rarely hospitable lands? Awareness of the common historic fate in which all Jews shared led her to abandon her cloistered life in the ivory tower, to hurl herself into relief and rehabilitation projects, and to use her poetic gifts to stir her lethargic co-religionists to a new birth.

The family into which Emma Lazarus had been born in 1849 was still adhering to rigid orthodoxy but assimilationist tendencies were beginning to make inroads upon the younger generation, as evidenced by one of her sisters marrying a Catholic and embracing the new faith. She herself in her early years had avoided Jewish themes. When at twenty-one she published *Admetus and Other Poems,* her interest lay in retelling in lyric forms the Greek tales of the King of Thessaly and of Orpheus and the medieval legends of Tannhäuser and of the saintly Lohengrin. At twenty-five, still reserved and unmarried, she retold in her novel *Alide* the story of Goethe and Friederike, the innocent, natural girl whom he loved but never married. Two years later, in 1876, *The Spagnoletto* was completed, a tragedy in five acts dealing with mid-seventeenth century Italy.

Not until after the appearance of George Eliot's *Daniel Deronda* in 1876, with its call for Jewish rejuvenation and ingathering in the Holy Land, did Emma Lazarus become aware that she no longer had to seek "heroic ideals in alien stock, soulless and far removed, in pagan mythology and mystic, medieval Christianity, ignoring her very birthright— the majestic vista of the past, down which high above flood and fire had been conveyed the precious scroll of the Moral Law." [5]

At first, the timid poetess could merely grope her way step by step but, as she gathered confidence in her power to lead and inspire, she began to stride more boldly until by 1882 she swept majestically onward and upward to the heights of prophecy.

Her Rosh-Hashanah poem of 1882 was a clarion call to her people to be reborn with the New Year. The future was full

[5] Emma Lazarus, *Poems,* Boston, 1889, I, 19.

of portent and promise. It was inviting Jews to renew ancient glory. She dreamed of a resurgence of Jewish creativity both in the hills of Judea and under the skies of Texas. The Jordan and the Rio Grande would be linked in a mystic chain, the rustle of Eastern palms and of broad Western prairies would unite in sweet rhythm and glad refrain. An age would dawn comparable to the Golden Age of Spanish Jewry when Jewish troubadours sang lyrics of ardent love for Israel, their eternal bride.

Fascinated by the medieval Sephardic poets Yehuda Halevi, Moses ibn Ezra, and Solomon ibn Gabirol, she undertook to translate them into English despite her inadequate knowledge of Hebrew. Fortunately, she was able to make use of the excellent German adaptation of the original texts by Michael Sachs in his *Religiöse Poesie der Juden in Spanien,* a volume which had also inspired Heinrich Heine. Her translation, which she completed in 1879, led Gustav Gottheil, Rabbi of Temple Emanuel of New York, to invite her to write religious hymns based on the Hebrew for Jewish Reform congregations who were increasingly using English in their rituals. She was willing to assist the rabbi but confessed that she had no real religious fervor in her soul. She was no Penina Moise, impelled by religious need and with gaze directed back to a glorious past. She was preparing to join in a call for a more glorious future for a revitalized Jewish people. She was working on a play *The Dance of Death,* which she completed before 1882 and in which she personified herself in the heroine Liebhaid von Orb.

In this distracted maiden, torn between love for a princely suitor who offered unfathomed joy and her devotion to a persecuted people who were about to undergo martyrdom, the poetess dramatized her own inner conflict between the radiant Anglo-American world of letters which beckoned and lured and the Jewish masses who were in desperate need of an articulate voice to give utterance to their agony and hope. Her decision was made: "I am all Israel's now. Till this cloud pass—I have no thought, no passion, no desire, save for my people."

With missionary zeal, the frail poetess undertook to defend her people against all detractors and defamers. When an article appeared in the April 1882 issue of *The Century Magazine* justifying the terroristic acts of the Russian mobs against their Jewish neighbors, she replied in the following issue of the periodical with a devastating attack upon the apologists for pogroms. She expressed her pride in belonging to a people that was the victim of massacres rather than to one that perpetrated massacres. She held that it required heroism to choose to remain a Jew when every bribe, spiritual and secular, was held out by modern society to persuade Jews to become converts to the dominant faith. On Ward's Island, New York, were quartered hundreds of homeless refugees, men of brilliant talents, scholars familiar with ancient and modern tongues. She had seen them huddled together, engaged in menial drudgery, but burning with zeal in the cause of Jewishness. These despoiled exiles were heroes and not degenerates. They were her brothers, despite their shabby dress and strange jargon.

In the spirit of this essay, she wrote a series of prose poems entitled *By the Waters of Babylon,* the last of which ended with the following invocation: "But thou—hast thou faith in the fortune of Israel? Wouldst thou lighten the anguish of Jacob? Then shalt thou take the hand of yonder caftaned wretch with flowing curls and goldpierced ears; Who crawls blinking forth from the loathsome recesses of Jewry; Nerveless his fingers, puny his frame; haunted by the bat-like phantoms of superstition is his brain. Thou shalt say to the bigot, 'My Brother,' and to the creature of darkness, 'My Friend.' And thy heart shall spend itself in fountains of love upon the ignorant, the coarse, and the abject. Then in the obscurity thou shalt hear a rush of wings, thine eyes shall be bitten with pungent smoke. And close against thy quivering lips shall be pressed the live coal wherewith the Seraphim brand the prophets."

Emma Lazarus was prepared to accept the burden and the blessing of a prophetess. She felt that the time had come for Jews to undertake vigorous and concerted action to reestablish themselves as an independent nationality. She asked them to awaken from their assimilationist delusions, to raise again the banner of the Jew, to let resound once more the battle-anthems that led them to victory over pagans and idolators and that ennobled them even in defeat, when, as the smallest of nations, they took up arms under Bar Kochba against the moral tyranny of the greatest of nations. The martial stanzas of her lyric "The Banner of the Jew" demanded of her lethargic Jewish contemporaries that they exchange their comfortable but unheroic life for a more difficult but more meaningful existence:

Oh for Jerusalem's trumpet now,
    To blow a blast of shattering power,
To wake the sleepers high and low,
    And rouse them to the urgent hour!
No hand for vengeance—but to save,
    A million naked swords should wave.

Oh deem not dead that martial fire,
    Say not the mystic flame is spent!
With Moses' law and David's lyre,
    Your ancient strength remains unbent.
Let but an Ezra rise anew,
    To lift the Banner of the Jew!

A rag, a mock at first—ere long
  When men have bled and women wept,
To guard its precious folds from wrong,
  Even they who shrunk, even they who slept,
Shall leap to bless it, and to save.
Strike! for the brave revere the brave!

In a lyric "The New Ezekiel," she prophesied that the dead bones of her people, whose sap was dried by twenty scorching centuries of wrong, would soon revive and take on flesh. Jews would resume a national existence on their hallowed soil. She tried to open Jewish eyes to the beauty and grandeur of the Hebraic past and to the opportunities that could arise for a Jewish future. If Jews were to experience a national revival, vast vistas would open up for all mankind. The historic group from whose hands dropped the seed out of which grew Christianity and Islam would again sow seeds for humanity's future growth.

Philip Cowen, editor of *The American Hebrew,* opened the columns of this influential periodical to her and invited her to outline in detail her ideals for reforming and deepening Jewish life. She did so in a series of sixteen epistles to the Hebrews. As against the extremes of religious petrification, on the one hand, and the gradual elimination of distinctions between Jews and their neighbors, on the other hand, she felt that the Jews were a distinct people and that they could best promote the advancement of all peoples by retaining their uniqueness and living it at the highest possible level of moral and intellectual eminence. If they were to serve as a beacon-light unto all the nations, they must furnish an example of healthy living by returning to the soil and accepting the dignity of labor as a Jewish article of faith. Jews needed brawn as well as brains, strong bodies as well as subtle minds. Their education must be geared to practical tasks, but not exclusively. The farmer, the mechanic, the tradesman, every Jew ought to devote his leisure hours to study for its own sake, since love of learning was a basic Jewish trait. Democratic solidarity must prevail. Every Jew must feel the sting of every wound and insult inflicted upon any of his kin anywhere in the world. He must rally to protect the victims of anti-Jewishness on all continents. He must work for the resettlement of a majority of the Jews in a national homeland. The possible breakup of the Turkish Empire might offer a splendid opportunity. Jews had only to unite, to watch, to wait and to be ready for action when the hour of national redemption struck. At such an hour, Jews would stream to the Holy Land from the lands of the Diaspora where they were denied elementary human rights. But from the emancipated countries of Europe and America, where Jews shared all the civil and religious privileges of their compatriots, idealistic pioneers would also be required who would give of their skills and serve as leaders and counselors.

The poetess envisaged the rise and growth of two strong centers of Jewish creativity, Palestine and America. In both lands Jewish faith would flourish, Jewish talent would thrive and Jewish culture would dispense gifts to the Eastern and Western cultures in a constant interchange with these no less valuable cultures in which it would be embedded.

Laurence Oliphant, the British diplomat, novelist, and non-Jewish pioneer of Zionism, reacted to the epistles of Emma Lazarus and asked her to get the American government's support for his Gilead project, the opening up of a Transjordanian region, north of the Dead Sea, for mass settlement by Jews. He had already obtained favorable reactions from British leaders such as Lord Beaconsfield and Lord Salisbury and from Jewish intellectuals such as Peretz Smolenskin and Samuel Mohilever. Was Emma Lazarus voicing American public opinion or dominant Jewish opinion in America?

Little did Oliphant know how negligible was the influence of the lyric dreamer upon American policy and how indifferent were her native, well-adjusted, prosperous, coreligionists to her breath-taking visions of Jewish national redemption in Palestine. The immigrants who were streaming from the Eastern European Pale to America's shores would have reacted more vigorously to her stimulating ideas, if they had known of them. But their language of communication was still Yiddish and not English. Decades were to pass before they were to attain to supremacy on the American Jewish scene and before they were able to embody the dreams of the Sephardic poetess Emma Lazarus and the thoughts of the Viennese aesthete Theodor Herzl in concrete deeds and mass activities.

CHAPTER V

LEGEND AND REALITY

With the beginning of mass immigration of Eastern European Jews in the eighteen-eighties, the reality of American Jewish life was bound to modify substantially traditional stereotypes. These stereotypes had not been based on actual contacts between Jews and non-Jewish creators of literature but were rather inherited from theological and fictional prototypes. The dominant theological prototype, imported by the Puritans, was the patriarchal Jew of the Old Testament, whose descendant was still supposed to have about him a gleam of ancient glory and an aura of angelic morality. The dominant literary prototype, by contrast, was the villainous Jew of the English motherland, as he had evolved during the centuries from Chaucer, Marlowe, and Shakespeare to Scott and Dickens. The German-Jewish peddler and the Russian-Jewish sweatshop worker bore no resemblance to either Father Abraham and Moses, on the one hand, or to Shylock and Fagin, on the other hand. Legend and reality were in conflict. Both writers and audiences had to be reeducated to accept the living human beings in their midst as more typically Jewish than the historic saints or the mythical bogies.

The New England poets had, on the whole, displayed a fondness for the patriarchal stereotypes and for Biblical subject-matter. Dramatists and novelists, however, were more addicted to the diabolical stereotypes and to modern themes.

The characteristics of the villainous Jew of stage and fiction were summarized by Edgar Rosenberg in his study *From Shylock to Svengali* as follows: "He was a fairly thorough-going materialist, a physical coward, an opportunist in money matters, a bit of a wizard in peddling his pharmaceutica; queer in his religious observances in so far as he still paid attention to them, clannish in his loyalties, secretive in his living habits, servile in his relations with Christians, whom he abominated; for physical signposts he had an outlandish nose, an unpleasant odor, and frequently a speech impediment also." [1]

In contrast to this villainous Jew, there was always his beautiful daughter, most attractive to Gentiles and wooed by them. Sometimes she was won by them and abandoned her faith for that of her successful suitor. At other times, she clung to her faith out of a sense of loyalty to her despised people and her unworthy father. But whether ending happily or tragically, the noble Jewess was and remained a paragon in word and deed. In English literature, the most famous of these Jewish heroines were Jessica, daughter of Shylock, in Shakespeare's *Merchant of Venice,* and Rebecca, daughter of Isaac of York, in Scott's *Ivanhoe.*

In American fiction, she was best portrayed by Nathaniel Hawthorne in the figure of Miriam in *The Marble Fawn,* 1860. This young lady, about whose origin many stories circulated, was to some extent modelled from a Jewess whom Hawthorne met in London. Her strange beauty stemmed from a certain rich Oriental character in her face. She was said to be the daughter and heiress of a great Jewish banker and to have fled from her paternal home to escape marriage to a cousin who had been selected for her because he too was the heir of another rich Jew. The purpose of the marital union was not the happiness of the couple but the retention

---

[1] Edgar Rosenberg, *From Shylock to Svengali,* Stanford, California, 1960, p. 35.

of the vast accumulation of wealth within the family. As an artist, Miriam preferred to sketch Jewish Biblical women. However, these women were heroines whose deeds in behalf of their people were cruel, bloody, demoniacal. Such a woman was Judith of Bethulia, who cut off the head of the Babylonian general Holofernes. Another was Jael, who drove a nail through the temples of Sisera. It was "as if Miriam had been standing by when Jael gave the first stroke of her murderous hammer, or as if she herself were Jael, and felt irresistibly impelled to make her bloody confession in this guise." [2] Miriam is aware that dark forces operated about her and within her. She tells Donatello, the Faun; "There is a great evil hanging over me! . . . It will crush you too, if you stand at my side. Depart then, and make the sign of the Cross, as your faith bids you, when an evil spirit is nigh. Cast me off, or you are lost forever." [3]

To Hawthorne, the Jews both at home and abroad were mysterious and exotic. In 1857, when in Italy, he visited the ghetto of Rome and described the Jewish district as the foulest and ugliest part of the city, as a place where thousands were crowded within a narrow compass and were leading a close, unclean, and multitudinous life, resembling that of maggots when they overpopulate a decaying cheese.[4] In his own immediate New England vicinity, he must have come across itinerant peddlers who roamed the countryside and in his story *Ethan Brand* he depicted such a German-Jewish immigrant who tried to make a living travelling with a diorama on his back and showing his tattered pictures to viewers at all hours of day or night. His gigantic, brown, hairy hand, with which he pointed out what purported to be cities, public edifices, ruined European castles, Napoleon's

[2] Nathaniel Hawthorne, *The Marble Faun,* New York, 1910, p. 33.
[3] *Ibid.,* p. 132.
[4] *Ibid.,* p. 327.

battles, and Nelson's sea fights, might have been mistaken for the Hand of Destiny. There was something uncanny about this eternal wanderer whom Ethan Brand recognized as a Jew of Nuremberg. Hawthorne reproduced this uncanniness but refrained from hinting at miserliness or excessive wealth. Apparently, a chance meeting with a peddling Jew, who was trying to make ends meet, led the novelist to the realization that not all Jews were members of a "golden brotherhood," as he had assumed on the basis of hoary legends and literary stereotypes.

American novelists were having difficulty in delineating Jewish peddlers and salesmen, since these, when encountered in the flesh, were not conforming to the stereotypes of fiction. They were not Fagins but fairly decent individuals and yet somehow different from the Yankee peddlers and hawkers. The Jewish salesman, depicted by Hamlin Garland in *Rose of Dutcher's Cooly,* 1895, was chubby-faced and no longer gaunt, smiling and no longer filled with resentment, a New Yorker by birth but equally happy amidst Chicago's hustle. While other characters had individual names, this Jewish person who lived in the same boarding-house was repeatedly referred to simply as the Jew. Only once was mention made of his name, Mr. Simons, when the heroine was informed that though the salesman was a Jew, "he's not too much of a Jew,"—a qualifying clause which was supposed to mitigate the stigma of his origin and to win sympathy for him as atypical of his group.

A German-Jewish salesman was also the central figure of a popular farce with melodramatic features which was the box-office success of 1881 in New York City and which continued to be performed season after season. It was entitled *Sam'l of Posen; Or The Commercial Drummer,* and its author was G. H. Jessup.

This play excellently illustrates the transition from earlier caricatures to later more realistic portraits of the Jew. Like preceding stage stereotypes, Sam'l retains the boundless energy and the irrepressible ambition to rise to the top and attain to wealth, but he differs from the established stage tradition by being scrupulously honest in all his dealings and ever faithful to the trust placed in him.

When in the first act Sam'l is given a temporary trial job as a stock clerk, he is absolutely sure of his ability to climb and he expects to own the business within a year. In the second act, which takes place a few months later, he has gotten to the position of being entrusted by his employer with the responsible task of transporting thousands of dollars worth of diamonds to a customer in New York. When the diamonds are stolen from him, he manages to get them back for the firm and to unmask the non-Jewish villain. He himself is certain that it pays to be honest toward everyone. He even goes out of his way to do good beyond the call of duty. When Mrs. Mulcahey, a mother of fourteen children, comes to pawn her shawl in order to buy medicine for her youngest child, Sam'l gives her the money, fills her basket with food, and then puts the shawl into it, muttering to himself in an aside: "A true Hebrew never goes back on the widows and orphans!"

The success of this play may be partly attributed to the fact that during the three or four years preceding its staging the Jews of New York had been at the forefront of controversy in press and literature, a controversy to which the Seligman-Affair had given rise.

Joseph Seligman was a prominent banker and a friend of President Grant. On passing Saratoga Springs with his family on May 31, 1877, he was refused a room at its largest and most fashionable hotel, the Grand Union, because he was a Jew. The humiliated banker brought this fact to the attention of the press. Judge Henry Hilton, braving the publicity, replied justifying the action. As executor of the estate of

A. T. Stewart, to whom the hotel belonged, it was his duty to conserve its value. Since hotels with Jewish guests were avoided by the best Christian clientele and therefore depreciated in value, he preferred to get along without Israelites as patrons or customers.

Soon battle lines were joined; newspapers took sides; and for three full years poems, orations, and pamphlets took up the issue and brought to the open insidious discriminatory practices which were beginning to mushroom in many communities. The most interesting defenses of the Jews were those undertaken by the novelist and poet Bret Harte, the preacher Henry Ward Beecher, and the atheist Robert G. Ingersoll.

Of the three, Bret Harte was the only one whose ancestry was partly Jewish. One of his grandparents was Bernard Hart, a member of a pioneering Canadian Jewish family. As a young man, he had come to New York in 1780, had prospered in business, and had participated actively both as an officer of the New York Stock Exchange and as a philanthropist and religious leader. He lived on until 1855, when he passed away at the age of ninety-one.

In his thirties, Bernard Hart was married for one year to a Christian mate, with whom he had a son Henry Hart, before separating and marrying into the prominent orthodox family of Rabbi Gershom Mendes Seixas and becoming a pillar of the synagogue.

Henry Hart's son, Bret Harte, was raised in a Christian home and normally did not react to Jewish matters. However, the Seligman-Affair did stir him to a satiric poem which appeared in June 1877, while the incident was being intensely debated.

The poem was entitled "That Ebrew Jew" and took issue with Hilton who, in a partial retreat from his earlier adamant stand, was claiming that he had no prejudices against Hebrews but was opposed only to Jews. Was an Israelite a Hebrew or a Jew?

The opening stanza referred to the rise to fortune of the Christian tradesman A. T. Stewart, who began as a petty shopkeeper and who ended as a department store owner and hotel proprietor. Though Hilton was not mentioned by name, he was easily recognizable, from the second stanza on, as the lawyer and friend of the tradesman.

There once was a tradesman, renowned as a screw,
Who sold pins and needles, and calicoes, too,
Till he built up a fortune—the which, as it grew,
Just ruined small traders the whole city through.
 Yet one thing he knew,
 Between me and you,
 There was a distinction
 'Twixt Christian and Jew.

Till he died in his mansion a great millionaire,
The owner of thousands, but nothing to spare
For the needy and poor who from hunger might drop,
And only a pittance to clerks in his shop;
 But left it all to
 A lawyer who knew
 A subtle distinction
 'Twixt Ebrew and Jew.

This man was no trader, but simply a friend
Of this gent who kept shop, and who, nearing his end,
Handed over a million—'twas only his due,
Who discovered this contrast 'twixt Ebrew and Jew.
 For he said, "If you view
 This case as I do,

There *is* a distinction
'Twixt Ebrew and Jew.

"For the Jew is a man who will make money through
His skill, his *finesse,* and his capital, too.
And an Ebrew's a man that we Gentiles can 'do'.
So you see there's a contrast 'twixt Ebrew and Jew."
    Ebrew and Jew,
    Jew and Ebrew—
    There's a subtle distinction
    'Twixt Ebrew and Jew.

So he kept up his business of needles and pins,
But always one day he atoned for his sins,
But never the same day (for that wouldn't do)
That the Jew faced his God with the awful Ebrew.
    For this man he knew,
    Between me and you,
    There was a distinction
    'Twixt Ebrew and Jew.

So he sold soda water and shut up the fount
Of the druggist whose creed was the Speech on the
    Mount;
And he trafficked in gaiters, and ruined the trade
Of a German whose creed was by great Luther made.
    But always he knew,
    Between me and you,
    A subtle distinction
    'Twixt Ebrew and Jew.

Then he kept a hotel—here his trouble began—
In a fashion unknown to his primitive plan.

For the rule of his house to his manager ran:
"Don't give entertainment to Israelite man."
  Yet the manager knew,
  Between me and you,
  No other distinction
  'Twixt Ebrew and Jew.

"You may give to John Morrissey supper and wine,
And Madame N.N. to your care I resign;
You will see that those Jenkins from Missouri Flat
Are properly cared for, but recollect that
  Never a Jew
  Who's not an Ebrew
  Shall take up his lodgings
  Here at the Grand U.

"You'll allow Miss McFlimsey her diamonds to wear,
You'll permit the Van Dams at the waiters to swear,
You'll allow Miss Decollete to flirt on the stair,
But, as to an Israelite, pray have a care.
  For, between me and you,
  Though the doctrine is new,
  There's a business distinction
  'Twixt Ebrew and Jew."

Now, how shall we know? Prophet, tell us, pray do,
Where the line of the Hebrew fades into the Jew?
Shall we keep out Disraeli and take Rothschild in?
Or snub Meyerbeer—and think Verdi a sin?
  What shall we do?
  Oh give us a few
  Points to distinguish
  'Twixt Ebrew and Jew.

There was One—Heaven help us!—who died in man's
    place,
With thorns on his forehead, but love in his face;
And when "foxes had holes," and birds of the air
Had their nests in the trees, there was no spot to spare
    For this "King of the Jews."
    Did the Romans refuse
    This right to the Ebrews
    Or only to Jews?

Henry Ward Beecher's sermon, entitled "Jew and Gentile," was delivered before his congregation during the very
same month in which Bret Harte's poem appeared. Beecher
told of his long friendship with the Seligman family, whose
behavior was above reproach. He then went on to eulogize
the Jews as unrivalled benefactors of the human race. He recounted the great Jewish achievements since they came upon
the historic scene. He pointed out that the promise originally
made to Abraham that in his seed would all the nations of the
earth be blessed had indeed been fulfilled. While the Greeks
may have carved better marble temples, the Jews carved better human beings, persons who hungered for righteousness,
who fought for liberty, who set an example of indomitable
courage in the face of adversity. "Are they in our poor-
houses? In which? Are they in our jails? Where? Are they in
our reformatories? Point them out. Do their women defile
our streets? You cannot find another people in America
among whom the social virtues are more rigorously taught
and observed than among the Israelites. . . . They are a
temperate people, and we are a drunken people. They are a
virtuous people, and we largely tend to be a lascivious people. They are a people excessively careful of their children,
and there is a great laxity among us in the education of the

household. We may well take lessons of them. They were the schoolmasters of our fathers, and we may well go to school to the same masters." [5]

Beecher's sermon made an emotional impact but did not change the facts of American life. Discrimination continued in fashionable hotels and summer resorts. At times, it was even openly acknowledged and defended. Austin Corbin, President of the Long Island Railroad, expressed his preference that Jews would not patronize his railroad even as passengers. Nor did he want them at Coney Island, which was to be developed as an exclusive resort for desirable people. When he tried to exclude the Jews from his Manhattan Beach Hotel in Brooklyn in 1879, they called upon their Christian friends to voice condemnation of his extreme action. Among those who responded was Robert G. Ingersoll, who castigated Corbin's attitude as bigoted, mean, disgraceful, reminiscent of the Dark Ages. Nevertheless, the practice, protested by some, defended by a few, and tolerated by many, continued until far into the twentieth century.

Lincoln Steffens, in his young days as a reporter, was sent by his editor to interview the proprietor of an hotel which excluded Jews and received the following explanation for the discriminatory practice: "I won't have one," said the proprietor. "I have had my experience and so learned that if you let one in because he is exceptional and fine, he will bring in others who are not exceptional, etc. By and by they will occupy the whole house, when the Christians leave. And then, when the Christians don't come any more, the Jews quit you to go where the Christians have gone, and there you are with an empty or a second-class house." [6]

In the original version of *The Rise of Silas Lapham,* which the novelist William Dean Howells printed in the *Century* magazine in 1884, he called attention to the unhappiness of

[5] H. W. Beecher, "Jew and Gentile," in *Menorah*, 1887, II, 203.
[6] Lincoln Steffens, *Autobiography*, New York, 1931, p. 244.

property-owners when Jews settled in their neighborhoods. This passage was omitted when the novel was reprinted in book form during the following year, partly because of the pressure of prominent Jews. The original text included the following conversation between Silas Lapham and his wife:

"It makes a difference in the price of property," replied the Colonel promptly. "But as long as we don't want to sell, it don't matter."

"Why, Silas Lapham," said his wife, "do you mean to tell me that this house is worth less than we gave for it?"

"It's worth a good deal less. You see, they *have* got in—and pretty thick too—it's no use denying it. And when they get in, they send down the price of property. Of course, there ain't any sense in it; *I* think it's all dumn foolishness. It's cruel, and folks ought to be ashamed. But there it is. You tell folks that the Saviour himself was one, and the twelve apostles, and all the prophets,—and I don't know but what Adam was— guess he *was*,—and it don't make a bit of difference. They send down the price of real estate. Prices begin to shade when the first one gets in."

Mrs. Lapham thought the facts over a few moments. "Well, what do we care, so long as we're comfortable in our home? And they're just as nice and as good neighbors as can be."

"Oh, it's all right as far as I'm concerned," said Lapham. "Who did you say those people were who stirred you up about it?"

Mrs. Lapham mentioned their name.[7]

After reading this passage, Cyrus L. Sulzberger, editor of the *American Hebrew*, wrote to Howells on July 12, 1885:

"As *The Rise of Silas Lapham* is about approaching completion and will, I presume, soon appear in book form, I beg

[7] *Century*, 1884, XXIX, 22–23.

to call to your notice a slur (Chapter II) upon a number of your readers and admirers—a slur as unmerited by the Jewish people as it is unworthy of the author. It is not alone upon the ignorant and uncultured of the Jews that you reflect, for neither 'the Saviour himself' nor the twelve apostles, nor the prophets, nor even Adam, were, so far as the records show, of that class which depreciated the value of property when they 'got in.'

"The introduction of the lines in question cannot even be excused on the ground that it serves a literary purpose, for no such end is accomplished. The sentiment is violently dragged in for no other ascertainable reason than to pander to a prejudice against which all educated and cultured Jews must battle. The literary leaders of a country have so great a power in fomenting or in repressing popular prejudice that I make bold to hope that in the permanent form in which *Silas Lapham* will no doubt soon appear, these objectionable lines will be omitted." [8]

Howells was in receipt of similar communications on the same subject from other Jews and therefore thought it more prudent to omit the controversial passage and also another one of like tenor later in the novel. He yielded reluctantly to a pressure which he did not feel was entirely justified, since he was stating a fact: property apparently did depreciate in value when a district became too Jewish. He recognized this fact and rebuked it as something civilized men should be ashamed of. Nevertheless, he struck out of his book the lines that might cause misunderstanding.

A year later, in 1886, he referred to this pressure in a conversation with Mark Twain, and the latter then related that his own experience with Jewish readers had been more fortunate. Indeed, he had been told by a Jewish friend that he

<hr>

[8] George Arms and W. M. Gibson, "Silas Lapham, Daisy Miller, and the Jews," *New England Quarterly*, 1943, XVI, 120.

"was the only great humorist who had ever written without poking some fun against a Jew." [9]

Mark Twain was proud of this record and in his essay "Concerning the Jews," he again quoted this Jewish friend: "A few years ago a Jew observed to me that there was no uncourteous reference to his people in my books, and asked how it happened. It happened because the disposition was lacking. I am quite sure that I have no race prejudices, and I think I have no color prejudices nor caste prejudices nor creed prejudices. Indeed, I know it. I can stand any society. All that I care to know is that a man is a human being—that is enough for me; he can't be any worse." [10]

Nevertheless, though enlightened intellectuals might be free of prejudices against Jews, hotel keepers and property owners had to reckon with the persistence of prejudices among large sectors of the American population. Robert G. Ingersoll deemed it outrageous that keepers of public establishments should brand an entire religious or ethnic group as unfit to associate with. "Every man should be treated justly and kindly, not because he is, or is not a Jew, or a Gentile, but because he is a human being, and as such, capable of joy or pain. If at any hotel a man fails to act in a decent and becoming manner, let him be put out, not on account of the nation to which he belongs, but on account of his behavior. Any other course is unjust and cruel." [11]

Ingrained prejudices did not, however, yield easily to appeals to reason.

Lafcadio Hearn, vacationing at Grande Isle near New Orleans in 1884, felt most uncomfortable because a majority of the vacationists at his hotel were Jews and he developed a violently antisemitic mood. Until this close contact with

[9] H. Smith and W. M. Gibson, *Mark Twain–Howells Letters*, Cambridge, Mass. 1960, II, 555.

[10] *Harper's Magazine*, September, 1899, p. 528.

[11] H. G. Ingersoll, *Letters*, New York, 1951, p. 683.

them, he had written pro-Jewish articles. Indeed, in the very same year, he had published the volume *Stray Leaves from Strange Literature,* in which he included six tales based on Jewish legends and Jewish folklore. Two years earlier, on July 9, 1882, he had retold marvellous tales from the Talmud in exquisite prose in an article entitled "A Peep Between the Leaves of the Talmud." A year before that, he had sung the praises of Lassalle, the Jew, in an article in the New Orleans *Item* of June 29, 1881. He called the socialist leader the Messiah of the Nineteenth Century and found the Germans unappreciative of the magnificent contributions made by their Jewish fellow-citizens. "And thus was a Jew worshipped by Freethinkers almost as another Jew is worshipped by Christians. Yet great as were the reforms obtained by Lassalle, unselfish as was his idealistic devotion to a grand Humanitarian purpose, deeply as the working-classes in Germany are indebted to him, neither Christians nor Freethinkers there seem at present inclined to remember that Lassalle and Heine too were Israelites. The aristocratic preachers are said to lead the rising against the Jews. Are they fearful, with good reason, lest that strange race might produce another terrible Heine and another Ferdinand Lassalle in the people's great Day of Judgment?" [12]

Despite such philosemitic sentiments, Hearn was so upset by the Jews he had to consort with in his hotel when on vacation that he wished there were no Jews in the world. While Jewesses were attractive and bewitching, the male specimens, card-playing merchants with German accents, were obnoxious and he was anxious to flee from them—"anywhere to escape from the shadow of the Jew. But the shadow pursueth me evermore." [13]

In 1885, Hearn wrote an editorial on the Jewish Question

[12] Lafcadio Hearn, *Occidental Gleanings,* New York, 1925, II, 172–173.
[13] E. L. Tinker, *Lafcadio Hearn's American Days,* New York, 1924, p. 369.

for the New Orleans *Times-Democrat* which the editor, Page Baker, refused to print because it was so abusive. It was probably based on the antisemitic diatribes of Edouard Drumont, whom Hearn was now prepared to accept as a reliable authority on Jews.

By 1886, Hearn recovered from his temporary prejudices against Jews, prejudices that erupted as a result of a few days' contact with a few unlovely Jews. He made amends by defending the Jewish group as on the whole far removed from the grotesque and villainous caricatures presented in fiction and on the stage. He recognized that unfortunately the Jew in tragedy and comedy had to be invariably shown as either hateful or absurd in order to satisfy audiences which had been raised on such literary fare for centuries. But Hearn no longer accepted the view that the real Jew was as repulsive as the imaginary Jew of the novelists and dramatists. He had come to the conclusion that the dominant stereotypes had no existence in any part of the real world. Jews were not usurers, thieves, murderers, or apostles, but normal human beings, indistinguishable in most respects from their neighbors. In that case, why should one present them on the stage as Jews rather than as Americans, Frenchmen, or Germans? "Why indeed? No one could give a rational and at the same time honest answer to that question. The truth is that the Jewish type proper disappeared with the demolition of the old ghettos; and that the Jews are now Frenchmen, Germans, Americans or Englishmen, like their fellow-citizens—nothing more." [14]

In later years, Hearn ceased to characterize his American contemporaries as either Christians or Jews. As a romanticist, he was not interested in emancipated Israelites but retained his literary interest in European ghetto-types, such as Leopold Kompert was nostalgically vivifying. Hearn recommended Kompert as the greatest Jewish story-writer of the

[14] Lafcadio Hearn, *Occidental Gleanings*, New York, 1925, II, 189.

age. Though unable to read the Bohemian Jewish narratives in the original German, he read them in a French translation, and adapted them for English readers.

While Jewish reality was making ever greater inroads upon American literature, writers who were not in frequent or intimate contact with Jews continued to regale American readers with Jewish bogies and moldy stereotypes. As late as 1899, Frank Norris, in his novel *McTeague* presented a Polish Jew who had not the slightest resemblance to the Polish-Jewish immigrants that were streaming into the mid-Western cities, but for whom Fagin of *Oliver Twist* might have served as model. As the personification of Jewish greed, Zerkow was introduced as follows: "He had the thin, eager, cat-like lips of the covetous; eyes that had grown keen as those of a lynx from long searching amidst muck and debris; and claw-like prehensile fingers—the fingers of a man who accumulates but never disburses. It was impossible to look at Zerkow and not know instantly that greed—inordinate, insatiable greed—was the dominant passion of the man. He was the Man with the Rake, groping hourly in the muckheap of the city for gold, for gold, for gold. It was his dream, his passion; at every instant he seemed to feel the generous solid weight of the crude fat metal in his palms. The glint of it was constantly in his eyes; the jingle of it sang forever in his ears as a jangling of cymbals." [15]

Greed was also the dominant trait of the international Jewish plutocracy which seized control of the world in Ignatius Donnelly's apocalyptic novel of 1890, *Caesar's Column, a Story of the Twentieth Century*. The author depicted the overthrow of civilization by an aristocracy of wealth which by the twentieth century was supposedly almost entirely of Hebrew origin.

Donnelly forewarned of gloomy days ahead if existing

[15] Frank Norris, *McTeague*, New York, 1899, p. 43.

tendencies in social and economic life were not checked before the end of the nineteenth century. He foresaw the possibility of a society which divided into two hostile camps, the camp of the capitalists, who would continue to grow ever richer and who would have great standing armies at their disposal, and the camp of the giant communistic organizations who would represent the poor among whom hatred and envy were bound to burn ever more fiercely. Ultimately, an explosion was inevitable. The longer the explosion was delayed, the greater would be its violence and devastation. With the collapse of the dominant dictatorship, anarchy was likely to take over and starvation would then wipe out the greater part of mankind.

Anticipating George Orwell's *1984*, Donnelly illustrated his thesis by means of phantasmagoric visions of an iron tyrannical rule in the twentieth century. The real government was by then in the hands of Israelite bankers, with kings, queens, and so-called presidents functioning as mere puppets, carrying on for the benefit of the financial coterie. The world had become Semitized. What Hannibal had failed to achieve, the subjugation of Latin and Germanic peoples to the Semitic merchants of Carthage, was successfully accomplished by the Israelite cousins of the Carthaginians. The nomadic children of Abraham had schemed their way from Palestinian tents to a power higher than all thrones. Before their august dominion, non-Jews lay as prostrate slaves.

How had all this come about? "It was the old question of the survival of the fittest. Christianity fell upon the Jews, originally a race of agriculturists and shepherds, and forced them, for many centuries, through the most terrible ordeal of persecution the history of mankind bears record of. Only the strong of body, the cunning of brain, the long-headed, the persistent, the men with capacity to live where a dog would starve, survived the awful trial. Like breeds like; and now the

Christian world is paying in tears and blood for the suffering inflicted by their bigoted and ignorant ancestors upon a noble race. When the time came for liberty and fair play, the Jew was master in the contest with the Gentile, who hated and feared him. They are the great money-getters of the world. They rose from dealers in old clothes and peddlers of hats to merchants, to bankers, to princes. They were as merciless to the Christian as the Christian had been to them. They said, with Shylock: 'The villainy you teach me I will execute; and it shall go hard but I will better the instruction.' The wheel of fortune has come full circle; and the descendants of the old peddlers now own and inhabit the palaces where their ancestors once begged at the backdoors for second-hand clothes; while the posterity of the former lords have been in many cases forced down into the swarming misery of the lower classes." [16]

One of the Russian Jews, a cripple who had been driven out of the synagogue, joined the Brotherhood of the Proletariat. With his ability and cunning, he was able to coordinate the American and European branches and become second in command. When the leader of the successful proletarian revolution, the great Caesar, celebrated the communist victory by an all night carnival, the Jewish Vice President fled in one of the large dirigibles with the treasure of the revolutionary regime. It was rumored that he proposed to make himself king in Jerusalem, to reestablish the glories of Solomon, and to revive the splendor of Judea, while the rest of the world went down to ruins and dissolved in anarchy.

Fortunately, a small group of idealists remained outside of the conflict. The novel could, therefore, end with their escape to an inaccessible spot in the heart of Africa. There a Utopian community was established by them based on Christian, democratic, and socialist principles. While barbarism

[16] Ignatius Donnelly, *Caesar's Column*, Chicago, 1891, pp. 36–37.

was sweeping the earth and human wolves prowled else-where, the small band of idealists in the Utopian village of Lincoln preserved the instrumentalities with which to restore civilization to the world at some future time.

The legend of Jewish wealth, Jewish cupidity, and Jewish power persisted in the literature of the eighteen-eighties and eighteen-nineties, even though the typical American Jew was by that time a peddler or a sweatshop worker. The fantastic fictions of Jewish bankers ruling the world was believed in, despite all evidence to the contrary, not only by the supersti-tious and the uneducated but also by some intellectuals of the highest American social and governmental circles. James Russell Lowell expressed the view that all bankers were Jews, that press and politics were dominated by Jews, that Jews had slipped into diplomacy and were becoming ambassadors, cabinet members, and even prime ministers, that they were emerging from ghettos and were inhabiting palaces and the most aristocratic quarters. Though admiring them as a race of great ability, he exaggerated their influence and power al-most to a pathological degree and suspected them of seeking to gain absolute control of governments and society.

A writer in the *Atlantic Monthly* recalled, in 1897, that when he met Lowell in Paris sixteen years earlier, he found that the subject of Jews was almost a monomania with this poet and diplomat. "He detected a Jew in every hiding-place and under every disguise, even when the fugitive had no sus-picion of himself. To begin with nomenclature: all persons named for countries or towns are Jews; all with fantastic, compound names, such as Lilienthal, Morgenroth; all with names derived from colors, trades, animals, vegetables, min-erals; all with Biblical names, except Puritan first names; all patronymics ending in *son, sohn, sen,* or any other version; all Russells, originally so called from red-haired Israelites; all Walters, by long descended derivation from wolves and foxes

in some ancient tongue; the Caecilii, therefore Cecilia Me-
tella, no doubt St. Cecilia too, consequently the Cecils, including Lord Burleigh and Lord Salisbury; he cited some old
chronicle in which he had cornered one Robert de Caecilia
and exposed him as an English Jew." [17]

After giving other illustrations of Lowell's obsession that
the insidious Jewish race had penetrated and permeated the
human family more universally than any other influence except original sin, the writer concluded his lengthy report of
the poet's conversations as follows: "Mr. Lowell said more,
much more, to illustrate the ubiquity, the universal ability of
the Hebrew, and gave examples and statistics for every statement, however astonishing, drawn from his inexhaustible in-
formation. He was conscious of the sort of infatuation which
possessed him, and his dissertation alternated between ear-
nestness and drollery; but whenever a burst of laughter
greeted some new development of his theme, although he
joined in it, he immediately returned to the charge with
abundant proof of his paradoxes. Finally he came to a stop,
but not to a conclusion, and as no one else spoke, I said, 'And
when the Jews have got absolute control of finance, the army
and navy, the press, diplomacy, society, titles, the government, and the earth's surface, what do you suppose they will
do with them and with us?' 'That,' he answered turning towards me, and in a whisper audible to the whole table, 'that
is the question which will eventually drive me mad.' " [18]

The most famous statement on Jews by Lowell, frequently
quoted as his tribute to them, must therefore be reinter-
preted as not necessarily stemming from any great admiration
for them. It was more likely dictated by awe and fear: "On a
map of the world you may cover Judea with your thumb,
Athens with a finger tip; but they still lord it in the thought

[17] H. E. Scudder, *James Russell Lowell*, Boston, 1901, II, 303.
[18] *Ibid.*, II, 305.

and action of every civilized man." [19] Although this statement by itself seems to equate Greeks and Jews as benefactors
of mankind, it assumes a different emphasis when related to
his other expressions about Jews. In reality, it confirms his
obsession that Jews were lording the world.

Similar obsessions stalked through the minds of his Boston
townsmen, Henry Adams and Brooks Adams. A letter by
Brooks Adams, under the date of July 26, 1896, stated as a
fact that England was as much governed by the Jews of Berlin, Paris, and New York as she was by her own native
growth. The writer suspected the existence of a vast syndicate
of Jewish bankers who controlled London and through London the entire world.[20] In the same year, Henry Adams
wrote, from Washington, that the Lombard Street Jews were
ruling England; from Milan, that the Jews were not sharing
the shock of the general panic but were bolstering stock-
exchanges and were carrying bankrupt governments with apparent confidence; from Paris, that Jew governments were in
charge there, also that "we are in the hands of Jews; they can
do what they please with our values." [21] This obsession continued to haunt him until the end of his life. As late as 1914,
he complained of the Jewish atmosphere that was developing
in Washington and of the difficulty of keeping Jews at a distance. "We are still in power, after a fashion. Our sway over
what we call society is undisputed. We keep Jews far away
and the anti-Jew feeling is quite rabid. We are anti-every-
thing and we are wild up-lifters; yet we somehow seem to be
more Jewish every day." [22]

With the streaming of poor, impoverished Jews to Amer-

[19] J. R. Lowell, *Harvard Anniversary Literary and Political Addresses*,
Boston, 1892, VI, 174.

[20] Thornton Anderson, *Brooks Adams, Constructive Conservative*, Ithaca,
N.Y., 1951, p. 60.

[21] Henry Adams, *Letters (1892–1918)*, Boston, 1930, pp. 98, 107, 111.

[22] *Ibid.*, p. 620.

ica's shores by the hundreds of thousands during the closing decades of the nineteenth century and the early decades of the twentieth, however, legends based on ignorance, prejudice, and long unquestioned assumptions were bound to give way in literature to a more accurate and more truthful appraisal of American Jewish reality.

CHAPTER VI

PERSISTENCE OF STEREOTYPES

The Jewish population of the United States doubled in the eighteen-eighties and doubled again in the eighteen-nineties, but the image of the Jew in American literature was still drawn to the largest extent not by them but by their non-Jewish contemporaries. The pioneering generation of Eastern European Jews on American soil used Yiddish as its main medium of communication and, except for Emma Lazarus, it found no adequate interpreter in the English tongue.

Henry Harland, who in the eighteen-eighties published four novels of Jewish life in New York, was not interested in the new immigrants but in the assimilating Israelites of German origin with whom he came in contact at the College of the City of New York. He attended this educational institution from 1877 to 1880. He also came under the influence of Felix Adler, then a young philosopher who was straining to break away from religious dogmatism. In the Society for Ethical Culture, Adler was gathering about himself a humanitarian group of Jews and non-Jews who sought to follow ethical ideals without at the same time accepting either Jewish or Christian rituals. Harland referred to such Jews as better educated individuals who were anxious to cast loose from their Judaism and to amalgamate with their neighbors in order to help form the American people of the future. His first novel, entitled *As It Was Written: A Jewish Musician's*

Story, appeared in 1885 under the pseudonym of Sidney Luska. This led readers and critics erroneously to assume that the author was of Jewish descent. Actually, he was descended from an English clock-maker and silversmith who had come from London to Connecticut on one of the tea-ships on the eve of the Revolution.

In two of his four novels, Harland preached a fusion of Jew and Gentile through intermarriage. In *Mrs. Peixada,* 1886, he resolved the misery of his Jewish heroine by marrying her to an Anglo-American lawyer. In *The Yoke of the Torah,* 1887, he showed his Jewish hero being driven to the point of insanity and death because an attempted union with a Gentile girl was frustrated by religious intolerance.

The former novel was well received by Jewish readers despite many deficiencies. Faced with two conflicting literary traditions in depicting Jewish male characters—the Jew as villainous and the Jew as patriarchal—Harland followed both by contrasting the monstrous Mr. Peixada, on the one hand, with the saintly Mr. Nathan, on the other hand.

Peixada was portrayed as a rich, old pawnbroker with a hawk's beak for a nose and a hawk's beak inverted for a chin. In between were two thin, blue, crooked lines across his face. They served as lips. The yellow fangs behind them shone horribly when he laughed. His eyes were two black, shiny beads, deep-set beneath black, shaggy brows, with the venomous malevolence of a leering demon aflame within them. His bald skull was kept warm by a red wig. His skin was wrinkled, dry, and sallow as old parchment. His voice was metallic, grating, cruel. His hands were writhing claws. Instead of fingers, he had long, brown, bony talons, with black, untrimmed nails.

To this toadlike person, the nineteen-year-old heroine Judith was given in marriage. If he had all the traits of the villainous stereotype, she had all those of the beautiful Jewess of romance: a suffering, silent face; a brow white as marble, crowned by black, waving hair; a nose and a chin modeled on the pattern of Juno; lips that were full and ruddy and tender; eyes that were translucent brown, eloquent of pathos and passion and mystery, and that sent an electric spark into the heart of whosoever gazed into them; hands that were shaped and colored to perfection and always animated; a voice soulful and exquisite like a clarion from heaven.

The plot of the novel was based upon Gutzkow's *Uriel Acosta.* Like the heroine Judith of the popular German tragedy, Harland's Judith was betrothed to the sixty-year-old pawnbroker because her father was heavily indebted to him and these debts could only be discharged by the marriage. The horrified girl had to go through with the ceremony in a sort of stupor, her brain dazed, her heart deadened. But her husband proved false to his part of the transaction. Instead of canceling her father's indebtedness as he had promised, he simply sold his claims and her father died bankrupt. From a living hell, Judith was saved by her husband's melodramatic murder and she ultimately ended as the happy wife of the Gentile hero Arthur Ripley.

When this novel was enthusiastically received in Jewish circles, Harland was encouraged to continue his narrative study of New York Israelites and intermarriage in his next novel *The Yoke of the Torah.* To his amazement, however, he found himself castigated for meddling in Jewish affairs by the very same circles. He was accused of instilling the poison of prejudice and the venom of malicious slander into the mind of the average American reader.

Harland had hoped that among liberal-minded Jews intermarriage would be accepted as a matter of personal choice and he had therefore inveighed in his novel against the intolerance of orthodox Jews, some of whom supposedly still clung to a bigoted notion that the most unpardonable sin in the eyes of the Lord was for a member of the Chosen People to marry a non-Jewess. Harland's principal character was a Jewish artist, Elias Bacharach, who fell in love with an ideal Gentile maiden and wanted to wed her. Jewish orthodoxy in the figure of a rabbinical uncle insisted, however, that the integrity of Israel must be preserved at all costs, even at the cost of individual happiness. Torn between love for the ideal Christian girl and the superstitious taboo of his people against intermarriage, the Jew got the better of the man. Elias stifled his love. He permitted his uncle, who had bowels of brass instead of bowels of mercy, to break off the marriage and to get him wedded to a mediocre Jewish girl with a snug sum of money as dowry. Thereafter, the unhappy Elias suffered all the hellish torture of remorse until his mind collapsed and death overtook him, thus atoning for his folly in bending under the yoke of the Torah and sacrificing love and happiness to satisfy an outmoded prejudice.

Harland's novel ran into a storm of criticism. The most violent reaction was voiced by Kaufmann Kohler, the champion of the liberal wing of Judaism. This rabbi of Temple Beth-El in New York protested against the author's pernicious influence upon the American scene. He found the Jewish characters in the narrative to be vulgar, uninteresting, and repulsive, while the Christian characters were painted in the most attractive colors. He accused Harland of disseminating a most dangerous libel in presenting the Torah as a declaration of perpetual war of clannish, exclusive, bigoted, intolerant, and superstitious Judaism against large-hearted, broad, and vigorous humanity. He warned the novelist not to court Haman-like fame but rather to steer clear of sensitive Jewish problems.

Harland defended himself by explaining that he had a warm love for the Jews but that, as a realistic writer, he had honestly depicted both laudable and low Jewish characters.

He declared his readiness to atone for any unintentional injury to his Jewish fellow-citizens by writing a fourth novel in which only higher and nobler German Jews would make their appearance.

In this fourth novel, *My Uncle Florimond*, 1888, the Jewish characters were unbelievably angelic. They went out of their way to do good. They made no distinction in their philanthropic deeds between their own co-religionists and their Christian neighbors or employees and they would not dream of opposing intermarriage.

This hastily written and poorly constructed novel was received in silence. The same Jewish press that had raised such a hue and cry over Harland's apparent antisemitism was indifferent to his philosemitism. He was deeply disappointed and ever thereafter he shunned the subject of Jewish-Gentile relationship. He had come to realize that this was too sensitive an area and too complex a subject for him to handle. He left America and joined aesthetic circles in Paris and London. As editor of the *Yellow Book,* organ of the English Symbolists and Decadents, he found a new field of activity and let his Jewish novels sink into oblivion.

Among non-Jews, Joaquin Miller, who visited Palestine in 1874, wrote several glowing tributes to the spirit of the Jewish people. He began his sketches of Palestinian life in *The Building of the City Beautiful* with a description of the enthusiastic reception accorded to the aging philanthropist Moses Montefiore in Jerusalem. In one of the "Songs of the Hebrew Children," he upbraided Russia for its hostility to the Jews. He held that the Russians had every reason to be grateful to the Biblical people and their descendants for taming the lawless Tartar blood and teaching moral conduct to skin-clad savages on the steppes. In another of these songs, he invited "Rachel in Russia" to leave the icy Volga for more hospitable America. In "A Song of Creation," he called upon those who jeered at the homeless, landless Jews to model their own family lives upon those of the Jews.

> Bear with me, I must dare be true.
> The nation, aye, the Christian race,
> Now fronts its stern Sphynx, face to face,
> And I must say, say here to you,
> Whate'er the cost of love, of fame,
> The Christian is a thing of shame—
> Must say because you prove it true,
> The better Christian is the Jew.[1]

Joaquin Miller's friend and America's foremost humorist Mark Twain published no less glowing tributes to the Jewish people in the essay "Concerning the Jews," which appeared in *Harper's Magazine* in September 1899. Beginning with a summary of all the marvelous qualities that commended the Jew as an ideal citizen, one who was quiet, peaceable, industrious, sober, honest, benevolent, unaddicted to high crimes and brutal dispositions, Mark Twain then raised the question as to why such a person was generally disliked. He volunteered the answer that the Jew was too intelligent for his neighbors, and this superior intelligence was resented. In the hard conditions imposed upon the Jew down the centuries, he could not survive without better brains and he had to keep these brains in good training and well sharpened or else starve. Prejudice against Jews was also intensified because he was everywhere substantially a stranger, despite efforts at assimilation, and strangers were normally disliked.

After suggesting that Jews might be able to ameliorate their condition by emulating the Irish-Americans and organizing politically, wherever they settled in considerable numbers, Mark Twain concluded with the following paean of praise: "If the statistics are right, the Jews constitute but one per cent of the human race. It suggests a nebulous dim puff

[1] Joaquin Miller, *Poetical Works*, New York, 1923, p. 529.

of star dust lost in the blaze of the Milky Way. Properly the Jew ought hardly to be heard of; but he is heard of, has always been heard of. He is as prominent on the planet as any other people, and his commercial importance is extravagantly out of proportion to the smallness of his bulk. His contributions to the world's list of great names in literature, science, art, music, finance, medicine, and abstruse learning are also way out of proportion to the weakness of his numbers. He has made a marvelous fight in the world, in all the ages; and has done it with his hands tied behind him. He could be vain of himself, and be excused for it. The Egyptian, the Babylonian, and the Persian rose, filled the planet with sound and splendor, then faded to dreamstuff and passed away; the Greek and the Roman followed, and made a vast noise, and they are gone; other peoples have sprung up and held their torch high for a time, but it burned out, and they sit in twilight now, or have vanished. The Jew saw them all, beat them all, and is now what he always was, exhibiting no decadence, no infirmities of age, no weakening of his parts, no slowing of his energies, no dulling of his alert and aggressive mind. All things are mortal but the Jew; all other forces pass, but he remains. What is the secret of his immortality?" [2]

The non-Jewish image of the Jew still alternated at the turn of the century between the two extremes of adulation and deprecation. The Jew was either angelic or diabolic. He was either the materialist whose God was Gold and whose basic motivation was greed or else he was the persecuted sufferer victimized by evil governments in the Old World and rushing to the shores of the New World in search of freedom. Sometimes he retained the contradictory traits of both images.

Charles W. Eliot, who was president of Harvard University from 1870 to 1909, was, like Mark Twain, an eloquent exponent of the philosemitic legend. In a memorable address

[2] Mark Twain, "Concerning the Jews," *Harper's Magazine*, Sept. 1899, p. 535.

on the two hundred and fiftieth anniversary of Jewish settlement in America, which he delivered in Boston's famed Faneuil Hall on November 29, 1905, he hailed the Jews as a freedom-loving group with lofty conceptions of God, man, nature and social justice. "If ever any race came hither in search of liberty and equality before the law and of the safety and prosperity which industry and virtue can win in a fresh land under just conditions, it is the Jews who have sought here freedom to worship God, freedom to live in peace, freedom to earn a livelihood by honest toil—all these liberties being denied them in the places whence they came." [3]

Eliot found America to be the ideal land for Jews, since here they were offered the opportunity to reap the fruit of their industry, frugality, and intelligence. Here all callings were open to them. Here they were not excluded from the professions, arts, and trades. Eliot called upon Americans of all other ethnic groups to welcome the Jewish group to a free competition in racial intelligence, morality, and honor and to recognize that the prodigious vitality of the Jew was due at bottom to a sublime religious idealism worthy of emulation.

Ten years later, Eliot reaffirmed his faith in the indestructible vitality and persistent idealism of the Jews. "In all generations and all environments the Jews have succeeded in competition with other races to a remarkable degree. Among a poor population they are less poor than their neighbors; among a free and prosperous population the Jews become richer and more prosperous than the average. Confined in ghettos they retain to an astonishing degree their health and vitality, helped doubtless by the dietary and sanitary directions given in their ancient Scriptures. Deprived of the right to bear arms in many countries and, therefore, unable to resist savage attack, they remain inextinguishable. Wherever

[3] C. W. Eliot, in *Addresses Delivered at 250th Anniversary of the Settlement of the Jews in the United States,* New York, 1906, p. 78.

they become prosperous they develop an extraordinary community feeling and take care of their own poor or unfortunate. In short, in all generations and in all their various environments they have exhibited and still exhibit a remarkable racial tenacity and vigor not due to any especially favorable material conditions, but to the rare strength and significance of their ideals." [4]

Eliot wondered what would happen to American Jews under the impact of increasing luxury, the worst destroyer of sound family life and national life. Would they be able to bear liberty as well as they had borne oppression? Would they resist the lure of materialism and continue to hold fast to their social, intellectual, and religious ideals?

These questions also troubled another keen observer, the Anglo-American novelist Henry James, after he gained insight into the currents of Jewish life in his native New York. In this metropolis he found the Jews bursting all bounds in their irrepressible vitality. He contrasted their grossness and materialism with their reverence for the intellect. He felt, however, that the immigrant Jews, primarily those of Eastern European origin, whether they were materialists or intellectuals, could not as yet claim brotherhood with native Americans but that the sons and daughters of these immigrants would reap in full the benefit of their parents' transplantation to American soil and would in time establish a free, unembarrassed, intimate relationship with the older stock of the population. Perhaps the genius of the Jews might even transform ever changing New York into a phantasmagoric New Jerusalem in the course of the twentieth century.

The new immigrants did indeed change the face of New York but they themselves were changed even more. With them a most fascinating chapter of American history and of Jewish history began.

[4] *Menorah Journal*, June 1945, I, 142.

CHAPTER VII

THE NEW IMMIGRATION

Mass Jewish immigration began in the eighteen-eighties and continued uninterruptedly until the First World War. Harold Frederic, in 1892, characterized this movement of Jews from Russia as *The New Exodus*. This exodus, stimulated by large-scale pogroms, economic distress, and harsh Czarist laws, was at first panicky and unregulated. It was not welcomed by the leaders of the American Israelites. There was widespread fear that the hard won social and economic status of the recently assimilated Israelites might be endangered. Their periodicals deplored the immigrants' lack of refinement and true spirituality despite adherence to orthodox Judaism. To forestall too great an influx of Russian Jews, the *Jewish Messenger*, on May 20, 1881, suggested that American Jewish missionaries be sent to Russia to civilize its Jews rather than to "give them an opportunity to Russianize us in the event of such a colossal immigration." [1]

A year later, Adolf Moses, an influential editor and respected leader of the Chicago Israelites, warned against applying the same yardstick in measuring Russian Jews as was applied towards German, French, or English Jews. The former were, in his opinion, semi-barbarians like their uncouth neighbors in the Czarist realm. What if these semi-

[1] A. I. Mandel, "Attitude of the American Jewish Community Towards East-European Immigration, As Reflected in the Anglo-Jewish Press (1880–1890)," *American Jewish Archives*, III, 1 (1950), 15.

Asiatic coreligionists did possess certain admirable traits such as piety, love of learning, compassion! Their psychology was still that of helots and barbarians. Their customs, morals, and language were far inferior to those of Jews who had profited from generations of sojourning on German soil before coming to America.[2]

Towards the end of this decade, Kaufmann Kohler, spokesman for American Reform Judaism, expressed the fear that the Russian Jew would drag American Judaism down from the honorable position it attained. He saw the Eastern Jew as a degenerate type of the splendid German Jew and called for the establishment of institutions for the elevation of these coreligionists, who were defective in education, lacking in culture, pauperized, and speaking a corrupt jargon of German.

Little did Adolf Moses, Kaufmann Kohler, and their circles of Israelites sense the idealism and moral stamina of these despoiled refugees who were spewed out of ghetto towns and into the filthy slums and ugly sweatshops of New York and Chicago, but who nevertheless continued to dream their Messianic dreams of mankind's salvation from exploitation, injustice, and serfdom. The Yiddish which these immigrants spoke and wrote was not a corrupt German but a sensitive linguistic medium which they were to develop to utmost refinement on the new soil. The recipients of the meager charity of the Israelite relief committees were not abject beggars but impoverished literate persons with poetic souls and a fanatic faith in orthodox, socialist, or anarchist ideals. Among them were David Edelstadt, the Yiddish poet, Jacob Gordin, the Yiddish dramatist, Abraham Cahan, the Yiddish journalist, and Dr. Charles Spivak, the Yiddish lexicographer and physician. They belonged to the *Am Olam* intellectuals, a group comparable to the *Bilu* pioneers. The latter reacted to

[2] E. Tcherikower, *History of the Jewish Labor Movement in the United States*, New York, 1943, I, 213.

the Russian Pogroms of 1881 by setting out for the land of Israel to found a new life close to the soil. The former left for America, urged on by a similar ideal: to establish themselves in agricultural colonies based on mutual aid. Although these colonies failed to prosper and although most of the Utopian visionaries soon drifted back to the cities and had to earn their bread not on farms but in sweatshops, nevertheless, their spirit interpenetrated the Jewish masses and gave organized direction to the immigrants' inarticulate aspirations. In time, this spirit gave rise to the great Jewish trade unions, which often served as models for the American Labor Movement.

Non-Jewish writers, such as Norman Hapgood, Hutchins Hapgood, Jacob Riis, Lincoln Steffens, and Robert Haven Schauffler, felt closer to these immigrant masses than did the Israelite philanthropists and communal leaders, among whom Michael Heilprin and Emma Lazarus were rare exceptions. In a lyric, entitled "Scum o' the Earth," Schauffler raised his voice in protest against those Americans, themselves descendants of immigrants, who called the newcomers rabble, refuse and scum o' the earth. These newcomers contained marvellous folk of great races, scions of philosophers, bards, and seers. The Jewish immigrant was hailed in these verses:

> Stay, are we doing you wrong
> Calling you "scum o' the earth,"
> Man of the sorrow-bowed head,
> Of the features tender yet strong,—
> Man of the eyes full of wisdom and mystery
> Mingled with patience and dread?
> Have I not known you in history,
> Sorrow-bowed head?
> Were you not the poet-king, worth

Treasures of Ophir unpriced?
Were you not the prophet, perchance, whose art
Foretold how the rabble would mock
That shepherd of spirits, ere long,
Who should carry the lambs on his heart
And tenderly feed his flock?
Man—lift that sorrow-bowed head.
Lo! 'tis the face of the Christ!

The vision dies at its birth.
You're merely a butt for our mirth.
You're a "sheeny"—and therefore despised,
And rejected as "scum o' the earth." [3]

The poet foresaw that out of such denigrated immigrants would arise children in whose frail arms would rest prophets and singers and saints of a future America.

Norman Hapgood, editor of *Harper's Weekly* and of *Collier's Weekly*, felt that the strenuous side of life, the ethical, abstract, spiritual striving was more ably represented by the immigrant Jews than by any other ethnic group and for that reason they were particularly interesting to him. In 1916, he wrote: "In New York City, it is from the Russian Jews, who are the mass of poor Jews in America, that the real contribution to American life is likely to come, because their aspirations are spiritual, their imagination alive. The Jews on the East Side are extraordinarily interesting. Often when I have been rather tired of the New York that everyone sees, I have gone down on the East Side to the theatres, clubs, cafés, and felt that I was in a universe that was young and full of hope." [4]

[3] H. F. Armstrong, *The Book of New York Verse*, New York, 1917, p. 247.
[4] Norman Hapgood, "The Jews and American Democracy," *Menorah Journal*, II (1916), 203.

Hutchins Hapgood treated with great sympathy and deep understanding a large variety of Jewish toilers, misfits, poets, and sidewalk philosophers who made the East Side so colorful and exciting. When Lincoln Steffens undertook the editorship of the *Commercial Advertiser,* he had Hapgood write a long series of serious articles about the Jewish denizens of the tenements. Abraham Cahan, who was gaining his most valuable journalistic experience on this English newspaper, introduced Hapgood, even as he had introduced Steffens, to the cafés of Canal and Grand Streets. There actors, playwrights, poets, scholars and artists congregated. There Hapgood met and etched pen-portraits of Jacob Adler, Bertha Kalisch, Jacob Gordin, Morris Rosenfeld, Abraham Liessin, Naphtali Herz Imber, David Pinski, and Jacob Epstein.

Hapgood later recast these articles for his books *The Spirit of the Ghetto,* 1902, and *Types from City Streets,* 1910. Epstein, who was then still an unknown, struggling artist, living in a tumble-down rickety building on the corner of Hester and Forsyth Streets, illustrated the former volume and received four hundred dollars for his many drawings, a sum which then seemed enormous to him and which enabled him to satisfy his dream of studying in Paris and ultimately to become one of the foremost sculptors of his generation.

Hapgood described Epstein as a ghetto boy who began his conscious American life with contempt for the Jewish past but who with growing culture learned to perceive the beauty of the Jewish traditions and faith. Thereupon, the young artist, reconciled to the spirit of his fathers, put into his sketches of Hester Street types an imaginative, almost religious, idealism; he showed his people in their suffering picturesqueness; he injected into the dark reality of their external life a melancholy beauty of spirit; he emphasized the humane expressiveness of their sensitive faces.

Hapgood himself saw charm in the ghetto and reported

sympathetically on the character, lives and pursuits of the East Side Jews. There he observed traditions and customs of medieval orthodoxy which were still retained in their purity and, juxtaposed to these, he found forms and ideas of modern life of the most extreme kind. Hapgood described the mature patriarchal immigrant who continued to follow deeply rooted habits, who sought consolation in the old religious rituals, who remained attached in his dreams and imagination to the old country.

Such a Jew congregated with his *landsleit* both to interchange reminiscences and to engage in mutual aid. He read his Yiddish newspapers and devoted himself to prayer, study, and worship during the hours he was not busy toiling. But Hapgood also described the immigrant child or the child of immigrant parents with its shrewd face and melancholy eyes. In such a child, he saw a mixture of almost unprecedented hope and excitement on the one hand, and of doubt, confusion, and self-distrust on the other hand. Three groups of influences were at work upon such a young person: the orthodox Jewish, the radiant American, and the Utopian Socialist. The violent contrast between the Jewish environment at home and the American environment on the street, between the religious education in the *Cheder* and the secular education in the public school, between values embedded in the past and values beckoning towards a glamorous future caused such a person to break away from the sway of parents, to become arrogant in his attitude towards them, and yet to some extent to regulate his life by their moral code. Seeking to bridge the chasm between himself and his forebears, he often found the answer in the cooperative ideals of socialism or in the libertarian ideals of anarchism. He joined debating clubs, ethical culture clubs, literary clubs. He became excited about new panaceas and enthusiastic about acquiring knowledge.

Hapgood placed great hopes upon the vanguard of these

young people, the Jews of the East Side who were beginning to enter American universities, who were retaining their strong ethical and spiritual characters, and who were devoting themselves to the work of fusing American ideals with the spirit at the heart of the Hebraic tradition.

In the volume *Types from City Streets,* 1910, Hapgood continued his studies of New York Jewish misfits, poets and philosophers, and throughout his later years, most notably in his controversy with Theodore Dreiser, he fought for greater sympathy and deeper understanding between the Jews and their neighbors.

Another keen observer of the teeming slums of New York's East Side was Jacob A. Riis, the friend of President Theodore Roosevelt and for many years a reporter for the *New York Evening Sun.* His observations were recorded in works of great sociological interest, such as *How the Other Half Lives,* 1890; *The Children of the Poor,* 1892; *Out of Mulberry Street,* 1896; *The Battle With the Slums,* 1902. He was most favorably impressed by the indestructible spirit of the Jewish immigrants. In these wanderers who had so long been homeless and degraded, he was conscious of a passionate longing for a home to call their own and a country to accept them as equals. America could be that home and that country. It would be a splendid home and a glorious country for their children. But for the adult newcomer, there was much suffering in store. Penury and poverty, dirt and disease were rampant in Jewtown. The flats of the Hebrew quarter were also the workshops. In the East Side apartments the whir of a thousand sewing-machines was audible, machines worked at high pressure from earliest dawn until mind and muscle gave out together. "Every member of the family, from the youngest to the oldest, bears a hand, shut in the qualmy rooms, where meals are cooked and clothing washed and dried besides, the livelong day. It is not unusual to find a dozen persons—men, women, and children—at work in a single small room." [5]

Riis was certain that such people would ultimately rise out of their poverty, because they were thrifty—they were the yeast of the slums—but at what cost in human values! "Thrift is the watchword of Jewtown, as of its people the world over. It is at once its strength and its fatal weakness, its cardinal virtue and its foul disgrace. Become an overmastering passion with these people who come here in droves from Eastern Europe to escape persecution, from which freedom could be bought only with gold, it has enslaved them in bondage worse than that from which they fled. Money is their God. Life itself is of little value compared with even the leanest bank account." [6]

Lincoln Steffens, in his young years as a reporter for the New York *Evening Post,* vied with Jacob Riis in ferreting out both the filth and the poetry of the slums. He saw the picturesqueness of the orthodox, bearded Jews and sensed both heart-breaking comedy and unmitigated tragedy in the conflict that raged between parents out of the Middle Ages and children of the streets of New York. His editor, now and then, received complaints from socially prominent Israelites. Once Steffens was asked to call personally upon a lady who wanted to know why so much space was given to the ridiculous performances of the ignorant, foreign, East Side Jews and none to the Uptown Hebrews of her circle. Steffens enlightened her about the comparative beauty, significance, and character of the Uptown and Downtown Jews. He himself became infatuated with the ghetto, nailed a mezuza on his office door, attended synagogue on Jewish Holy Days, fasted on Yom Kippur, and thrilled to the awesome solemnity of the ancient liturgy. His Jewish friends scoffed at him for his

[5] J. A. Riis, *How the Other Half Lives,* New York, 1890, p. 107.
[6] *Ibid.,* p. 106.

ardent admiration of the orthodox liturgy. But Israel Zangwill understood him far better and, when this English novelist came from London to New York in 1898, he asked this
non-Jewish reporter to be his guide for a survey of the East
Side.

Steffens, in a letter to his father dated December 10, 1898,
described a typical evening with Zangwill: "I gave a little
dinner over in the ghetto last night to I. Zangwill, the English novelist, who, a Jew himself, has written the most beautiful modern stories of ghetto life. Among my guests, all Jews,
were Abraham Cahan, the writer of New York ghetto stories,
and a Morris Rosenfeld, who is a Yiddish poet whose works
have recently been translated and printed in English. After
dinner we went to the Jewish theater, met all the actors and
then went to an East side café." [7]

Zangwill's visit to New York influenced him to write his
drama *The Melting Pot,* a title which became a slogan for
many years. In this play, staged in 1908, Zangwill pleaded for
a reconciliation in the New World of the antagonisms and
animosities that were rending the Old World apart. He projected as his protagonist David, a young Russian Jew, whose
parents had been murdered by an antisemitic nobleman in
the course of a Russian pogrom. David had escaped to New
York. Here he met and fell in love with Vera. In the course of
the dramatic action, he discovered that she was the daughter
of this Jew-hating aristocrat. However, in the great Melting
Pot of America, love triumphed and prejudices were discarded. The play concluded with this vision:

> *David:* There she lies, the great Melting Pot—Listen!
> Can't you hear the roaring and the bubbling? (he
> points east). There gapes her mouth—the harbor
> where a thousand mammoth feeders come from the

---

[7] Lincoln Steffens, *Letters,* New York, 1938, I, 133.

> ends of the world to pour in their human freight
> . . . . Celt and Latin, Slav and Teuton, Greek
> and Syrian,—black and yellow—
> *Vera:* Jew and Gentile—
> *David:* Yes, East and West, and North and South, the
> palm and the pine, the pole and the equator, the
> crescent and the cross—how the great alchemist
> melts and fuses them with his purging flame! . . . .
> Ah, Vera, what is the glory of Rome and Jerusalem
> where all nations and races come to worship and
> look back, compared with the glory of America,
> where all races and nations come to labor and look
> forward! [8]

The operation of the Melting Pot upon children at the turn of the century was most vividly described in the stories of Myra Kelly, an elementary school teacher of Irish birth who spent the greater part of her short life on New York's East Side. She was born in 1875 and died in 1910. Her father was a physician who practiced in Downtown New York. His patients and her pupils included many refugees from pogroms.

Her earliest story was *A Christmas Present For a Lady.* The interest it aroused induced her to continue recording her observations of her pupils and their parents. These stories, full of kindness and sentimentality, taught sympathy and understanding. The best of them were collected in the volumes *Little Citizens,* 1904, *Wards of Liberty,* 1907, and *Little Aliens,* 1910. In her tales she emphasized the transmutation of the foreign-born children into little Americans in thought, feeling, and behavior.

In the introduction to *Wards of Liberty,* she acknowledged her own limitations and the difficulties she experienced in

[8] Israel Zangwill, *The Melting Pot,* New York, 1909, p. 96.

penetrating into the souls of these young Jews: "The deepest can never be written out by one of an alien race. The lives being lived in those crowded streets are so diverse, so different in end and in aim that no mere observer can hope to see more than an insignificant vista of the whole seething, swarming mass of hope, disillusion, growth and decay. The opening through which I saw my vista was the school-room. I taught these babies and I loved them. The larger problems of maturity passed far from Room 8, but their shadow crossed its sunshine. This was inevitable in a community where all the life of a family, eating, sleeping, cooking, working, illness, death, birth, and prayer is often crowded into one small room." [9]

The best narrative in this volume was entitled *A Soul Above Buttons*. Its main character was a nine-year-old boy who was known as "The Boss." When his father died, he took over the so-called business, having learned the details by acting as his father's messenger. He got his mother and his half-witted sister to work for him and soon enlarged his establishment even further by including three broken-spirited refugees, who paid for their board and lodging by their ceaseless labor. He himself would bring home the piles of clothes from the factory in order to have his employees sew buttons on the coats. Soon he discovered that, if he could read and write English, he could also get gents' vests for finishing. The pay would be better. And so he registered for the First Reader Class. There he was impatient with the teacher. He felt he had no time "to fool" with other subjects of the school curriculum. After two weeks of hard work learning to read, his teacher awarded him a certificate of merit. He wanted to know where he could have it cashed. Besides, he wanted to be paid for his classroom work, sewing and making mats and book-marks. When the teacher tried to explain that these

⁹ Myra Kelly, *Wards of Liberty*, New York, 1907, p. VIII.

were educational exercises, he refused to accept her explanation and organized a strike of the children. When the strike
was broken by the teacher's diplomacy, he quit school, after
calling his classmates a bunch of scabs, and returned to his
buttons.

The novels that dealt with the generation of immigrant
children who grew up between 1880 and 1914 stressed the
contrast between the bright, happy atmosphere of the public
school and the dank gloom of the supplementary Jewish
school or *cheder*. The novelist Samuel B. Ornitz, in *Haunch
Paunch and Jowl*, 1923, depicted the several lives that Jewish
boys at the turn of the century led simultaneously: "First
there was the queer relationship of American street gamins to
our old-world parents. Indeed, an ocean separated us. And
distance does not encourage confidings and communings, but
creates misunderstanding and leads to contempt and intolerance. Many of us were transient, impatient aliens in our parents' homes. Then there was that strict, rarefied public school
world. The manners and clothes, speech and point of view of
our teachers extorted our respect and reflected upon the
shabbiness, foreignness and crudities of our folks and homes.
Again, there was the harsh and cruel *cheder* life with its atmosphere of superstition, dread and punishment. And then
came our street existence, our sweet, lawless, personal, high-
colored life, our vent to the disciplines, crampings and con-
finements of our other worlds." [10]

Far more gloomy is the description of immigrant boyhood
in Henry Roth's novel *Call It Sleep*, which had as its basis the
author's own recollections of his early years. His hero David
Schearl arrived as a child in 1907, the year of the largest Jewish immigration, and grew up in Brownsville and the Lower
East Side. What a contrast between his boyhood amidst the
stench, the filth, and the screams of his tenement home and

[10] S. B. Ornitz, *Haunch Paunch and Jowl*, New York, 1923, pp. 30–31.

the boyhood of a Tom Sawyer or a Huck Finn amidst the wide open spaces along the Mississippi! The darkest hours were those spent in the *cheder* under the tutelage of the Hebrew teacher, Reb Yidel Pankower. This pedagogue, whose traits had already evolved into a stereotype in Yiddish literature and were to haunt American fiction until the mid-century when he became an historic anachronism, was depicted as follows: "He was not at all like the teachers at school, but David had seen rabbis before and knew he wouldn't be. He appeared old and was certainly untidy. He wore soft leather shoes like house-slippers, that had no place for either laces or buttons. His trousers were baggy and stained, a great area of striped and crumpled shirt intervened between his belt and his bulging vest. The knot of his tie, which was nearer one ear than the other, hung away from his soiled collar. What features were visible were large and had an oily gleam. Beneath his skull cap, his black hair was closely cropped." [11]

The rabbi's main teaching instrument was a short-thonged cat-o'-nine-tails. His voice was menacing. Scared silence locked all mouths when he seated himself. He cursed and slapped. He fastened the pincers of his fingers on the cheeks of a howling pupil. He wrenched a boy's head from side to side. When the panicky boy, tears streaming down his cheeks, explained that his misreading of a Hebrew text was caused not by ignorance but by darkness, the rabbi exploded: "May your skull be dark and your eyes be dark and your fate be of such dearth and darkness that you will call a poppy-seed the sun and a caraway the moon. Get up! Away! Or I'll empty my bitter heart upon you!"

Henry Roth and Samuel B. Ornitz recorded their reminiscences of their childhood years decades later when a more realistic approach prevailed. However, the first Jewish novelists who wrote for an English reading audience at the opening of

---

[11] Henry Roth, *Call It Sleep*, New York, 1934, p. 289.

the century were much more sentimental in their treatment
of the new material. In the stories of Jewish immigrant life
by Bruno Lessing, James Oppenheim and Montague Glass,
there was sunshine amidst sadness and kindness amidst
cruelty.

Bruno Lessing was the pen name of Rudolph Block, a
journalist associated with the Hearst newspapers for more
than a quarter of a century. In his collection of tales *Children
of Men*, 1903, he mingled humor with pathos. He showed
warm humanity surviving amid the clamor of sewing machines where men and women were needed merely as hands
to serve the ceaselessly whirring devils. In such a shop, the
pale girl who once lived amidst orchards and forests near
Odessa was dying of consumption but was still continuing
her daily routine that kept starvation from her door. But her
fellow-worker, shortly before her end, was able to let her experience hours of joy gazing at a Corot landscape and reliving
happy memories of flowers and trees, even if he had to steal
this valuable painting from the museum. In another shop,
Erzik and Sarah sit side by side along the assembly line and
are happy amidst the buzzing, humming, and droning, because they are in love. They marry; they continue to work in
the same factory throughout the many hours from dawn to
dusk; they are content with their lot in life. Mother Politsky,
the fish vendor of Hester Street, finally sells a fish for the Sabbath to the rabbi at half price because he enchants her with
his parables even while they are engaged in bargaining.
Queer Scharenstein sings at his machine on hot summer days
when others gasp for breath. He is in free America after en-
during the horrors of a pogrom abroad. He is in a land
guarded by the beloved Statue of Liberty.

James Oppenheim, who was primarily a poet rather than a
novelist, attempted in the sketches centering about Dr. Rast,
the title hero of his early book published in 1909, to portray

the new immigrant Jews of Eastern European background in their quaintness, queerness, shabbiness, and above all goodness. He did so by having them pass through the East Broadway office of a kind, German-Jewish physician who chose to work in their midst, alone and obscure, a healer of their feverish bodies and injured souls. To anyone who might complain of the lack of drama and heroism amid the squalid tenements, Dr. Rast could counter: "Man, you can't look at a lighted window of a tenement at night, without seeing the outline of a whole novel—a whole tragedy or comedy. Why, the city is simply flooded with material. Every face that goes by is marked by a whole history. Every day there are greater dramas unfolded right down East Broadway than Shakespeare even got the scent of." [12] Yet, once even Dr. Rast was fed up with the drama of the nauseous crowds, the dirty streets, the stinking tenements, and the daily grind. He felt tempted to get out to Connecticut, where he could practice in a beautiful cottage amidst delightful woods and brooks and lovely neighbors who were peaceful, happy, and never in a hurry. However, when his office bell rang and he was called out in the middle of the night to a patient, he realized what his presence, his love, his service, his skill meant to the helpless creatures behind dank walls, in cellars, in garrets, in factories. These creatures would sink into quicksands and be among the debris of society if he and the other modern men of God, the settlement workers, the nurses, the general practitioners would not give them a helping hand. And so Dr. Rast continued his unending battles with disease and death on New York's East Side. He loved this hive of humanity and trudged through the muddy gutters and along the dull brick-red walls to his holy task. He was content to be an old-fashioned doctor, to lay his healing hand on the filth of the world's flesh and his comforting heart and soul on bruised

[12] James Oppenheim, *Dr. Rast*, New York, 1909, p. 5.

hearts and broken souls. His patients trusted him and put their precious lives into his keeping. It was up to him to return these lives to them safe and sweet and sound. Beneath the callous crust of every person, he saw something full of miracles and glory and wonder. Beneath the meanness, the clash, the greed, the pavement pettiness, there were bared to him deeper layers, the love that breathed through all, the reminder of a Brotherhood to be. He knew it was good to work hard and to be tired at night; it was good to eat one's supper at one's own table; it was good to suffer and then to be free of pain; even at its worst human life was rich and warm.

In the awesome presence of death, this understanding physician brought back groping Americanized children to their Yiddish-speaking parents. To Esther, the medical student who was ashamed of her parents' broken English and dull jabber of Yiddish, he applied the scalpel of truth and awakened her conscience. He pointed out to her that, despite her American polish, she was reacting with a brain and body and soul that stemmed from Russian Jews. Her foreign-mannered father had more essential talent, learning, character and breeding than she had. How else could he dream his bright vision of making a doctor of his daughter? How else could he uncomplainingly and unhesitatingly trudge about selling newspapers from dawn to dusk, in the hot summer and the terrible winter, in order to give his children a higher education, peace, joy, plenty? A mother who wore her eyes out on piece-work so that her daughter might be free of the sweat and dust of life certainly deserved reverence and not scorn.

In one of Dr. Rast's Jewish colleagues, a pure scientist who inoculated himself with disease germs in order to test an antitoxin, Oppenheim anticipated and may even have supplied the model for Professor Max Gottlieb, the Jewish scientist in Sinclair Lewis's novel *Arrowsmith*. This teacher and researcher was regarded by his colleagues as an atheistic Jewish crank but his pupil Arrowsmith worshipped him and followed his example of absolute devotion to pure science.

While Oppenheim depicted the poetry and the idealism of the immigrant generation as its men and women faced sickness and poverty and death, Montague Glass concentrated on the kindness, fascination, and strange beauty that filled the daily, competitive struggle for economic survival with drama. His was the tragi-comic realm of the Jewish garment industry, in which little, brave, cunning persons were emerging from the status of workers to that of struggling manufacturers and marginal businessmen and were filling the New York atmosphere with their loud presence and creative manipulations.

As a lawyer with a predominently Jewish clientele, Glass knew this social sector best and in the sketches of *Potash and Perlmutter,* which began to appear in 1910 and which had a great vogue for more than a decade, he reproduced its queer, quaint habits with tolerant kindness and gentle humor. These sketches dealt with the ventures and adventures of two partners who faced and successfully overcame innumerable obstacles in their combined effort to manufacture and sell cloaks and suits. There was the smart Jewish lawyer Henry D. Feldman, who had a habit of quoting abstruse Latin phrases to impress his clients and who thus did impress them not only with his learning but also with his infallibility. He never employed a word of one syllable if it had a synonym of three or four syllables. However, when it came to money matters, he could be colloquial to the point of using slang. When he drew up a contract, it was for keeps and only he himself knew how to break it. There was the conservative partner Abe Potash, who was able to salvage some profit out of almost every deal and who constantly managed to get his more venturesome partner Morris Perlmutter out of the difficulties in which the latter involved the firm because of a more trusting good-naturedness.

The dialogue and the thinking of the many characters were drawn from real life and the vocabulary was a picturesque English behind which a Yiddish substratum peered through, even though the only foreign expressions included by the author were German ones introduced by the German restaurateurs of the East Side.

So accurate and authentic was the author's insight into the bizarre intricacies of the garment trade that many readers assumed Montague Glass was himself engaged in it. His reply, when questioned on this matter, was: "I have never been in any business but the law business, which in New York City is the trouble department of every other business in the directory from 'architectural iron work' down to 'yarns, cotton and woolen.' I was associated with a firm whose practice was largely of a kind called 'commercial' and many of their clients were engaged in the women's outer garment business. From this source I derived some knowledge of the cloak and suit business, but not enough to prevent me from getting into technical difficulties." [18]

While the novels and sketches of Montague Glass now have largely entertainment value, since they do not penetrate into tragic, lonely depths, Abraham Cahan, in his best novel, *The Rise of David Levinsky*, 1917, did see through the superficial hustle and bustle of the same Jewish garment industry and did unlock deeper recesses of Jewish immigrant souls caught up in a whirl of apparent success.

Cahan, whose greatest achievement was the founding of the *Jewish Daily Forward* in 1897 as the organ of the Jewish Socialists and directing its editorial policies from 1902 until his death in 1951, also made his mark as an English journalist during the Muckraking Era. He published his first English

[18] A. B. Maurice, *The New York of the Novelists*, New York, 1916, p. 67.

tale of the New York ghetto as early as 1896 under the title *Yekel*. It was enthusiastically acclaimed by William Dean Howells and Hutchins Hapgood but it found few readers and was soon forgotten. It was followed by other stories in English and in Yiddish, but not until more than two decades later did his realistic masterpiece appear and not until 1960, on the centenary of its author's birth, did it attain its widest vogue.

The title-hero David Levinsky, had arrived as a young immigrant from a Russian townlet in 1885, three years after his author, and had worked, starved, struggled, until the four cents with which he landed became in the course of three decades more than two million dollars and he himself was recognized as one of the two or three leading men in the cloak-and-suit trade in the United States. Nevertheless, when this erstwhile Talmudic student of Antomir surveyed the metamorphosis he had gone through, his station, power, and worldly success seemed to him devoid of significance, while his boyhood in the lowest depths of poverty, vividly recalled, had aspects of holiness.

David Levinsky had come to New York with a multitude of steerage passengers, all of whom had lustrous visions of an enchanted America. His daydreams of a magnificent entry into a new world whose thoroughfares were strewn with nuggets of gold gave way to a sense of helplessness and awe as he had to worry about shelter and food from the very moment of landing. Instead of stumbling upon gold on his first walk, he came upon a poor family which had been dispossessed for non-payment of rent and whose household goods were piled on the sidewalk.

The young immigrant David began as a basket-peddler, with collar-buttons and garters as his sole stock, graduated soon to push-cart peddling with remnants of dress-goods, linen and oil-cloth as his wares, worked his way up to ever

higher economic strata, especially after he learned the trade
of cloak-making. In the process of Americanization, his piety
deteriorated and his religion fell to pieces. On his first day his
forelocks were trimmed. Within a few weeks his sprouting
beard was shaved. Before long, the last threads that bound
him to orthodox Jewish living snapped and he sank into the
maelstrom of sensuality. But the yearning for knowledge persisted. As he had earlier sought to be learned in Talmudic
studies, so he now wished to be a college man. In his eyes, a
college diploma was a certificate of moral as well as intellectual aristocracy. City College, toward which so many immigrant youths aspired, became the synagogue of his new life,
the temple of highest learning. During his slack seasons as a
cloak-maker, he applied himself to the study of subjects required for admission to college. He found geometry deeper
than Talmud and an interesting mathematical problem more
delicious than the best piece of meat. However, when an opportunity presented itself to him to enter the cloak business,
he proved faithless to his scholarly ideal and turned to moneymaking. At first, his was a hard struggle for business survival.
Competition was keen and merciless. But, as he toiled on, day
and night, with wits and brawn, his business hummed and
leaped; he rose in affluence; the jingle of gold pouring into
his lap constantly increased. At the same time, he felt his
heart congeal, loneliness grip him, and desolation creep upon
him. In retrospect, his gloomiest past was dearer to him than
his brightest present; his sense of triumph was coupled with a
brooding sense of emptiness and insignificance.

The envied millionaire finally summed up his own evaluation of his achievements in these words: "At the height of my
business success I feel that if I had my life to live over again I
should never think of a business career. I don't seem to get
accustomed to my luxurious life. I am always more or less
conscious of my good clothes, of the high quality of my office

furniture, of the power I wield over the men in my pay.
. . . I can never forget the days of my misery. I cannot escape from my old self. My past and my present do not comport well. David, the poor lad swinging over a Talmud volume at the Preacher's Synagogue, seems to have more in common with my inner identity than David Levinsky, the well-known cloak-manufacturer." [14]

Though Cahan passed severe judgment upon this unscrupulous go-getter, he did not dehumanize him or strip him of a conscience. David Levinsky was only temporarily made dizzy and giddy by his rise to wealth. He was still aware of a moral yardstick by which to measure individual and social behavior. Gnawing remorse and loneliness accompanied his apparent success as an exploiter. Nostalgia for the warmth and kindness of his humbler days and longing for the intellectual life he had forfeited broke in upon the barren splendor of his luxurious years. Despite his many faults of character, he aroused sympathetic interest. He was the Jew gone astray, dazzled by the tinsel values of his unhealthy environment but aching for the abandoned Jewish values of his forefathers.

Abraham Cahan, as editor of the most influential Yiddish newspaper and as a leading figure in the Jewish Socialist movement, participated actively in the struggle of the workers to improve their condition by mutual cooperation, he supported their strikes with his pen and with his oratorical gifts, he comforted the beaten and defeated toilers with ever new hope, he exulted with them when their efforts finally reached a victorious climax in the organization of the great Jewish trade unions on the eve of World War I. The most dramatic victory was achieved after "The Uprising of the Twenty Thousand," in 1909, the strike of the New York dressmakers and shirtwaist-makers, mostly Jewish girls, who

[14] Abraham Cahan, *The Rise of David Levinsky*, New York, 1917, p. 530.

fought for three long months against strike-breakers, gang-
sters, police, magistrates, and starvation, until they at last
won out. Florence Converse's novel *The Children of Light,*
1912, Arthur Bullard's novel *Comrade Yetta,* 1913, and
James Oppenheim's novel *The Nine-Tenths,* 1911, were inspired by this event.

The struggle of American workers throughout the land to
organize and to better their lot had always found sympathy
and support among Jewish warriors of the pen. As early as
1901, the year of the founding of the United States Steel Corporation, Isaac Kahn Friedman, scion of a prosperous Chicago family, called attention to the horrible condition of the
steel workers in his novel *By Bread Alone.* The hero of this
book, like the author, became a convert to Socialism, obtained a job in the steel mills, led a losing strike which was
attended by violence, and concluded that only through more
peaceful political action could workers expect to advance toward a longed for Cooperative Commonwealth.

Generally, however, the Jewish writer could describe more
intimately and more accurately the battle for economic survival among Jewish workers than among non-Jewish Americans. The effort of the immigrant generation of Chicago to
emerge from sweatshop conditions into which they were
plunged upon their arrival in this mid-Western metropolis
from the eighteen-eighties on was the subject of Beatrice
Bisno's novel *Tomorrow's Bread,* 1938, a novel which followed in the wake of *The Rise of David Levinsky.* She too
showed the younger immigrants turning away from the traditional rituals of Orthodoxy and espousing Anarchism, Socialism, Trade Unionism. She too showed the young idealists
ready to starve and die for the new panaceas even as their fathers had suffered for clinging to a more ancient faith. But
she also pointed out that once the breach with the older views
was effected, then the entire wall of taboos disintegrated and

crumbled; free love replaced the so-called archaic attitude of marital possessiveness. Nevertheless, thirty years after the pogrom-fleeing, penniless immigrants arrived in Chicago, their radical ideals were also in a state of decay. The Jewish workers and agitators had become manufacturers, real-estate operators, *allrightniks*, opulent, dull, ostentatious. After three decades of fighting for a variety of causes, the hero found himself entrapped in bourgeois smugness, imprisoned in a spiritual vacuum of material luxury, stranded among Oriental rugs, expensive lace hangings, shiny furniture, and Ming vases—utterly unhappy. America, which shone before him and his kindred in the eighteen-eighties as the Promised Land had indeed fulfilled its promise of plenty and freedom but still had not brought him happiness.

A hungry, hope-inspired, dream-intoxicated Jewish generation was gradually yielding to a prosperous, disillusioned, self-hating generation.

Chapter VIII

THE PROMISED LAND

The Promised Land was the title of an autobiography by Mary Antin which created a literary sensation when it appeared in 1912. It told of a young Jewish girl who immigrated with her parents from Russia to Boston in 1894 at the age of thirteen, of her successful assimilation to American ways and of her happy acceptance into American society.

In her native Plotzk, Mary Antin was aware all the time that she was living in exile. She was made to feel that the world was divided into Jews and Gentiles. The former were restricted to the Pale of Settlement and had to suffer indignities and disabilities. In the Boston of the closing nineteenth century she discovered what it meant for a Jew to be at home. In Plotzk she had prayed to God to lead her out of oppression, for there even children, if they were Jewish, felt the lash of oppression and hostility. There Gentile children could do as they liked with Jewish children and not fear punishment. There one accepted taunts and ill-usage from neighbors as one accepted the weather. There one had to know how to dodge and cringe and dissemble if one were to survive. There little girls had old, old faces and eyes glazed with secrets. There free schools were non-existent and, even if one were willing to pay for a higher education, one faced the quota system which restricted the admission of Jewish candidates, also special examinations for Jewish students and low ratings against which there was no appeal. School life was an incessant struggle against injustice, dishonest marking, spiteful treatment, and unmerited insults from teachers, educational authorities, and classmates.

Mary Antin's hope and longing had been fulfilled. She had been delivered from bondage and it was of this deliverance she testified in her book. She documented her faith that in America every child of the slums owned the land and all that was good in it. Seen through her eyes, America was fair and kind and splendid. In America the arch of heaven soared above every head and a million suns shone out for every star. Education was free and opened wide doors for vast opportunities. All occupations were respectable and all persons were equal. Her optimism was infectious. Her enthusiasm was boundless. For her, integration into America meant sloughing all Jewish traits, customs, beliefs, and habits of speech that harked back to a pre-American past. She advocated such a course for others to follow, just as she herself had done. She offered herself as a typical rather than as a unique case, as an illustration of the golden opportunities in store for the courageous who plunged wholeheartedly into the Melting Pot and let themselves be remolded: "I was born, I have lived and I have been made over. Is it not time to write my life's story? I am just as much out of the way as if I were dead for I am absolutely other than the person whose story I have to tell. Physical continuity with my earlier self is no disadvantage. I could speak in the third person and not feel that I was masquerading. I can analyze my subject, I can reveal everything; for *she* and not *I* is my real heroine. My life I have still to live; her life ended when mine began." [1]

Her Jewish life with its medieval vestiges ended, so Mary Antin imagined, when she plunged into the twentieth century, married a non-Jewish professor of paleontology, made her home in an upper middle class suburb of New York, and

[1] Mary Antin, *The Promised Land*, Boston, 1912, p. XI.

mingled with Americans of Mayflower vintage. She ended her autobiography, written in the first year of her marriage, with the joyous words: "America is the youngest of the nations and inherits all that went before in history. And I am the youngest of America's children, and into my hands is given all her priceless heritage, to the last white star espied through the telescope, to the last great thought of the philosopher. Mine is the whole majestic past, and mine is the shining future." [2]

Alas, her later years belied her earlier optimism. In 1920 the professor who personified for her the ideal Gentile left for China and stayed there more than a quarter of a century far from his wife and daughter. Mary Antin's brief years of opulence and celebrity were followed by many hard, glamorless, lonely years as a social worker eking out a bare living. Then she sought refuge in vague mysticism and in an increased attachment to religion.

Rabbi Abraham Cronbach, who was in touch with her during her later years, when she suffered from impaired health and financial stringency, reported in his *Autobiography* that "the atheist of *The Promised Land* had, amidst deprivation and suffering, discovered the reality of God." [3]

While Mary Antin, immediately upon landing in Boston, could enter into the best schools and develop her talents under the beneficent encouragement of sympathetic teachers, Anzia Yezierska, who landed in New York at the age of sixteen, was denied such an opportunity. She too had begun life in the Russian Pale amidst extreme poverty and constant fear of a pogrom. She too had dreamed of free schools, free colleges, free libraries, where she could learn and keep on learning, where she could lift up her head and laugh and dance

[2] *Ibid.*, p. 364.
[3] Abraham Cronbach, "Autobiography," *American Jewish Archives*, April 1959, p. 41.

and soar like a bird in the air, from sky to sky, from star to
star. Unfortunately, what awaited her on the East Side was
not sunshine and singing and a teacher's cheery smile but
rather cheerless narrow streets of squeezed-in houses, a sweatshop with foul air where she had to sew dresses for a pittance,
the fish-smell of Hester Street, filth and dirt and raucousness.
Her orthodox father, unlike Mary Antin's freethinking father, continued to live with his Talmudic folios, to practice
Old World rituals, and to accept poverty as his family's God-
given lot on earth. But his daughter rebelled. She ran away
from home. She sought to scrape together bits of joy and
crumbs of secular learning. She experienced ecstasy and despair, kindness and cruelty, hunger of the heart and an all-
consuming passion for beauty. From obscurity and poverty
she was for one brief moment lifted to fame and riches as the
Cinderella of Hollywood and was shortly thereafter again
plunged into penury and ugliness.

She published her first story in 1915, when she was already
thirty, and she established her reputation as a talented realist
with her first collection of stories, *Hungry Hearts,* in 1920.
Most of her tales and sketches in this and her succeeding five
volumes dealt with the adjustment of the Jewish immigrant
to America, an America which even amidst bitterest agony
still remained also for her the Promised Land. "Inside the
ruin of my thwarted life, the *unlived* visionary immigrant
hungered and thirsted for America. I had come a refugee
from the Russian pogroms, aflame with dreams of America. I
did not find America in the sweatshops, much less in the
schools and colleges. But for hundreds of years the persecuted
races all over the world were nurtured on hopes of America.
When a little baby in my mother's arms, before I was old
enough to speak, I saw all around me weary faces light up
with thrilling tales of the far-off 'golden country.' And so,
though my faith in this so-called America was shattered, yet

underneath, in the sap and roots of my soul, burned the deathless faith that America is, must be, somehow, somewhere. In the midst of my bitterest hates and rebellions, visions of America rose over me like songs of freedom of an oppressed people." [4]

The golden country to which Anzia Yezierska's immigrant heroes and heroines and victims reached out in their deepest aspiration was a country of spiritual idealism and social justice and not an El Dorado whose streets were paved with gold and where exploitation lined the pockets of exploiters. "I refuse to accept the America where men make other men poor—create poverty where God has poured out wealth. I refuse to accept the America that gives the landlord the right to keep on raising my rent and to drive me in the streets when I do not earn enough to meet his rapacious demands. I cry out in this wilderness for America—my America—different from all other countries. In this America promised to the oppressed of all lands, there is enough so that man need not fight man for his bread, but work with man, building the beauty that for hundreds of years, in thousands of starved villages of Europe, men have dreamed was America—beautiful homes—beautiful cities—beautiful lives reaching up to higher, ever higher visions of beauty. I know you will say what right have I to come here and make demands upon America. But are not my demands the bread, the very life of America? What, after all, is America, but the response to the demands of immigrants like me, seeking new worlds in which their spirit may be free to create beauty? Were not the Pilgrim Fathers immigrants demanding a new world in which they could be free to live higher lives? Yes, I make demands —not in arrogance, but in all humility—I demand—driven by my desire to give. I want to give not only that which I am, but that which I might be if I only had the chance. I want to

[4] Anzia Yezierska, *Hungry Hearts*, Boston, 1920, p. 174.

give to America not the immigrant you see before you—starved, stunted, resentful, on the verge of hysteria from repression. I want to give a new kind of immigrant, full grown in mind and body—loving, serving, upholding America." [5]

In her autobiography, *Red Ribbon on a White Horse*, 1950, Anzia Yezierska sought to find an underlying meaning to her jagged existence with its turbulence and rapid changes of fortune. Her first book, *Hungry Hearts*, was praised by critics and esteemed as good literature. But it did not sell. The income of two hundred dollars, which she received as her total royalties, was soon spent on food and rent and she again faced starvation and eviction from her one room apartment in the slums. Suddenly, as she was trying to satisfy her hungry stomach with stewed-over tea leaves, a telegram arrived with the fabulous news that Hollywood wanted movie rights to her book. In order to have the carfare to the movie agent's office, she pawned her mother's shawl for a quarter, the shawl that served her as a blanket by night and a cover for her cot by day. She learned that she could have ten thousand dollars at once and an additional magnificent salary in Hollywood upon getting there. A heaven of splendor and ecstasy seemed to have opened up to her, the Cinderella of Hester Street. However, when she did arrive in the glamorous California movie colony and did find herself the sensation of the hour and was headlined as the sweatshop waif turned into a Hollywood princess, she felt like a beggar who drowned in a barrel of cream. Given an office in the same building as Will Rogers, Rupert Hughes, Elinor Glyn and Gertrude Atherton, she was completely bewildered, entirely beyond her depth, unable to endure the strain of living up to the artificial Hollywood existence. Her inspiration dried up. Though dined and wined by Samuel Goldwyn and offered a fabulous contract for future scenarios by William Fox, she fled back to

[5] Anzia Yezierska, *Children of Loneliness*, New York, 1925, pp. 27–28.

the real world she knew, to the poverty of New York, to genuineness.

Three decades later, after she had barely survived the Great Depression and its aftermath, she still had no regrets for having turned her back upon a life of artificial glamor and having preferred a life of truth to her inner self. She came to realize that so-called success, failure, poverty, riches, were but values of the market place and had no relationship to ultimate reality. The values of her father, whom she had always fought and from whose world she had sought to escape, were the true values that gave meaning to existence. "Now, all these years after his death, the ideas he tried to force on me revealed their meaning. Again and again at crucial turning points of my life, his words flared out of the darkness. 'He who separates himself from people buries himself in death. . . . Can fire and water be together? Neither can godliness and the fleshpots of Mammon. . . . Poverty becomes a Jew. . . .' He didn't feel himself poor. Poverty had never starved him as it had me. Having nothing only drew him closer to God. Homelessness, hunger, exile—Jews have survived them for thousands of years. What was there to fear in a shabby coat? He walked the earth knowing that the kingdom, the power, and the glory were in his own heart; and no worldly prizes could swerve him from his chosen path." [6]

This final understanding to which the scarred novelist attained in the autumn of her life was always present in the work of Alter Brody, her East Side neighbor. He also came in early years from a Lithuanian village. He too had to make the difficult transition from his native Yiddish to the new tongue of whose cadences he was enamoured and which he soon mastered to perfection. He too depicted the new reality as coarse, hard, merciless, and yet interpenetrated by a strange beauty. However, he never suffered from a sense of frustration in his

[6] Anzia Yezierska, *Red Ribbon on a White Horse*, New York, 1950, p. 218.

family circle, as did Anzia Yezierska, even when he was wedged in a Cherry Street flat amidst aunts, uncles, cousins, boarders, and boarders-in-law. In his verses he harmonized the shrieking dissonances of the squalid alleys and dingy tenements. In the poems of *A Family Album*, 1918, he emphasized the boyhood delights that he experienced in his native townlet on a twig of the Vistula, he stressed the Sabbaths when every Jewish face shone with a Sabbath newness rather than the weekdays filled with care and fear. He had no resentment towards his progenitors. He showed his immigrant mother as a tired-faced woman bending over the washtub, working with ever diligent hands for her ten children, loving them with infinite patience, battling for them with poverty, disease, and death, and seeing these children cast off, ignore, and deride her old faith as a foolish fable.

In the folkplays of the American Jew, entitled *Lamentations*, 1928, Brody lit up hidden recesses of the Jewish soul. Without using a single Yiddish word, he caught the authentic intonations of Yiddish-speaking men and women on New York's East Side, in Harlem and the Bronx, and reproduced these intonations in the English medium: a conversation in the night between a husband and wife in a bedroom back of a candystore; a dialogue between two old women about their children during a recess in the Atonement Day Services in the synagogue; an interchange of phrases and sighs that lightened the burden of sorrow-laden hearts.

In the lyric *Ghetto Twilight*, Brody caught the mood of the Jewish East Side as no poet writing in English before him, as only the Yiddish social lyricists had as yet grasped:

> An infinite weariness comes into the faces of the old
>   tenements,
> As they stand massed together on the block,
> Tall and thoughtfully silent,

In the enveloping twilight.
Pensively,
They eye each other across the street,
Through their dim windows—
With a sad recognizing stare,
Watching the red glow fading in the distance,
At the end of the street,
Behind the black church spires;
Watching the vague sky lowering overhead,
Purple with clouds of colored smoke
From the extinguished sunset;
Watching the tired faces coming home from work,
Like dry-breasted hags
Welcoming their children to their withered arms.[7]

Samuel B. Ornitz, who grew up in this ghetto district at the same time as Brody and Yezierska, saw about him neither kindness nor beauty. Though he later attained to eminence as a Hollywood script writer, he remained an eternal rebel against the established order whose excrescences he witnessed in his young years. His most successful novel *Haunch Paunch and Jowl*, 1923, dealt with the rise of an East Side boy who became a crooked politician, a corrupt judge, a cynical pillar of society. The depiction of the cruel struggle for existence in the sweatshop era before 1914, when only the strongest and most unscrupulous could advance to the top of the heap, was a dreary chronicle of social climbing, fortune hunting, political scheming.

Through one of the minor characters, a physician, Ornitz justified his own approach as that of a critic who was undertaking a house-cleaning and was attempting to rid the hardworking, clean-living, simple, law-abiding Jewish masses of the handful of riffraff, the scum that awakened unpleasant as-

[7] Alter Brody, *A Family Album*, New York, 1918, p. 39.

sociations in the minds of non-Jews. "I will take the sick ego
of my people to the clinic. I know I will be called the enemy
of my people, hounded, cursed, spat upon, disowned even by
my own family, ridiculed, called a renegade, a turn-coat, the
paid tool of the antisemites, excoriated, left without peace.
But I have got to go ahead, see ahead." [8]

Ornitz favored the abandonment of all vestiges of Jewish
separateness, getting rid of the foul fungus of the ghetto,
becoming an integral part of the American nation. He held
that, if Jews retained their paranoic tendency to regard themselves as God's Chosen People, they faced the danger of again
being yellow-badged, of again arousing distrust, dislike and
persecution among their neighbors. The quickest way of ending Jewish isolationism was by intermarriage. By bringing in
the saving tonic of new blood, by mingling and mixing, Jews
would no longer stand out as hysterical and neurasthenic;
they would cease to be money-chasers and dream-chasers,
fanatics, radicals, and *allrightniks;* they would become normal individuals.

The term *allrightniks* was just then becoming popular as a
designation for the Jewish nouveaux-riches and Ornitz gave
the following description of them: "Allrightniks: plump and
fat women who blandished the extremes of the latest styles in
clothes, trying to outvie one another; and were never seen
without a blending array of diamonds on ears, breasts, fingers
and arms . . . . the men were always businessmen—business
was their cult, hobby, pastime—their life. Did they collect in
little groups on a social evening, then they discussed the fascinating details of some speculation or enterprise. They interpreted life in terms of moneymaking. Their faces were
puffed and sleekly pale; their bellies stuck out as the show
windows of their prosperity. Invariably you found them
chewing fat cigars; their middle fingers ablaze with many-

[8] S. B. Ornitz, *Haunch Paunch and Jowl,* New York, 1923, p. 200.

karated solitaires: eye openers. . . . The women played poker in the afternoon and in the evening came together to gossip and flaunt clothes and diamonds, mentioned significantly what they paid for this and that, complained of their servants, to whom they left the care of their children, and told risqué stories: their talk was a hysteric din, and their laughter unrestrained . . . . while in the adjoining room, their husbands, loud-mouthed and coarse-humored, gathered to play stud-poker or pinochle for high stakes. The game was not the thing: they were charmed by the gamble." [9]

The decay of the Jewish immigrant generation under the influence of sudden wealth or crushing poverty, first adequately described by Abraham Cahan and continued by Yezierska and Ornitz, remained a fertile subject for the realistic novel that flourished between the two World Wars and reached a climax during the years of the Great Depression.

[9] *Ibid.*, p. 295.

Chapter IX

TWENTIETH CENTURY JEWISH POETS

Not until the decade of the First World War was the impact of American poets of Jewish origin significant for the development of American literature. In the nineteenth century, no Jewish writer of verse with the exception of Emma Lazarus rose above mediocrity. But even her influence did not extend beyond her coreligionists, save for her sonnet engraved on the Statue of Liberty. Penina Moise composed her hymns solely for the Jewish ritual and her lyrics on general themes hardly penetrated further than her small Charleston circle. Adah Isaacs Menken owed her fame far more to her glamorous personality and her daring acting than to her slender volume of lyrics.

The immigrant generation of Eastern European origin did include ever since the eighteen-eighties poets of fine talent but their medium of expression was Yiddish and not English. Of their early poets the most gifted were David Edelstadt (1866–1892), Joseph Bovshover (1873–1915), Morris Rosenfeld (1862–1923), and Morris Vinchevsky (1856–1933).

Only Bovshover published a few good poems in English before he was shrouded in spiritual darkness at the age of twenty-six. His poem *To the Toilers* anticipated Edwin Markham's *Man with the Hoe*. It appeared under the pseudonym of Basil Dahl in Benjamin R. Tucker's Anarchist journal, *Liberty*, in 1896.

Morris Rosenfeld's Yiddish lyrics of the sweatshop were available to English readers as early as 1898. He owed this good fortune to the fact that in the preceding year his *Song Book* had attracted the attention of Leo Wiener of Harvard University, who was a professor of Russian, a lover of Yiddish, and the father of Norbert Wiener, the mathematician and cyberneticist. He reviewed this book in *The Nation*, a widely read and influential weekly. Other articles then appeared in the *Boston Transcript*. Interest in the poet of the slums reached a climax with the publication of Rosenfeld's *Songs from the Ghetto* in an English transliteration and an English prose rendering by Leo Wiener. New York newspapers sensationalized the emergence of a genuine poet in the exotic Judeo-German jargon of the immigrants. Periodicals in French and German then spread his reputation to foreign countries.

At the turn of the century, Solomon Bloomgarden (1870–1927), who wrote under the pen name of Yehoash, Abraham Wald (1872–1938), whose works appeared under the pseudonym of Abraham Liessin, H. Rosenblatt (1878–1956), and Joseph Rolnick (1879–1955) were making the transition from didactic social poetry and propagandistic verse to the impressionistic, individualistic lyric which was to become dominant after 1905. In 1907, *Die Yunge* erupted upon the American Yiddish scene, preaching art for art's sake, deëmphasizing content, straining for perfection of form, and leading the Yiddish muse out of its parochial hamlet and onto the world scene.

No English poet of Jewish origin who appeared in America before World War I could vie in talent with these Yiddish lyricists. The native Jewish generation was largely mute. The few who did publish volumes of verse eschewed Jewish themes. Arthur Guiterman, the New York poet, who was born of American parents in Vienna in 1871 but who was educated in New York's public schools and in constant contact with Jewish fellow-students at the City College, began with light verse in 1907, published fifteen volumes of verse until his death in 1943, but left not a single Jewish poem of value. Franklin P. Adams, who began in 1902 with the light love poems *In Cupid's Court,* wrote on innumerable themes but scrupulously avoided Jewish ones. His early rondeaus, triolets, villanelles, ballades and sonnets betrayed the influence of France and England but not of Jewish spiritual territory. He became better known with the verses of *Tobogganing on Parnassus,* which appeared in 1911. His next collection, entitled *In Other Words,* 1912, contained a poem on "The Exile of Erin," in which he sang the praise of the Irish immigrant lass Maggie O'Ryan, who after a month on the new soil was again cheerful and gladsome, thriftily at work, faultlessly dressed, completely integrated in her American environment.[1] But Adams was completely oblivious of the Jewish immigrants who daily passed before his eyes and never permitted himself to mention them in a single line. His "Lines On the Sabbath," in this volume, dealt with the Christian Sabbath and not the Jewish. They recounted the joys and diversions of a Sunday afternoon.

For many years Adams edited *The Conning Tower* in *The New York Mail,* then in *The New York Tribune,* and longest of all in *The New York World,* a column in which he accepted and edited the verse of other people as well as his own. The best of these poems were published in 1926 as *The Conning Tower Book* and in 1927 as *The Second Conning Tower Book.* Every one of these literary contributions was entirely devoid of references to Jews or Jewish events. His selected songs of thirty years, which appeared in 1936 under the title *The Melancholy Lute,* contained a poem on Benjamin Franklin which began with the lines:

[1] F. P. Adams, *In Other Words,* Garden City, New York, 1912, pp. 129–130.

"O Muse American, assist me,
And elevate my pinions to the sky!" [2]

It was to the American muse and not to the Jewish that he ever turned for inspiration. His American visions began with Christopher Columbus, the discoverer of the New World, and swept on to the heroes and heroines of the contemporary scene but he completely overlooked Jewish personalities or Jewish achievements. He hailed Noah Webster's American Dictionary as a tremendous Declaration of Independence, for it set down authoritatively words that the new country felt ashamed of and apologized for until they appeared in this book. But for Franklin P. Adams—F.P.A., as he was known daily to hundreds of thousands of readers—the secret shame of his Jewishness was never bared in a declaration of independence. His nobility of soul made him, the satirist and eternal mocker, stop short of satirizing or mocking his origin. He never uttered a word of defamation about Jews as did some Jewish self-hating poets of his generation. He was merely silent.

Equally silent about his Jewish coreligionists and fellow-citizens was the poet Stanton A. Coblentz, who wrote daily feature poems for *The San Francisco Examiner* until 1920, when he left his California home and settled in New York. His twelve books of poetry and eight books of prose roamed far from the Jewish field and even in the anthologies of modern lyrics which he edited he avoided including poems on Jewish subject-matter by others.

The poet and novelist John Cournos, who was born in Kiev, Ukraine, during the pogrom year of 1881, as the offspring of Hassidim and of Cabalists, and who began his American career in 1891 as a newsboy in Philadelphia, jeered and taunted as a dirty sheeny in the City of Brotherly Love,

---

[2] F. P. Adams, *The Melancholy Lute*, New York, 1936, p. 79.

ultimately reacted to his Jewish origin far more vigorously and far more negatively by having himself baptized and thus escaping all association with an undesired ancestral community of fate. In *An Open Letter to Jews and Christians*, 1938, he even pleaded with his former coreligionists to accept Jesus as the apex and the acme of Jewish teaching.

Joseph Auslander, a poet of fine sensitivity, included in his first volume of poetry *Sunrise Trumpets*, 1924, verses "To a Nun," to the medieval "Yseult," to the guillotined "Marie Antoinette," and to a fabled queen of ancient Egypt "In the Temple of Nofertari," but not a single reference that would identify him, who was born of Jewish parents in Philadelphia, as a Jew. The figures of the great Age of Romance floated before his eyes and he struck his lyre like a medieval troubadour or, as Padraic Colum characterized him, "a troubadour who had slipped into the New World." [3] Was this lyricist really unaware of the glory and martyrdom of his own forefathers or of their contemporary offspring even while he displayed keenest insight into the glory and martyrdom of many peoples, past and present? He was not deficient in perception. He merely retained within his complex personality inhibitions that he could not overcome. He, who was educated at Harvard and at the Sorbonne, who lectured on poetry at Columbia University and who was poetry editor of the *North American Review*, merely preferred to remain mute about this facet of his being which linked him with denizens of the slums and children of the ghetto.

The extreme absurdity to which this poet attained in his eagerness to avoid any reference to Jews even when it was almost unavoidable can best be illustrated by an examination of his lyric salutes to the European peoples that were occupied by the Nazis and whom he hailed in 1943 in his volume *The Unconquerables*. He paid poetic tributes to the undying spirit of the French, Czechoslovaks, Norwegians, Poles,

---

[3] Joseph Auslander, *Sunrise Trumpets*, New York, 1924, p. XI.

Dutch, Belgians, Greeks, Luxembourgers, and Yugoslavs. He had verses of compassion for the Finns and the British, the heroes of Dunkerque and the Chetniks of the Balkans. But he did not include a single verse of compassion for Jewish suffering or a single word of praise for Jewish resistance.

In recounting German savagery in Poland, Auslander was intensely eloquent but maintained deep secrecy about the fact that the victims of this savagery were primarily Jews:

Write down the whole horrible inventory
Of murder and massacre and plunder:
Record the appalling story
In all its minutiae, howsoever gory—
The sacking of each home, each laboratory,
Each library, church, convent, museum—the ripping asunder
Of beds, the burning of books, the carts groaning under
Their daily hauls,
The people falling flat on their faces
From bullets or hunger, in all kinds of places,
The blood-splattered walls,
The knocking on doors in the night,
The driving like cattle, the faces dead-white,
The vast slaughterhouse from which there is no flight;
Executions en masse
By electric shock or lethal gas,
Or, lined up along self-dug trenches,
And shot in the back of the head,
Or rotting in labor camps, or dropping dead
In the streets with their incredible stenches;
The women parcelled out as wenches
For the pleasure of privates and officers—precise blueprint of extermination
Of the Pole by every vicious device of annihilation.[4]

[4] Joseph Auslander, *The Unconquerables*, New York, 1943, p. 27.

In this recording of the entire horrible inventory, Auslander makes no mention of synagogues burned but only of churches and convents; he gives no hint of ghetto walls or extermination camps for Jews; he leaves the impression that every vicious device of annihilation was directed against these victims because they were Poles and not because they were Jews.

What a contrast between Auslander's silence on Jewish suffering even during the years of the holocaust and Maxwell Bodenheim's outcry in the "Poem to Gentiles," a poem of 1944 which began with the accusing lines:

> The butchering must be wholesale and the smell
> Of dead Jews must be strong enough to drift,
> Like vastly stifled echoes of a yell,
> Before the easy, widespread protests lift.
> How many of them are sincere? [5]

Bodenheim was a master of modernistic technique, a hedonist in life and art, a rebel against social conventions, a Bohemian who wandered on many erring paths in search of elusive beauty, a symbolic representative of Greenwich Village culture until he was murdered. He never shunned unpopular causes and he pioneered in the treatment of unconventional themes. One of his earliest lyrics dealt with a Jewish pushcart peddler, who was not depicted sensationally as an object of pity or adoration but rather etched as a living, breathing human being who made up part of the New York landscape. This majestic poem, entitled "East Side: New York," appeared in Bodenheim's first volume of poems, *Advice*, 1920:

> An old Jew munches an apple,
> With conquering immersion
> All the thwarted longings of his life
> Urge on his determined teeth.

[5] Thomas Yoseloff, ed., *Seven Poets in Search of an Answer*, New York, 1944, p. 15.

His face is hard and pear-shaped;
His eyes are muddy capitulations;
But his mouth is incongruous.
Softly, slightly distended,
Like that of a whistling girl,
It is ingenuously haunting
And makes the rest of him a soiled, grey background.
Hopes that lie within their grave
Of submissive sternness,
Have spilled their troubled ghosts upon this mouth,
And a tortured belief
Has dwindled into tenderness upon it. . . .
He trudges off behind his push-cart
And the Ghetto walks away with him.[6]

Louis Untermeyer characterized Bodenheim's world as one of dreams and bright unreality—an escape from the real world to which he was unable to make any adjustment—and he sensed in Bodenheim's lyrics the racial austerity of the Jew manifesting itself beneath the lavish, tropical imagery.[7]

American Jewish poets who wrote in English were not usually recruited from the ranks of the immigrant generation and they, therefore, did not reflect the reality in which these newcomers lived. The poets were either respected members of the second generation on American soil who had made good their escape from the metropolitan ghettos or else wayward Bohemian artists who seemed indifferent to applause or calumny and hence touched only now and then upon piquant and picturesque aspects of the Jewish scene without attempting to penetrate into deeper levels. The poets with a dedicated Jewish approach were in a minority and made little or no impact upon the general American literary move-

[6] Maxwell Bodenheim, *Advice*, New York, 1920, p. 32.
[7] Louis Untermeyer, "The Jewish Spirit in Modern American Poetry," *Menorah Journal*, VII (1921), 127.

ments. Some like David P. Berenburg and Elias Lieberman were unread. Others found an audience in limited Jewish circles, and only temporarily. There was Charles Reznikoff, historian and scholar, whose first volume, *Poems*, appeared in 1920 and was followed by many other volumes of prose and verse, fiction and drama, none of which had a wide vogue despite their magnificent imagery and warm symbolism. There was Louis I. Newman, rabbi, orator, and poet, whose *Songs of Jewish Rebirth* appeared in 1921 and his *Joyful Jeremiads* in 1926. These were soon forgotten while his *Hasidic Anthology*, 1934, and *Talmudic Anthology*, 1939, long retained popular favor. There was Philip M. Raskin, who began with *Songs of a Jew* in 1914 and of whom Charles Angoff said that he not only "Caught the loneliness of the Jewish soul and its dark pessimism and its resigned ironical outlook on life but he also caught its cosmic playfulness, its high mockery of the vicissitudes of life, its impregnable pride in its own integrity." [8] There was Jesse Sampter, whose lyrics of Zion were recited upon their publication in the nineteen-twenties and nineteen-thirties and rarely since, even though she was among the pioneering American women who not only sang of a nighing rebirth of Israel but herself actually experienced this rebirth when she settled in the young Kibbutz of Givat Brenner.

The only poet who participated in a major way in America's lyric upsurge on the eve of World War I and thereafter and who at the same time sought inspiration both in the Jewish past and in the Jewish forces that streamed within him was Louis Untermeyer, the author of more than seventy volumes of prose and verse, short stories, travel books, parodies, essays and critical anthologies.

Untermeyer was a third-generation American of German

[8] Charles Angoff, "Impressions of Contemporary Jewish American Poetry," *Jewish Book Annual*, XV (1957), 29.

Israelite ancestry. His paternal grandfather emigrated from Bavaria and his maternal grandfather from Alsace. His father regarded himself as a Yankee and his mother regarded herself as a Southerner. The poet, who was born in 1885, was so deeply rooted in Americanism that he did not have to struggle to attain an American personality. He merely accepted his Americanism and his Jewishness as the destiny assigned to him at birth and he lived this destiny without struggling against it or boasting of it.

When Untermeyer joined the radical magazine *The Masses* in 1912, he submitted as one of his early contributions a poem on Moses, whom he envisaged as a divided soul, liberator and lawgiver, half realist and half philosophical anarchist. Although this long poem was rejected by the editors, Floyd Dell and Max Eastman, he continued with this theme until it ultimately ripened as his novel *Moses*, 1928.

In an essay on the Jewish spirit in modern American poetry, Untermeyer distinguished between three tendencies present in the poetry written by Jews. The first was the poetry of exaltation, of mystical fervor and vision, of Messianism. The second was the poetry of disillusionment, of bitter irony and driving restlessness. The third was the poetry of exultation, of sheer physical joy and thanksgiving. Untermeyer saw in James Oppenheim an almost perfect example of the first type. Despite the fact that Oppenheim did not normally choose his subjects from the Bible or Jewish folklore, his approach was definitely Biblical. "His literary ancestry can be found in the psalms of David, the denunciations of Jeremiah, the confident fervors of Isaiah. His is the spirit of the prophet-poets, the spirit that declares 'Cry aloud, spare not, lift thy voice like a trumpet!' In Oppenheim is united the old iconoclasm and the older worship; his books read like the work of a challenging minor prophet with a flair for analysis. . . . Here is a poetry that searches even as it sings; an attempt to diagnose the twisted soul of man and the twisted epoch that conditions it." [9]

Untermeyer himself belonged to the second type, whose finest exponent in modern times had been Heinrich Heine. Indeed, the strongest literary influence in the shaping of Untermeyer's personality came from this German poet. This influence was already apparent in Untermeyer's earliest book of lyrics, *First Love,* 1911. It remained with him ever thereafter. It found expression in a superb volume of translations of Heine's *Poems,* 1917, and in the two volume biography *Heinrich Heine: Paradox and Poet,* 1937. The spirit of the dying Heine was reproduced brilliantly and pathetically in the "Monolog from a Mattress," one of Untermeyer's best poems.

Untermeyer saw Heine as a sensitive Jew not unlike himself but born in a savagely antisemitic country rather than in a democratic one like America, which was far more tolerant of ethnic and religious dissent. He traced many of Heine's paradoxical traits back to his birth. Superficially Heine became a Christian-German lawyer, a French journalist, an expatriated cosmopolite, but in the deepest reaches of his soul he still remained a Jew.

Untermeyer did not take Heine's Hellenism too seriously. Peering into his own soul, he found that the Greek ideal of art for art's sake did not satisfy him but that the Hebraic ideal of art for life's sake did. He then read this Jewish ideal also into Heine. He formulated his own vision of the Jew as poet in these words: "From the first prophet-priests who compiled the Books of Moses to the obscure rhapsodist who wrote the Psalms, the vision was always a democratic one. These Jews identified themselves with their songs; their confident egoism as message-bringers lifted them above their pre-

[9] Louis Untermeyer, "The Jewish Spirit in Modern American Poetry," *Menorah Journal,* VII (1921), 122–123.

occupations as artists; and when they exalted God they were celebrating what was godlike and powerful in men. Before the Jews would acknowledge Beauty, it would have to stand shoulder to shoulder with them, work among them, drink, sweat, suffer and become part of their daily desires and dreams; to them it could never be merely its own excuse for being." [10]

This characterization of Jews as artists he was prepared to accept for himself. But he bristled when D. H. Lawrence in a letter of 1926 referred to him as "Der ewige Jude." In the same letter to Mabel Dodge Luhan, Lawrence continued: "Plus ça change, plus c'est la même chose: that is the whole history of the Jew from Moses to Untermeyer." While feeling rather flattered by this association with Moses, the American poet was deeply hurt to be dubbed a wandering Jew. Angrily he remarked in his autobiography: "But what did Lawrence know of me? Or Moses? Or the Jews?" Untermeyer then levelled an attack upon Lawrence for the latter's undemocratic views, for his belief in the divine right of natural aristocracy, the right of one individual to wield undisputed authority over others. "Here was the real split between Lawrence and myself. As a Jew I could not accept dictatorially inspired authority; freedom was not a 'detestable negative creed,' but something for which one never ceased fighting. The Jew suffered because he constantly denied divine authority in mortal man; he was hounded, put to the rack, beaten and broken because he refused to take power for granted. The Jew doubted perfection, and agonized himself to make something, anything, better. He was hurt (literally) not because he could not adapt himself to strange people, but because he dared to believe he could help them, even when they did not want to be helped. It was not merely the itch to

[10] Heinrich Heine, *Poems,* New York, 1923. Preface by Louis Untermeyer, p. VII.

reform; it was a constant *Weltschmerz,* a sad but stubborn moral yearning. He pitted himself foolhardily against inertia. Doomed by his very nature to resist complacency, which he identified with rigidity and death, the Jew offended those who did not wish to be roused. The objections to him were logical. He was, in the strictest sense, an agitator; he excited and irritated those who wanted no change. From the point of view of those who prayed never to be disturbed, the Jew was truly a disturbing element. The Jew might well have expected the reaction. He should have remembered that the pioneer is ridiculed by the stay-at-home, the disturber is cast out, and the prophet is stoned." [11]

Although Untermeyer never denied his Jewishness and normally did not go out of his way to stress it, he did make a point of emphasizing it during an audience with Mussolini in Rome in 1935, when the latter was at the height of power. Untermeyer then told the Fascist dictator: "I am not a politician. I am not always a poet. But I am undeniably a Jew." [12]

In the lyric volume *Roast Leviathan,* 1923, Untermeyer versified Jewish legends of Jephtha and Solomon and Istehar, the beloved of the Seraph Shemhazai. Blending irony and pathos in the title poem of this volume, he depicted two Jews who could put up with the jeers of this world because they found comfort in blissful dreams of Judgment Day when they and all the starving Chosen of God would feast on Roast Leviathan and listen to the Deity himself expounding the Torah.

In prefatory remarks, Untermeyer disowned his friendly critics who insisted with a well-meant euphemism that his poems were Oriental in quality. He told them that the poems were specifically and frankly Jewish. They were Jewish not only in subject matter but also in their peculiar mixture of

[11] Louis Untermeyer, *From Another World,* New York, 1939, pp. 322–323.
[12] *Ibid.,* p. 360.

fantasy and irony. In the opening poem, "Lost Jerusalem," he described the typical Jew as a cross between a monarch and a mourner, dark-eyed and dismal but proud with an insolent sort of grace, at once rebellious and resigned. When the news broke during World War I that Jerusalem had been taken by Allenby's forces and that therefore, under the Balfour Declaration of 1917, this meant freedom for the Jews at last, the poet's alter ego questioned whether restoration to Jerusalem was really the ultimate fulfillment of the Jewish goal for which their many generations had bled. Were not Jews also God-makers and God-breakers, bearers of light, freedom, faith, and tolerance to the whole world? Were they to skulk back home and be a light only for themselves? Yet, on the other hand, was not the alternative equally unthinkable: to continue forever as the Ishmael and scapegoat among the peoples of this earth?

In an ironic poem "Ishmael," Untermeyer reacted vigorously to a news despatch that several of the European nations under the stress of war made the concession of no longer debarring Jewish soldiers from attaining the rank of officers:

> Again the wanderer starts out
> To alien battles, and we see,
> Beneath the welter and the rout,
> The same persistent irony.
>
> He goes, too dumbly to be grim,
> Down to the dead, the chosen ones;
> While nations that rejected him
> Accept his flesh to stop the guns.
>
> Plunged in a war he never sought,
> Hurled at his brothers' gaping lines,
> Blinded, bewildered, scattered, caught,
> An unexpected promise shines.

He stops. The blessing seems too great.
Then, with a final, welcoming breath,
He goes to meet a brilliant fate,
And die, perhaps, a captain's death!

Pariah, outcast—he delights
In struggles that should drive him mad.
He lives upon despair, and fights
To save a home he never had.[13]

Untermeyer's *Roast Leviathan* was dedicated to the poetess Jean Starr Untermeyer to whom he was then married and in whom, he felt, the ancient music had found a living voice. However, one searches in vain throughout the early volumes of this Jewish poetess, *Growing Pains,* 1918, and *Dreams out of Darkness,* 1921, for any themes or characteristics that would identify her in any way with Jewishness. Not until 1927, when her lyric volume *Steep Ascent* appeared, did she include a poem in which she accepted her kinship with the Biblical people. In the stanzas of "According to Scripture," she gloried in this kinship and vowed to hold it dearer than daily bread. In her *Later Poems,* which appeared in 1958, forty years after her first volume, she took leave of the Gods of her youth and recognized that deep within her personality Sinai, and not Hellas, was dominant. In the poem "The Kaddish," she sought to recapture accents of the ancient Hebrew prayer, even though the ancestral language was strange to her. She was at last aware that to be in communion with her people was life and that to stand apart was death. From Venus with her capricious ardor, the poetess had come home to Jehovah.

Among the American writers of Jewish origin who came to the fore in the nineteen-twenties, Robert Nathan impressed his contemporaries primarily as a novelist and attention was

[13] Louis Untermeyer, *Roast Leviathan,* New York, 1923, pp. 135-136.

frequently called to his inclusion of Jewish characters in his
narratives and to his modernization of the Biblical story of
Jonah in 1925. But there was only limited knowledge of his
achievements as a poet. In a decade of blatant lyric mani-
festos and experimentation, his gentle verses, small in quan-
tity and using conventional stanzaic forms, were passed over
in comparative silence by critics. But Louis Untermeyer, discoverer of poetic talents, wrote of Nathan's second volume:
"Violence and self-glory are wholly absent from Mr. Nathan's
even lines. There is no belligerence or blatancy in this volume. There is, on the other hand, a little sadness, a little
shrugging whimsicality, and much of wisdom. Underneath
the simple contours, one can not fail to detect that grief for
an apathetic world, that racial and unrewarding sympathy
which the Germans call *Weltschmerz*." [14]

Nathan's books of verse began with *Youth Grows Old*,
1922, and *A Cedar Box*, 1929. Although the former volume contained lyrics on Israel's exile and on the funeral of a
Jew and the latter volume a poem on Noah and the beautiful sonnet beginning with the line "Thebes and Jerusalem
are in your eyes," it was in the sonnets of 1935 and in *A Winter Tide* of 1940 that Nathan bequeathed memorable Jewish
verses. Written during the Hitler period, when the poison of
antisemitism lapped the shores of all continents, Nathan did
not shout angry protests against a world gone awry. He rather
implored the God of pity and of love to return to this earth
and not to abandon it to the devilish powers of evil and darkness. God seemed to have chosen the Chosen People to wear
again the crown of pain, the briar branch of scorn. God hung
around their shoulders His scrolls and none who were born as
Jews were able to escape the poison of His grace. Experiencing sorrow from birth, hated and homeless, they themselves

[14] Robert Nathan, *A Cedar Box*, Indianapolis, 1929. Foreword by Louis
Untermeyer.

never learned to hate, they never yielded to evil, they continued to guard the wells of pity, of the heart.

The lyrics of *A Winter Tide* contained admonitions to the
Germans not to put Jews in ghettos or to undertake to wall
up the Jewish spirit. The Jewish scapegoats who were being
driven into the desert would somehow survive in the barren
wastes and would ultimately return to browse again in the
weeds of ruined gardens, while the pompous young and old
members of the *Herrenvolk,* who were flinging their hands
upward, shouting "Heil" and living by the sword, would in
the long run perish by the sword. The poet called for the
unity of Jew and Christian against the modern worshippers
of new Baalim. Judaism was the root and Christianity the
flower of the divine plant.

> Shall the flower deny the root, or the root the blossom?
> They are one, one growth, one planting, now and for-
> ever.
> Before them was nothing; and after them will be noth-
> ing.[15]

In the poem "Moses on Nebo," Nathan had Moses contem-
plate sadly the vista of the coming centuries and confess that
what he saw was not what he expected from his friend God.
He had hoped to lead his people out of Egypt to a land of
their own but they were wandering on and on down the generations still homeless and hearthless.

> David and Jesus, children of my bones,
> Have you nowhere to bid us welcome home? [16]

In "Prayer for Exiles," the poet invoked God's help for the
forlorn children of Israel set adrift in an unfeeling world:

> Almighty Spirit who has shaped our truth,
> Within whose awful hand the sparrow rests,

---

[15] Robert Nathan, *A Winter Tide,* New York, 1940, p. 25.
[16] *Ibid.,* p. 21.

Whose angels in the heavens of our youth
With holy mercy comforted our breasts,
Father and friend, whose voice melodious
Sang through the thunder in the cloudy dome,
Take to Your heart which weeps for all of us,
These children very small and far from home.
These are no soldiers weighted with a sword,
These are but babies fed with bitter bread;
Their only roof and dwelling is Your word,
Your love the only pillow for their head.
Watch over them and guard them all forlorn,
Far in the west amidst the alien corn.[17]

The mood of this prayer was the mood of his sad novel *Road of Ages,* 1935, whose theme was the exile of the Jews from all lands. Only the Mongols offered them a haven in the Gobi Desert. These unhappy people were therefore forced in the mid-twentieth century to undertake the long trek across Europe and Asia, conversing in all the languages of the world, beaten by students, robbed by the peasants, and assaulted by the police of every country. At first, in the midst of their distress, they still kept alive their differences of opinion. Communists fought socialists and capitalists, orthodox worshippers disputed with atheists, those who had once been citizens of the West could not easily get along with Chassidim of the East. But under the goad of suffering, they were gradually welded into a unity, they found their way to their Jewish selves, they would establish in the desert a new Israel where everybody would be friends.

Nathan, the descendant of Colonial Sephardic Jewry—one of his ancestors was the revered Revolutionary patriot Rabbi Gershom Seixas—and Louis Untermeyer, the descendant of pre-Civil War Israelites, expressed in their prose and verse a far more positive approach to the Jewish past, a far deeper

[17] *Ibid.,* p. 42.

understanding of the Jewish present and a far greater faith in the Jewish future than did the no less talented but only semi-integrated children of the Eastern immigrants, the unhappy second generation Americans who were fleeing from ghetto memories, wallowing in self-hatred, and inflicting much hurt upon themselves and their kinsmen before their recovery set in. The emotional and spiritual insecurity of this generation, its frustrated idealism and its sneering cynicism, its mighty striving and its horrible excrescences were explored in the realistic novel of the nineteen-twenties and nineteen-thirties.

Chapter X

THE JEW IN NON-JEWISH FICTION

The Jew depicted in American fiction before the Eastern European mass immigration still bore in the main the traits of the stereotypes that stalked through British fiction. The muckrakers of the closing nineteenth century discovered the quaint Russian-born Jew of the slums and the sweatshops. The radical novel of the early twentieth century introduced the Jewish agitator who was active among the younger immigrants as socialist, anarchist, trade-unionist, Utopian visionary. The sentimental novel mirrored the pathos and the comedy of the Jewish family from the precocious breadwinning children to the outlandish impractical patriarchs. But it was the realistic novel between the two world wars that best portrayed the increasing complexity of the Jewish scene, the dissonances and frailties of the Americanized successors of the pioneering immigrants.

Both Jewish and non-Jewish writers made use of the medium of fiction to come to grips with Jewish reality. To some non-Jewish novelists like Robert Herrick, Willa Cather, Edith Wharton, Ernest Hemingway, Thomas Wolfe and Theodore Dreiser the Jew was still inscrutable, uncanny, or monstrous. To other non-Jewish novelists like Dorothy Canfield Fisher, Sinclair Lewis, John Dos Passos, John Hersey and Richard Wright, he was more pleasant and sympathetic.

Reviewing in June 1930 the presentment of the Jew in American fiction of the preceding decade, Florence Kipper

Frank summarized the attitude of a group of novelists of old American stock who resented the intrusion of the Jewish influence into the sphere of American culture. "They know that there is only one sort of Jew—the bounder Jew. Robert Herrick's novels contain him in contemptuous reference. Willa Cather has devoted a bitter story to the Jewish bounder, Ernest Hemingway has done his portrait in *The Sun Also Rises*. Edith Wharton recognizes only this Jew. For these writers, he is a symbol of modern social disintegration. Here, they say in effect, is what our subtle and discriminating Anglo-Saxon culture has come to—this contact with a type that is influencing and yet can never understand our values." [1]

This vulgar Jew of obtrusive manners was no longer an East Sider but had made his way to the more fashionable districts of Park Avenue or Riverside Drive and was hobnobbing with the socially elect. Edith Wharton described this glittering, bejewelled, distasteful upstart as follows: "A short man with a deceptively blond head, thick lips under a stubby blond mustache, and eyes like needles behind tortoise shell-rimmed glasses, stood . . . . bulging a glossy shirtfront and solitaire pearl toward the company. 'Don't this lady dance?' he enquired, in a voice like melted butter, a few drops of which seemed to trickle down his lips and be licked back at intervals behind a thickly ringed hand." [2]

Hemingway's Robert Cohn in *The Sun Also Rises*, 1926, had no trace of this vulgarity and yet he too was an unpleasant, ridiculous figure. He too tried to infiltrate old-stock American circles where he was not really wanted. A member through his father of one of the richest Jewish families of

---

[1] F. K. Frank, "The Presentment of the Jew in American Fiction," *Bookman*, LXXI (1930), p. 274.
[2] *Ibid.*

New York and through his mother of one of the oldest, he had grown up without any Jewish consciousness and had been sent to a military school, where he prepared for Princeton. Not until he got to this fashionable college did anyone make him feel that he was a Jew and therefore did not quite belong among the respectable and the socially elite. This experience made the friendly young man shy and bitter. To counteract a budding feeling of inferiority, he took up boxing. Although he really disliked this sport, he learned it painfully and thoroughly. It gave him a sense of physical achievement and of belongingness. Nevertheless, others still looked upon him as an outsider and an intruder. Despite a hard stubborn streak in his personality, which made him persist in wooing a society which at best barely tolerated him, he was not happy in its midst, miserable outside of it, and made others uncomfortable by his presence.

Hutchins Hapgood, an ardent defender of the Jews, tried to convince Hemingway that it was an error to depict Robert Cohn as the typical Jew. In a letter of May 27, 1937, Hapgood wrote to the novelist: "I don't know whether you know the Jews very intimately or not, but, if you do, you must have been impressed with their extreme sensitiveness. . . . Your character of Cohn in *The Sun Also Rises* is a remarkable picture of a human being. I know the man who served as a sitter to you for the portrait, know him very slightly, and it is a striking fact that only on the slightest acquaintance he affected me the same way as he affected the other characters in your book. Without doing or saying anything that I could fairly resent, he yet made me feel uncomfortable the two or three times I was with him. But he made me uncomfortable not because he was a Jew but because he was the man you call Cohn. It has never seemed to me to be fair to put into an unfavorable picture of a human being the factor of race as a causal relationship. It is certainly something which one cannot expect the Jews to like." [8]

Hapgood found a dynamism and vitality both among Jewish intellectuals and artists and among the Jewish masses, such as he never experienced among any other group of people. While the reserved, genteel writers sneered at these human beings as an unpleasant lot, he knew them to be colorful, tumultuous, vigorously alive, delightfully intense.

When Thomas Wolfe came from Harvard to New York, he also found among Jews thrilling excitement, richness, color, genuineness, indestructible hope. When he walked along Second Avenue by day or prowled there during long, lonely nights, he discovered in this Broadway of the East Side Jews the better Broadway, a Broadway with the warmth of life and the thronging sense of community. After a generation of eating the bread of misery and of dwelling in habitations unfit for swine, Jews were emerging undefeated, opulent, mocking, insatiate, having a glorious time.

Wolfe was torn between his admiration for the Jews among whom he was constantly thrown and a deep-seated hostility towards them that harked back to childhood prejudices. In his boyhood days at Asheville, North Carolina, he often joined his playmates in the grand sport of spitting upon Jewish lads, shouting coarse epithets at them, and even torturing them. It was fun to pounce upon a little "kike," to harry him down alleys, over fences, across yards, into barns, stables, until he escaped into his own house. It was good to have a Jewish scapegoat around, somebody weak, somebody to badger, somebody at whom the flood of ridicule might be directed from which one might himself suffer otherwise.

After his New England years, where he was disgusted by what he termed the dry sterility and juiceless quality of the

[8] Hutchins Hapgood, *A Victorian in the Modern World*, New York, 1939, p. 535.

Puritan inheritance, Wolfe plunged into the whirl of New York and found himself surrounded by admiring Jewish students, loved by a Jewish woman, and admitted into the circles of wealthy Jewish businessmen and sophisticated Jewish aesthetes.

When as a young instructor he entered his classroom at Washington Square College of New York University, he imagined that "the girls, the proud and potent Jewesses with their amber flesh, schooled to a goal of marriage, skilled in all the teasings of erotic trickery, with their lustful caution and their hot virginity pressed in around him in a drowning sensual tide; with looks of vacant innocence and with swift counterglances of dark mockery." [4]

When he escaped from the classroom to the glittering salons of the intellectuals and the patrons of arts and letters, he also encountered there a predominance of Jews and soon tired of their constant talk about art and literature. He found them weary with the excess of knowledge, arrogant in the consciousness of their own superiority despite their apparent grovelling before Christians, oversensitive to criticism of their people. They were forever arguing, jibing, shrieking, shouting, swarthily jeering and sneering: their words were sharp and cutting, impregnated with unpleasant aggressiveness.

When he took refuge from all this turmoil in the love of a brilliant, artistic, assimilated, rich Jewish woman, he was at first intoxicated by her. She nurtured his talent, she helped him to his initial success as a novelist, she spread his fame, she introduced him to cultivated Jewish men and to their elegant, fashionably gowned, exotically lovely wives. He found a princely quality in the men and admired their fiercely Oriental pride in their identity and their vast pride in the toil and intelligence which had brought them their opulence. He

[4] Thomas Wolfe, *Of Time and the River*, New York, 1935, p. 479.

found, or rather he imagined he found, the Jewish women, the curve of their bodies and souls still unbroken, ready to receive him within the sea-gulf of their passion. "Female, fertile, yolky, fruitful as the earth, and ready for the plow, they offered to the famished wanderer, the alien, the exile, the baffled and infuriated man, escape and surcease of the handsome barren women, the hard varnished sawdust dolls, the arrogant and sterile women, false in look and promise as a hot-house peach, who walked the streets and had no curve or fruitfulness in them." [5]

Wolfe's intoxication with his Jewish beloved, however, did not last, and in his disappointment he soon reverted to his ingrained prejudices against Jews. He then reviled the Jewish men as dark-faced, beak-nosed plutocrats from whose pores goose-grease oozed and who ironically looked on while their wives and daughters yielded undulent bodies to the embraces of Gentile lovers. Suffering from the delusion that Jewish women were crafty Jezebels out to get Christians into their clutches, he regretted that he had ever allowed himself to become so deeply involved with one of them and wished that she and all of them would stick to their own kind.

There were, however, lucid moments unclouded by passion when Wolfe recognized the absurd contradictions in his distorted image of the Jew and he satirically summed up the thought-associations that crossed his mind when confronted with Jews: "The Jews hate the Christians, and they also love them. The Jewish women seduce the pure young Christian boys because they love them and want to destroy them, and the Jewish men, cynical and resigned, look on and rub their hands in glee because they hate the Christians and also love them, too, and want to destroy them because they feel such sympathy and pity for them, and yet say nothing because they get an obscene sexual satisfaction from the spectacle, and be-

[5] Thomas Wolfe, *Of Time and the River*, New York, 1935, p. 480.

cause their souls are old and patient, and they have known that their women were unfaithful for seven thousand years, and they must suffer and endure it." [6]

In his last year, Wolfe tried to make amends for his unreasoned hostility towards Jews, after he witnessed their mistreatment in Hitler's Germany. In the novel *You Can't Go Home Again*, which appeared posthumously in 1940, he described with considerable sympathy a Jewish lawyer who was trying to flee Germany in 1938 and who was caught by Nazi guards at the border. But this belated halfhearted penance could not undo the hurt that his novels had wrought in the relations between Jews and non-Jews during the years of the Great Depression.

Far greater hurt, however, was inflicted at this time by Theodore Dreiser, the realistic novelist who was reputed to be a great liberal. This reputation was justified because of his stand on many political and social issues. It was not justified on the basis of his attitude towards Jews.

It is true that this novelist, who was later to write the great masterpiece *An American Tragedy*, published, in 1918, a Jewish tragedy, *The Hand of the Potter*, which had a pleasant Jewish character, a patriarch of stern integrity. However, the basic theme of this play, the murder of an Irish girl of eleven by the abnormal twenty-one-year-old son of this patriarch, was anything but pleasant. There was no special reason why Dreiser had to inject the factor of race into this sex slaying, especially since sex murders were far rarer among Jews than among other sectors of the population.

Dreiser's basic thesis was that a person could not help being what he was any more than a fly could help being a fly and not an elephant; a person should therefore be judged by his acts and not by his nature and disposition, for which he was not at all responsible. Were Jews then as Jews by nature

[6] Thomas Wolfe, *The Web and the Rock*, New York, 1938, p. 594.

and disposition disposed to such mental and sex aberrations? Obviously not. What motivation was there then for the author to project the demented criminal as Jewish and the innocent victim as a Gentile girl fresh from confession? Was it really essential for Dreiser to bring back to the consciousness of American readers hoary medieval bugaboos? Dreiser went further. He presented the keeper of the furnished rooming-house in which the murderer hid out as a Shylock who even in the presence of the corpse lamented the loss of three weeks rent and tried to collect the owed sum from the grief-stricken father. To this Shylock, Dreiser gave an attractive young Jessica in accordance with an outmoded anti-Jewish literary tradition. Nor did Dreiser refrain from using for his Jews the derogatory synonym "kikes," even putting this expression into the mouths of a Jewish character. It was a designation he himself resorted to in his private correspondence with Gentile friends, generally spelling it "kykes."

As early as September 20, 1920, he was referring to Jews as "kykes," in a letter to the critic H. L. Mencken. In another letter, two years later, he wrote to Mencken on November 5, 1922: "New York to me is a scream—a Kyke's dream of a Ghetto. The lost tribe has taken the island." [7] However, it was more than a decade later, upon Hitler's ascent to power that Dreiser gave public expression to his unfriendly feelings towards Jews. As one of the editors of the periodical *American Spectator*, he suggested a symposium on the Jewish question. He maintained that not only in Germany but throughout the world the Jews were too successful, too clever, too dynamic, too aggressive in their personal and racial attack on all other types and races. The time was ripe to discuss what handicaps might best be imposed upon them and what limitation to their numbers might be desirable in the realm of commerce and in certain practical professions such as law.

[7] Theodore Dreiser, *Letters*, Philadelphia, 1959, II, 405.

Dreiser's fellow-editors George Jean Nathan, Ernest Boyd, James Branch Cabell, and Eugene O'Neill agreed to participate in such a symposium. Only the first of these was Jewish and his contribution was limited merely to a few clever, poisonous remarks. When Dreiser suggested that the Jews might try to nationalize themselves and cease to be wanderers over the face of the globe and when Eugene O'Neill added that to the Jews might be given a territory as large as the United States, a territory extending from the Atlantic to the Indian Ocean and from the northern border of South Africa to or including the Congo, Nathan interjected: "You visualize, Dreiser, one of the most extensive territories in the world inhabited and run by Jews. You believe that they would, by their genius, presently establish themselves as one of the most successful national enterprises in the present world. Within two years, I contend, the dominating element of that population would have joined the Episcopalian Church."

Ernest Boyd, alone among the editors, refused to stigmatize or jest about the Jews. Indeed, he pointed to the basic contradiction in Dreiser's views. How could Dreiser claim, on the one hand, that Jews differed markedly from their neighbors and tended to remain aloof, and assert, on the other hand, that they were not really aloof and that, given sufficient time, they might take over the dictatorship of the United States and of all the nations in whose midst they dwelt, a situation which the novelist could not envisage as comfortable or pleasant for the non-Jews?

Dreiser held that it would be beneficial both for Jews and for non-Jews if the former removed themselves to a land which they could develop into a distinguished nation. "I would ask the Jew with all his ability and his wealth and admiration of power, with all the genius he shows when he enters an alien land and becomes a powerful factor in its welfare, or its domination, I would ask him, I say, personally to consider whether in just plain fairness to nations that want to be themselves, that don't care to be dominated by a church or race or theory of life, and are not, in short, as clever as he is, why he shouldn't step up before the peoples of the world and ask for just such a territory in which to develop a nation of his own and with which he could deal on the basis of his genius in all lines. With the Jews nationally so placed, we could deal, just as they could deal with every other nation in the world. And by degrees all should benefit from their very great ability to organize and construct. What I cannot understand is their present objection to doing so. But this may be the result of their scattering in historic times, and it may, for all we know, be presently overcome by the Jew himself."

This view of Dreiser, as Eugene O'Neill correctly noted, was not far removed from the opinion of Zionists such as Ludwig Lewisohn. It was probably closer to the opinion of Jewish Territorialists like Israel Zangwill. What readers of the "Symposium," which was published in *American Spectator* in September 1933, could not fail to sense, however, was that Dreiser was espousing these views not out of kindness of the heart but rather out of a desire to remove a group he disliked as far as possible from America's shores. To neutralize Jewish influence by one means or another—was this not the Nazi program?

Hutchins Hapgood, who ever stood on watch in defense of Jews, immediately sent a letter to the magazine protesting against the expression of opinions in this liberal organ which might increase Fascist tendencies in the United States. He followed up with a second letter. Neither was published. Ernest Boyd as Managing Editor turned both communications over to Dreiser, who thereupon replied to Hapgood in two long letters reiterating and justifying his antipathy to Jews. In the first letter of October 10, 1933, he accused the Jews of being money-minded, very pagan, very sharp in practice, and lacking fine integrity. Liberalism was too weak to deal with them. "Left to sheer liberalism as you interpret it, they could possess America by sheer numbers, their cohesion, and their race tastes. . . . The Jew insists that when he invades Italy or France or America or what you will, he becomes a native of that country—a full-blooded native of that country. You know yourself, if you know anything, that that is not true. He has been in Germany now for all of a thousand years, if not longer, and he is still a Jew. He has been in America all of two hundred years, and he has not faded into a pure American by any means, and he will not. As I said before, he maintains his religious dogmas and his racial sympathies, race characteristics, and race cohesion as against all the types of nationalities surrounding him whatsoever."

In his second letter of December 28, 1933, Dreiser made the suggestion that the various nations should call an international conference with all Jewry and therein thrash out all the problems worrying so many of the nations as well as the Jews, and by wise counsel on the part of all concerned reach an acceptable program. Jews were mistaken in attempting to establish themselves in the bosom not of one country but of almost all countries. Dreiser was certain that nations would prefer not to annoy or persecute the Jews but rather to furnish them loans and assistance to get out and to start an independent glorious career as a reconstituted nation. This was not barbarism or antisemitism, but a sensible solution. If this proved impractical, Dreiser offered a second possible solution, a program of race blending, such as George Bernard Shaw had advocated. Let every Jewish male be forced to marry a Gentile female, and every Jewish female a Gentile male. There would thus be solved in a comparatively short space of time the vexing question of how the Jew was to be disposed of among the various races and nations of the world.

The publication of Dreiser's letters in *The Nation* on April 17, 1935, by Hapgood under the heading "Is Dreiser Antisemitic?" gave rise to a storm of indignation. *The New Masses,* organ of the Leninists who were claiming Dreiser as their adherent, called upon him for an explanation. After much hesitation and continual shifting of position, he finally consented to issue a statement on April 22, 1935, that Lenin's views on the Jewish question met with his approval. He was against Jewish capitalists but not against the interests of the Jewish workers. He was not responsible for any use the Nazis might make of his letters. He had nothing to do with Hitler or Fascism. He accepted the principle that communism would equitably solve the relations of man.

This equivocal statement, which did not repudiate his earlier letters, made necessary a further conference between Dreiser and his leftist friends, among them Corliss Lamont, James W. Ford, John Howard Lawson, and Michael Gold. They begged him to withdraw the antisemitic opinions expressed in his letters and to dispel the fog of confusion and bewilderment caused by his unexpected outburst of racial prejudice. When Dreiser stuck to his attitude that, as an individual, he had a right to say what he pleased, Michael Gold published a tirade against him in *The New Masses* on May 7, 1935, under the heading "The Gun is Loaded, Dreiser!" Gold recalled that he had once guided Dreiser around on a tour of the East Side when the novelist was gathering material for a play about Jews, *The Hand of the Potter.* Was this the same Dreiser who was now repeating so airily many of the familiar slogans of Hitler and Streicher? Surely Dreiser, the fighter for human liberty, would soon see the error of his ways.

Dreiser maintained public silence. In a letter to Sergei Dinamov on June 27, 1935, however, he made clear that his attitude was unaltered. "I have not changed my viewpoint in regard to the Jewish programme in America. They do not blend as do the other elements in this country, but retain, as they retain in all countries, their race solidarity and even their religion—here particularly. . . . But, after all, I did not make the Jewish problem, and am not compelled to solve it, but, as all Jews realize, it is a problem here in America, as elsewhere, only they will not discuss it, and they have no programme to offer." [8]

Ironically enough, in the same year in which Dreiser was running into so much trouble because of his antisemitism, his books were banned in Germany. He feared that this was being done because for some reason many people believed that he himself was a Jew. Did the Germans believe this because he had once written a Jewish tragedy—*The Hand of the Potter*—which had quite a run on the German stage? He wondered what could be done to alter the German viewpoint towards him. "Of course if my books are being banned because of their psychological or social merits or demerits I have nothing to say. But I would like to know that I am not being banned for being racially something that I am not." [9]

When Heywood Broun asked Dreiser if he could list his name among those protesting against sending an American team to the Olympic games in Berlin so long as the Nazis were persecuting Catholics, Negroes, and Jews, Dreiser replied in the negative in a letter of January 7, 1936. He questioned whether it was just to compel one race of people to associate against its will and inclinations with another.

Not until 1944, a year before his death, when the war against the Nazis was drawing to a successful conclusion, did Dreiser speak out against the German treatment of Jews. In a broadcast beamed to the German people, he mentioned the thousands upon thousands of helpless and often heroic Jews.

[8] *Ibid.*, II, 747.
[9] *Ibid.*, II, 715.

By that time, however, the consequences of antisemitism were apparent in the extermination camps and every American liberal had dissociated himself from the philosophy underlying the Nuremberg race laws.

Unlike Dreiser, the novelist F. Scott Fitzgerald recognized that Jews were neither devilish nor angelic but merely a segment of American society, part of the multiracial panorama. In *The Great Gatsby,* 1925, he attempted a kaleidoscopic image of New York society during the decade of normalcy that followed the First World War. This was the Prohibition Era abounding in liquor smugglers and racketeers. In the Jewish underworld figure Meyer Wolfsheim with the flat-nose and tiny eyes, whose living model was Arnold Rothstein, Fitzgerald created a New York character who was no worse than the other characters of his circle or than the Great Gatsby himself. There was nothing contemptible about him, nothing small except his physical size. He was credited with having fixed the Baseball World Series of 1919. According to Fitzgerald, respect was due to one who could thus play with the faith of fifty million people—with the singlemindedness of a burglar blowing a safe.

In his unfinished novel *The Last Tycoon,* upon which Fitzgerald was working when he suddenly died of a heart attack on December 21, 1940, he attempted to portray the Hollywood world that had just been through the Great Depression. Since Jews played an important role in Hollywood, he included Jewish characters in this novel. There was Manny Schwartz, the middle-aged Jew with the exaggerated Persian nose and oblique eye-shadow; he had come a long way from some ghetto and had integrated into the American scene just as completely as had the Irish and the English. There was Monroe Stahr, the paternalistic last tycoon; he had also managed to climb out of a thousand years of Jewry and had become, or thought he had become, a pure rationalist.

On the whole there was little that could be pinpointed as Jewish about his personality save perhaps that he did not know how to get drunk properly. He was a warm, normal human being, far more pleasant than his non-Jewish partner Brady. There was nothing weird or morbid or depressing about him. He stemmed from an ancient culture but he was not living in it any longer; he was not influenced by its moral taboos, religious rituals, or family traditions; his Jewishness had dwindled to a vague memory.

Among American novelists Dorothy Canfield Fisher was most outspoken in defense of Jews during the difficult decade of the Great Depression and the rise of Hitler. Her novel *Seasoned Timber,* published in 1939 on the eve of the Second World War, was a fiery declaration of her faith in fundamental democratic principles, a fervent plea to her fellow-countrymen not to be complacent in the face of the irrational attacks then being levelled against Jews the world over.

The hero of the novel is a quiet, self-effacing principal of a Vermont academy, an educator who would have preferred not to be involved in politics. However, he suddenly finds himself caught up in the contemporary whirlpool of political currents when a New York multimillionaire, a trustee of this preparatory school, dies and leaves a will bequeathing a million dollars to the academy on the condition that it exclude forever pupils of Jewish origin.

To accept this bequest would mean yielding to race prejudice and to abandon basic American ideals of human equality. Yet, the temptation not to refuse such an enormous sum was strong, since the community was impoverished by the Depression and could be reinvigorated by the prospect of immediate prosperity.

A new trustee for the academy is to be elected. His vote would decide the issue. The Vermont town is thus faced with the Jewish question as the main issue of the school election.

For a while, race prejudice runs rampant throughout the community. A farmer declares that he would not even sell a cow to a Jew dealer. A housewife recalls that a Jew once cheated her many years ago and resents being reminded that the cheater was an Armenian Christian and not a Jew. A teacher states that she never liked Jews, Irish and French Canadians. Another teacher holds that the time has come to break with nineteenth-century egalitarian sentimentalism and to embrace the new reality of the twentieth century which had come to the fore in Nazi Germany. The principal's brother, a convert to the new race theories, feels that shutting Jews out of the school was no great hardship; indeed, hanging was too good for them. A businessman argues that antisemitism was growing stronger all over the world and that the small community should not stand up against this tidal wave. The few Jewish pupils normally admitted to the academy could go to another school in a neighboring town. Meanwhile, enormous economic advantages would accrue to his own town as word got around that it did not welcome Jews. Respectable, cultivated, well-bred American families with real money would flock there to buy or rent summer-homes, real estate would rise in value, and affluence would return to storekeepers.

The counterattack against prejudice is spearheaded by the school principal. He sees race prejudice as one of the tentacles of an octopus that fastened itself on some parts of the world, strangling the heart out of some countries. Unless this hideous snake-like tentacle was quickly cut off, it would wrap itself about the only thing of value the Vermont town still had—its honor, its tradition of fair play. The question at issue was not whether one liked or disliked Jews but whether equality of rights and equality of opportunity were to be denied to a group of Americans because their looks or mannerisms differed from those of the majority.

The principal is called a Bolshevist by opponents. He is suspected by a reporter to have some Jewish blood in his makeup. But he sticks to his views. When the votes are finally counted, he wins out and the bequest is rejected, thus affirming doctrines which had prevailed since the founding of the Republic.

In addition to *Seasoned Timber,* the novelist included Jewish characters in three of her short stories and treated with sympathetic understanding six prominent American Jews in her biographic sketches, *American Portraits,* 1946. These six were Bernard Baruch, Felix Frankfurter, Rose Schneiderman, Arthur Hays Sulzberger, Louis Finkelstein, and David Lilienthal.

In the short story "The City of Refuge," included in the volume *The Real Motive,* 1916, the novelist told of a great Jewish actor who came to America from Russia and who, after settling as a gardener in a small town, could not be tempted by his impresario to return to New York to make lots of money.

In the short story "The Artist" in the volume *Hillsboro People,* 1915, the novelist depicted a Jewish art dealer who had fine understanding for a non-Jewish painter.

In the short story "Professor Paul Meyer, Master of the Word" in the volume *Raw Material,* 1923, the novelist presented a Jewish philologist who became involved as a handwriting expert at the Dreyfus trial. When he testified in favor of Dreyfus, jeering antisemites invaded his classroom and hurled filthy epithets at him. He reacted with great dignity. Without striking a melodramatic attitude, he merely waited patiently for the noise to abate, so that he could continue with his philological explanation. "He looked at his assailants, the chalk ready in his bony fingers, and from him emanated so profound a sense of their entire unimportance, of the utter ephemeral quality of their emotion compared to the life of the consonant he was about to discuss at the black-board . . . . that little by little they were silenced. Their furious voices flattened out to an occasional scream which sounded foolish even to their own ears. They looked at each other, got up in a disorderly body and stamped out of the room." [10]

The philosopher David Baumgardt recalled, among the many unsung deeds of this novelist and humanitarian, her arranging summer vacations at the homes of Vermont farm-ers for Jewish refugee children who had escaped from Ger-man and Austrian oppression. He also noted her refusal to endorse the anti-Zionist program of the Council for Judaism and publicly declaring her great interest in Zionism.[11] This fearless champion of New England liberalism remained a steadfast friend and admirer of the Jews throughout her long life and amidst all the currents of change at home and abroad.

Dorothy Canfield Fisher's insight into the neuroses pro-duced in Jews by the irrational attitude towards them of the bigoted and the unthinking was paralleled by her compas-sionate insight into the warping of the Negro soul by preju-diced and unthinking Whites. The latter prevented the de-velopment of healthy personalities among their countrymen whose skin was of a different hue than their own by imposing physical barriers and psychological obstacles that could not be hurdled. In the introduction to Richard Wright's harrow-ing novel *Native Son,* which she penned in January 1940—a few months after her novel *Seasoned Timber* appeared, she pointed out, even as she had done in her own novel, that American society created ideals for its youth—to fight injus-tice fearlessly, to cringe to no man, to choose one's own life

---

[10] Dorothy Canfield, *Raw Material,* New York, 1923, p. 134.

[11] David Baumgardt, "Dorothy Canfield Fisher: Friend of Jews in Life and Work," *American Jewish Historical Society Publications,* XLVIII (1959), 254–255.

work, to resist affronts to human dignity—and then American society made it impossible for some youths because of their race or color to live up to these national ideals. As a result, neuroses and unhealthy behavior-patterns emerged.

Richard Wright's novel plumbed depths of the Negro soul beyond the reach of non-Negro writers. He looked into his own heart and exposed the bewilderment of a human being who found an unbridgeable contradiction between ideals preached and reality experienced. Perhaps the only non-Negroes who could fathom the spiritual hell in which resentful millions lived shut off because of the color of their skin from America's vaunted equality of opportunity were the Jews who could also look back upon a long history of unjustifiable discriminations and oppression in many lands.

Wright, therefore, had a Jewish lawyer undertake the defense of the Negro murderer Bigger Thomas, the main character of the novel. The white-haired, understanding lawyer braved the misrepresentations of the press, the vituperations of the angry mob and the scorn of the respectable classes because he saw in the apparent criminal caught in the clutches of the white man's law a person against whom society, the true criminal, had sinned and whom it had then driven to despair. With the weariness of old wisdom, the Jew fought the temporarily hopeless fight and accepted defeat as a passing setback in the long drawn out war for human justice and decency.

The non-Jewish realistic novel between the two world wars tried to mirror Jewish reality as part of the American scene. But just as Negro reality could best be probed by Negro writers like Richard Wright who experienced its glow and pain in their very flesh, so too Jewish reality was interpreted at deepest levels by the articulate, talented Jewish writers of this period.

CHAPTER XI

JEWISH AFFIRMATION

Between the two world wars Jewish life increased in complexity and difficulty even while the environmental forces of assimilation kept nibbling away at Jewish essence. At the same time antisemitism, which could formerly be dismissed as a mild irritant, began to take on virile forms as poisonous Nazi doctrines drifted across the Atlantic. Sensitive Jewish writers reacted in a variety of ways ranging from a truculent reaffirmation of their Jewishness to angry outbursts of self-hatred. Some rebounded from the wall of prejudice which they ran into unexpectedly by taking refuge in Zionism or returning to ancestral traditions while others joined in the vociferous attacks against Jews by self-depreciation and self-vilification.

Among the former the most influential were Ludwig Lewisohn and Maurice Samuel while the latter included apostles of Communism, undisciplined psychoanalysts and clowns of Hollywood and Broadway.

Lewisohn, who was born in Berlin in 1883 and brought to the United States at the age of seven, loved America with a passionate, desperate and hopeless love. When he discovered that his overtures were not reciprocated by the America of his dreams, he voiced his bitterness at his rejection in essay after essay, in novel after novel, and above all in his autobiography *Upstream*, 1922.

Lewisohn saw his own experiences not as unique but as

typical. He was, in his eyes, a living symbol of Jewish destiny
in America. He sprang from a family to whom Jewishness was
peripheral. In the Prussian capital, his parents had felt themselves to be Germans first and Jews afterwards. On arriving in
Charleston, South Carolina, they wanted to become Americans wholly and entirely or at least to raise their son to be as
American, as Southern, as un-Jewish as possible. In this, they
temporarily succeeded. Despite the snobbishness of native
Charleston society and their own isolation from non-Jewish
neighbors, their brilliant son was not excluded from the normal activities of other young Americans during his adolescent
and college years. Upon graduation, he looked forward to an
academic career as a professor of English. But when he came
to Columbia University to take his graduate work, he was
shocked to learn that special difficulties beset a person of Jewish birth and was advised to change his professional objective.
At first he was numbed by this discovery that in the land of
the free there prevailed discrimination against fellow-citizens
because of their ethnic origin. Had he deluded himself that
he was at home? Was he an exile and an outcast in the New
World even as his forefathers had been in the Old World?
Was discrimination universal, even if more subtly applied
and not openly conceded in refined circles? "We boast of
equality and freedom and call it Americanism and speak of
other countries with disdain. And so one is unwarned, encouraged and flung into the street. With exquisite courtesy, I
admit. And the consciousness of that personal courtesy
soothes the minds of our Gentile friends." [1]

Unable to break into academic life—not until he was past
sixty did he obtain a professorship at Brandeis University—he
turned to literature. Called upon to translate the German
novelist Jacob Wassermann, he came to know the latter's
suffering because of German antisemitism and he found

[1] Ludwig Lewisohn, *Upstream*, New York, 1922, p. 124.

many similarities between Wassermann and himself. Germany was the great laboratory of the assimilationist experiment. This experiment had, in Lewisohn's opinion, shown the bankruptcy of the assimilationist ideal. Was it necessary that the same experiment be repeated and that several American generations be sacrificed to foreknown humiliation and predictable disaster? All other peoples accepted their historic traits, present characteristics, and national aspirations with satisfaction and joy. Could not Jews do likewise? Could they not reverse their direction from self-negation to self-respect, from sickness to health, from attempted evasion of destiny to joyous creative activity? There were no abstract human beings. Every man lived in a culture. The American culture and the Jewish were not synonymous. They inhabited the same space. They were constantly in contact with each other and influenced each other. But they were not the same. "The conclusion then which my contact with Jews justified and confirmed was this: to rise from my lack and confusion into a truly human life, a life with its right relation to man and God, to the concrete and the universal, it was necessary for me to affirm in quite another fashion than I had yet done the reintegration of my entire consciousness with the historic and ethnic tradition of which I was a part. My Gentile friends and comrades were instinctively integrated with their own. That completeness and assurance could, alas, never be the portion of my Jewish generation. But I believed that, when I had achieved that integration as far as possible, I would no longer need or want to ask: What do you live by? What ultimate satisfaction sustains you? I would not ask. I would know. I would live the secret and it would be mine too. And I may say at once that that belief has proved itself to be wholly true." [2]

[2] Ludwig Lewisohn, *Mid-Channel*, New York, 1929, p. 24.

Lewisohn saw the Americanized Jews as hybrids and the texture of their lives as poor, colorless, thin. The root of their sickness lay in their flight from themselves. He wanted them to arise from their humble genuflections before Anglo-Americanism and to demand the right to cooperate creatively as Jews in strict proportion to their numbers in the American civilization amid which they lived. Jews should be Jews. They should react as Jews in a pluralistic America and should not be forced to carry on an unnatural, restless, alienated, self-denying existence in a conformist, monocultural America. "The Jewish problem is the decisive problem of Western civilization. By its solution this world of the West will stand or fall, choose death or life. But it is not the Jew's problem; it is the Gentile's. The wound is not in our side, O Gentiles whom we love, whose world we love and live in and would help to save—it is in yours. . . . You have all beauty—how poor are we Jews in that compared to you! You have all knowledge. You have no gift for righteousness, for humanity, for peace. And the result is that with all your beauty, your Shakespeare and your Beethoven, and with all your knowledge and with your unimaginable inventions wherewith you transmute into miracles the substance of the ancient earth and sail the air as though it were a lake, you lapsed in this high noon of time in your World War into the foulest barbarism of the ages, slaughtering and being slaughtered like the beasts of the jungle, blackening each other's souls with insensate lies like savage children and gravely recording these stupid lies in your amusingly solemn pacts and covenants. And you go on and on manufacturing your engines of war and your poison gases and fomenting your foolish hatreds and rivalries and strutting truculently before each other's eyes, careless, apparently, whether by barbarous catastrophes yet unheard of you destroy this marvelous civilization which you have builded with your gifts. You act like brilliant but evil children." [3]

Perhaps it might be best for Jews to leave the suicidal West and to betake themselves to their own physical soil where they could achieve national renewal. Out of the depths of Jewish consciousness Zionism had rearisen as a mass movement. It was seeking to give concrete expression to the hope that never ceased to beat in Jewish breasts. In Zion there would emerge a more moral state, the state of the future, the cultural state, the state of peace, the state that would restore the preserved of Israel and be a light to the Gentiles. There Jews would be at home. By concentrating on the upbuilding of Zion and by becoming wholly absorbed in this constructive work, American Jews would be redeemed from supineness, they would be salvaged from the morass of assimilationism, they would be cured of the sloth of their hearts.

For a quarter of a century Lewisohn wrote, spoke and fought for his ideal of Zionism and for a dignified affirmation of Jewish worth and Jewish rights in America. In this activity he found an able literary and forensic ally in Maurice Samuel, perhaps the most effective popularizer of the Zionist philosophy in America prior to the founding of the Jewish State.

Maurice Samuel was born in Roumania in 1895. He spent his boyhood in Manchester, England, and his adult years since 1914 in New York. At home both in Jewish culture and in Anglo-American culture, he tried to maintain an equilibrium between both but before long he could not hide from himself the fact that this zestful bicultural experience which enriched his personality also harbored dangers and required constant reexamination and reappraisal. He did so in provocative volumes beginning with *You Gentiles*, 1924, and *I, the Jew*, 1927, continuing with *Jews On Approval*, 1931, and

[3] *Ibid.*, pp. 303–304.

The Great Hatred, 1941, and reaching a climax in *The Gentleman and the Jew,* 1950.

Samuel arrived at the conclusion that Jewish and Gentile approaches to ultimate questions were antithetical and that antisemitism was not a Jewish problem but an affliction of the Gentile soul to which Jews had to accustom themselves. It was the expression of the pent-up rage of amoral man towards the group which imposed morality upon him in the form of a Christian offshoot of Judaism. It was the Great Hatred of the Pagan soul in Occidental man for the Jewish-Christian jailor who had bound it with the fetters of moral law and imprisoned it within the confines of ethical precepts. It was a furtive form of resentment against Jesus the Jew and his system of beliefs, for which his living kinsmen were coresponsible. It was not caused by Jewish misbehavior and would not be erased by Jewish saintliness. It was a Gentile obsession and could not be cured by logic. Jews had to learn to live with it. They had to accept the simple truth that they were born as Jews and they would be kept as Jews by the force of circumstances. Let them, therefore, make a virtue of necessity and live their Jewishness. Let them make Jewishness their channel to humanity.

Samuel makes a basic distinction between the Jewish and the Gentile ideal of man. The Jewish ideal, also in its Christian variant, was a society of cooperative human beings who aimed at moral perfection as the ultimate goal and who saw in goodness and holiness the justification for their persistence on earth. The Gentile ideal, on the other hand, was a society which accepted competition, rivalry, combativeness, as the basis of life and which saw the highest exponent of nobility in the sportsman, the knightly gentleman, the chivalrous warrior, the honorable killer, the individual and the group lusting for power. The Gentile ideal, which harked back to primitive Germanic and Viking standards of conduct, was still dominant and Christianity was but skin-deep. In the coming atomic age, however, it would be necessary for competitive man, pagan man, to give way to cooperative man, the Jewish-Christian man, if the human species is to survive. The moral principle would have to triumph over the power principle.

During the three decades between the Balfour Declaration and the establishment of the Jewish state, Samuel devoted his major thinking, writing, and speaking to Zionism. "The spirit which was born in Palestine between twenty and thirty centuries ago, which has recorded itself in the Bible, which has given personality to that country, was driven forth alive, in the person of the group which it invested. Had that spirit died in exile, there would have been nothing more to say. But it did not die. . . . It still lives, still suffers, still compels the lives of men and women. Its demand for a return to the place of its birth is not fictitious." [4]

Samuel believed that in Israel Jews would succeed in building a moral commonwealth, a unique group-existence, a cooperative society, a non-competitive nationalism. American Jews could not only help in this Jewish venture on their ancient soil but they could also bring to America and to the entire Occident the message of the moral form of group-life which their kinsmen and coreligionists were recreating in the land of the original Jewish covenant. This form of life, first proclaimed by the Biblical Prophets and retained as a Messianic vision throughout the centuries of dispersed exile, was Israel's destiny. Taught to other peoples by example, this Jewish form of life could effect the liberation of the human species from the mechanical cycle of nature, from the purely biological response to the environment. It could dispel the shadow of fear which overhung the entire earth as a result of the new scientific capacity for destruction. It could arrest im-

[4] Maurice Samuel, I, the Jew, New York, 1927, p. 209.

pending doom by making man more decent and nations more moral.

While Maurice Samuel and Ludwig Lewisohn, ably seconded by Judah L. Magnes, Jacob de Haas, Louis Lipsky, Marvin Lowenthal, Milton Steinberg, Horace M. Kallen, and other warriors of the pen were trying to win Jewish public opinion to an acceptance of Zionism as the answer to the tensions which persisted between Jews and non-Jews, literary exponents of Jewish negation and literary purveyors of Jewish self-hatred were also influencing readers by means of talented best-sellers and were asking coreligionists to turn a deaf ear to all pleas for Jewish national rebirth. These brilliant, witty Jewish iconoclasts and scoffers were recruited mainly from the ranks of second-generation Jews who were in revolt against their immigrant parents and whose flight from Jewishness led them to embrace communistic, hedonistic and aesthetic panaceas.

Chapter XII

THE UPROOTED AND THE ESTRANGED

The nineteen-thirties was the decade of the uprooted and the estranged Jewish intellectuals, the children of Eastern European immigrants who became articulate in the English tongue, Jewish saplings that had wrested themselves loose from the cultural earth of their fathers and transplanted themselves in the rich soil of their adopted culture. In the process, however, their roots were severely damaged and their healthy growth impaired. Stunted Jewish souls sought to regain soundness and spiritual equilibrium by embracing esoteric philosophies. Revolting against both American and Jewish realities, they took refuge in hedonism, aestheticism, communism and psychoanalytic self-dissection.

Two novels which appeared in 1929 on the eve of this decade anticipated the wasteland in which this generation was to roam. They were David Pinski's *The House of Noah Eden* and Myron Brinig's *Singermann.*

Pinski was a Yiddish dramatist and novelist who was born in Russia in 1872 and who came to America in 1899. For thirty years he observed and participated in the changing Jewish panorama. As editor of the influential Yiddish periodical *Die Zukunft,* he sought to stem the tide of estrangement from Jewish values. But the tide was overpowering. By 1929 he had come to fear that it would overwhelm the last resisters to assimilation and he wrote his genealogical novel both as an analysis of the worsening Jewish situation and as a warning of impending greater decay. This novel immediately became available to English readers in translation but it was not widely read and its prophetic message was unheeded.

Pinski portrayed three generations of a Jewish family which emigrated to America in the eighteen-eighties from a little town in Lithuania. He showed the difficulties encountered by the first generation, which nevertheless continued to lead a traditional life. He then showed the estrangement of the Americanized children, who fell under the spell of the brighter, freer, gayer life which opened up before them, full of golden opportunities but also full of perilous allurements. He showed the aftermath of this estrangement, the inner decay resulting from the attempt to get along without God and without strong roots in the world of the forefathers. Each of these Americans of Jewish origin ended as a detached fragment in the body of America, living a lonely life and dying a lonely death. Their ultimate lot was despair and self-annihilation.

An equally grim picture of the morass into which second-generation Jewish Americans were heading emerged from Myron Brinig's novel, *Singermann,* the story of a Roumanian Jewish family that had originally immigrated to America on the eve of the Balkan War. After a short stay in Minneapolis, its members moved to Silver Bow, Montana, Brinig's fictitious name for Butte, Montana. Here they opened a department store. Father and children worked hard to get ahead. Moses Singermann's store was the first to open in the morning and the last to close up shop at night. Gradually, however, under the influence of the alien spirit of this mining town, the children drifted away from parental authority. The oldest son Joseph married a Jewish girl who was attracted to Christian Science. She tore him away from his last links to Jewishness when she insisted on keeping the store open on the Day of Atonement. The daughter Rachel was no longer willing to give her parents a deciding voice in the choice of a mate for herself. She hearkened to the call of passion and succumbed to the fascination of an adventurer and bigamist. The second son, who was of an artistic temperament, tried to introduce a Christmas tree into the Jewish store. This resulted in a quarrel with his horrified father and led him to leave for a new community. After a few months in the completely non-Jewish town of Spokane, he returned defeated and dispirited to his father's store in Silver Bow. The third son succumbed to sensualism, married a prostitute, and tried to integrate her into his Jewish family. But she soon got tired of this strange Jewishness and ran off to California. Another son became a prizefighter. The youngest son went off to school at a distant community. The closely-knit family was shattered to fragments and scattered in all directions.

While Brinig and Pinski wrote of Jewish decay and degeneracy, sad at heart and worried about coming days, other Jewish novelists gloated at the loss of traditional values and looked to communism to bring salvation to a troubled world and efface the distinctions between Jews and non-Jews. Michael Gold's *Jews Without Money,* 1930, ushered in the Jewish proletarian novel of this decade.

Born in New York in 1894, Gold grew up on the East Side amidst filth and poverty. At twelve, he was sent to work in a dark, suffocating factory. Self-educated, he found emotional fulfillment in agitating for radical causes. By 1930, he had risen to the editorship of *The New Masses* and was preaching communism. His novel was hailed as a pioneering product of proletarian literature and was translated into fifteen languages. It presented the Jewish religion as a collection of superstitions fed to the gullible masses. Gold knew Jews, so he claimed, who believed in red, green, and blue devils. He recalled that his own parents believed in demons that had to be exorcized by rabbis. His landlord was a pillar of the synagogue but preferred prostitutes as tenants because these paid three times the normal rent. The miracle-working, imported rabbi of his neighborhood was a fat, dull-faced, lazy individual who gorged himself with delicacies provided by starving believers and who deserted his poor flock for a better paying pulpit in the Bronx. The entire neighborhood was a jungle where wild beasts in human shape prowled—perverts, kidnappers, firebugs, rapists. There sons of tubercular Jewish immigrants lost their Jewish timidity. There they learned to steal, to tease prostitutes, to shoot crap, to torture cats and, above all, to fight. Jewish education was a superfluous accomplishment, a long rigmarole of Hebrew prayers hammered into the heads and ribs of unhappy pupils by emaciated, orthodox ignoramuses. The only hope of escape from Jewish jungle existence lay in a workers' revolution and the establishment of international communism. Gold therefore ended his novel with a hymn to the Messianic realm of the classless society whose advent he believed to be imminent.

Gold's novel served as a model for others. Albert Halper's early novel *The Chute,* 1937, had a similar basic structure and a similar negative attitude toward the Jewish past and present. Halper too was a second generation Jew. His birthplace was Chicago and his novel dealt with a Chicago Jewish family. His hero, the talented son of immigrant parents, had his heart set on a career as architect. But family poverty compelled him, after graduation from high school, to start work in a mail-order house. There he was but a cog in an immense wheel. There he came to know the maze of belts and rollers and the chute that enabled the firm to operate efficiently. The chute was described as an immense mouth into which merchandise was pouring like lava, rushing into troughs. From this mouth the merchandise zoomed forth with a roar and at the bottom one hundred packers assembled the orders and packed them for parcel-post. The hero hated his job and prayed for deliverance. But whence was deliverance to come? Obviously not from the old and tired believers in ghosts of the past, in religious taboos, but from the militant fighters for a better social and political order to replace the status quo. Such a struggle would give more meaning to young lives than the Jewishness of immigrant forebears, a Jewishness of picturesque Anglicized Yiddish curses with which the novel opened or a Jewishness of greasy meals with which it closed.

Halper introduced his hero's Jewish father as belching and groaning and chanting his morning prayers, of which the following incantation was typical: "May the street wither to the size of a cough-drop, may Jehovah shrivel up the sidewalks, may my creditors be stricken with apoplexy over their morning coffee, may it rain rocks and knock out all the landlord's teeth! In plain language, a black eye on all my enemies!" [1] The Jewish mother was presented as ailing, whining, and helpless. Uncle Julius was rich but niggardly and heartless, since he did not want to take on the additional burden of seeing his nephew through college.

The most outrageous scene of the book was the final one which depicted a wedding, supposedly typical of most Jewish weddings. After pushing the bride and groom under the *chuppa,* the rabbi warmed up to his work, chanting, rocking on his heels and twitching his nose. "In the depths of his bristling reddish beard his red mouth was in rapid motion, like the mouth of a struggling fish. He muttered and he chanted, and the harsh light of the room danced on the little round black cap upon his head. Throwing his head back on his neck, which was as thick as a wrestler's, he forced his gutteral Hebrew words out like an endless stream of chunky box-cars rattling along." [2] The most important part of the wedding

[1] Albert Halper, *The Chute*, New York, 1937, p. 4.
[2] *Ibid.*, p. 534.

was, of course, the wedding-meal and the author went into details about every course, the greasiness, the gobbling, the grubbing and grunting, the guzzling of the Jewish wine. Then followed the haggling of the rabbi for his fee until he extracted the last dollars from his bridegroom-victim.

Halper never considered himself to be a Jewish writer. He claimed that he never thought of the Jewishness in his works, that he merely strove for an honest and moving picture of his world, as he saw it. And yet, he saw it through the eyes of a member of the self-hating Jewish generation that came to literary maturity in the decade of the Great Depression. By the end of this decade, he was in retreat from his negative evaluation of his ethnic kinsmen as were so many of his radical contemporaries.

In his novel *Sons of the Fathers*, 1940, he treated with considerable sympathy a Jewish family which was forced to move out of a Chicago neighborhood because the children of school age were taunted, harried and tormented by their classmates. He depicted Jewish ceremonies and institutions with reverence. He no longer saw anything absurd in the housewife going by horse-car to the kosher butcher two miles away to get her meat or for all the members of the family tramping on foot for three miles to get to a synagogue for the High Holidays. For the Passover Seder all the children returned home, even the travelling salesman from a distant town. The Hebrew that the father now intoned was no longer guttural and food was no longer the main attraction of Jewishness. "From his naturalized American lips issued Hebrew, an old world language, somberizing the room with its rich and mournful cadences. And though none of the children understood a word that their father said, they had the feeling that they were in a synagogue. Every year their father sat upon a pillow during this service and every year, though enticing food lay within hands' reach, they forgot for a moment the prospect of eating as a feeling of solemnity stole into the room." [3]

It is true that the novelist's knowledge of the Seder ceremony was very limited. The order of the Hagadah-prayers was inverted and the traditional Four Questions were put at the end rather than near the beginning, but at least there was no longer a superior mocking of all things Jews held holy, there was an awareness of the historic richness encased in Hebrew, a tongue as good as Arabic. Halper's scorn was reserved for Yiddish. His travelling-salesman, serving in the army during World War I, was one of the soldiers parcelled out to Jewish homes to attend a Seder and again heard Hebrew. "Unlike the gutteral Yiddish, a bastardized language, which, originating in the German ghettos centuries ago, had come to be the language of a dispersed people, the words spoken by the host were like jewels. In contrast to the Yiddish tongue, the Hebrew sounded like Arabic, austere in its texture, each syllable and inflection woven into a richly patterned fabric, glittering with ornamental tones. Coming under the spell of the service, the people present became conscious of their race. A feeling of the misery and the glory of their forefathers came over them. Egypt was again in their bones. Here they sat, petty merchants drudging away in small, mean towns of the South. Here they sat, part of a race which crawled the four corners of the earth like ants, grubbing to exist, submissive, segregated from the life of the community, despised— and tolerated." [4]

Edward Dahlberg was even more uprooted and estranged from Jewishness than was Halper. He was born in Boston in 1900, committed to a Catholic orphanage at the age of five, transferred seven years later to a Jewish orphan asylum, where he remained until he was seventeen, and then left to shift for

---

[3] Albert Halper, *Sons of the Fathers*, New York, 1940, p. 129.
[4] *Ibid.*, p. 352.

himself. Among his occupations he listed having been a Western Union messenger boy in Cleveland, trucker for the American Express, driver of a laundry wagon, cattle drover in the Kansas City Stockyards, dishwasher in Portland, Oregon, potato peeler in Sacramento, bus-boy in San Francisco, longshoreman in San Pedro, clerk in a clinic. These experiences gave him a wealth of material for novels. In 1934, he published his narrative *Those Who Perish,* in which he dealt with the rise of reactionary forces and the effect upon American Jews. These were in search of a faith they could not find and yet they could not escape their Jewishness, try as they might.

Isidor Schneider believed that escape was possible by attaching oneself to the cause of the proletariat and realizing oneself in work for the poor, the humble, the underprivileged. *From the Kingdom of Necessity,* 1935, was his novel of a Jewish family's migration from a Galician townlet to New York. Largely autobiographic, it concentrated on the maturing of a sensitive boy who grew up on the East Side and Harlem amidst poverty and loneliness, his search for belongingness, and the realization that, even after love and success came to him, he was still unrooted and homeless. His ultimate insight was expressed in the final paragraph of the novel: "He had set out from the kingdom of necessity; he had found a way out, the escape from his class, only to find that, outside, he was homeless. He was to learn that no one enters the kingdom of freedom alone. He would return to his class. With it, he would march, taking his place in the advancing lines, in the irresistible movement of the masses of mankind from the kingdom of necessity to the Kingdom of Freedom." [5]

The cause of the proletariat exercised a powerful fascination for many Jewish writers during the decade of the Popu-

[5] Isidor Schneider, *From the Kingdom of Necessity,* New York, 1935, p. 450.

lar Front. It fulfilled their need for a Messianic objective and most of them later suffered bitter disillusionment when their romantic idealization collapsed under the impact of Stalinist reality. But there were other writers who drowned their homelessness in wine, women, and song or at least in writing about these hedonistic possibilities. Chief of the self-hating Jewish hedonists was young Ben Hecht, author of the novel *A Jew in Love,* 1931.

Though born in New York City in 1894, Ben Hecht began his career as a journalist in Chicago during the First World War, was successful with his first novel *Erik Dorn,* 1921, and with the play *The Front Page,* 1928, which he co-authored with his journalistic colleague Charles MacArthur, and reached the height of his popularity in the nineteen-thirties and nineteen-forties as motion picture writer and producer.

In *A Jew in Love,* Hecht's Jewish self-hatred, which was later to boomerang as raucous Jewish self-assertiveness, led him to paint only unpleasant Jewish characters. His principal hero, Jo Boshere, born Abe Nussbaum, was introduced in the very first sentence of the novel as a dark-skinned little Jew with a vulturous face, a reedy body and a sense of posture. Another Jew glittered with ennui, obscenity and sophistication. All were disfigured by the ugly stamp of Jewishness. They had sausage faces or were bulbous, diabetic half-monsters.

Unlike Michael Gold's proletarian Jews without money, Hecht's hero Boshere had won a million dollars in the stock market and steered clear of entanglement with poor Jews. His wealth enabled him to dispense with the pathological Jewish sensitiveness that had clung to him from his adolescence. He could at last boast of his cosmopolitanism, of his mingling only in a society in which the individual counted and not his ancestry. He no longer had to espouse asceticism. He could devote himself entirely to the pursuit of pleasure.

Since woman was the choicest vessel of pleasure, his erotic experiences formed the main content of his days and nights. He had a wife, a reddish tinted, green-eyed Jewess, who wore her Paris gowns like a matronly harness. He also had a mistress, a neurotic younger Jewess, whom he could at will torment, caress, insult, adore, and deceive. In addition, this conceited libertine engaged in several side line affairs with other women, including non-Jewish ones. He could be a supreme egoist and uninhibited hedonist because he had shed his Jew-consciousness, which he defined as the consciousness of not being a normal social human being. He recommended that the first step which a Jew with brains should take in emancipating himself from his race of didactic imbeciles must consist of a frank recognition of the simple normal fact that he was ashamed of his pariah origin.

The Hitler decade proved to Hecht that he could not escape his Jewishness and so by 1941 he arrived at the opposite extreme of Jewish self-assertiveness. In a defiant article entitled "My Tribe Is Called Israel," he called upon all Americans of his formerly self-hating breed, who had never thought of themselves as Jews, to rise up in defense of Jewish rights and Jewish values which were under violent and apelike attacks. He himself did penance for the wounds he inflicted upon his people by sensational activities as American spokesman for extreme Zionism, by raising millions of dollars for the Irgun, and by writing the bellicose book *A Guide to the Bedevilled*, 1944, and a series of less passionate but more artistic short stories about good Jews.

One such story, entitled "God is Good to a Jew," told of the rehabilitation of a Polish Jewish refugee upon arrival in America and discovering that goodness, kindness, and compassion were tendered even towards a Jew.

Another story, entitled "Death of Eleazer," began with the murder of four Jews by a German shoemaker named Pfefferkorn. Rabbi Eleazer suspected the murderer to be a Gilgul of the infamous Pfefferkorn who was born in Moravia five centuries earlier and who was still unburied. When the rabbi sought to exorcize the murderous demon within Pfefferkorn, he was himself killed by the shoemaker's axe. Brought to trial for the murder, Pfefferkorn found public opinion swinging in his favor, as the American Nazis cast him in the role of a martyr of Jewish machinations. He was facing acquittal when at the last moment he beheld an apparition of Eleazer and in terror he confessed to the crime.

Hecht's brief moment in the limelight as a Jewish warrior of the pen came to an end with the bombing and sinking by Jews in Tel-Aviv's shoals of the *Altalena,* the ship which had been bought, outfitted and armed largely by his herculean efforts. The disbanding of the Irgun cooled his enthusiasm for further crusading efforts in behalf of Jews and, as a scarred and disillusioned veteran, he reverted to the hedonism and self-destructiveness of his earlier years. In his book *Perfidy,* published in 1962, he gave expression to his final bitterness and frustration.

In the nineteen-thirties, Hecht's diatribes against Jews spawned many disciples. The most gifted of these was Budd Schulberg, who overtopped the popularity of Hecht's novel of self-hatred with his own novel of this genre, *What Makes Sammy Run?,* 1941.

As the son of a Hollywood producer, Schulberg was intimately acquainted with the internecine struggles in the movie industry and the role of the Jews who got to the top in this struggle. Such a Hollywood Jew was Sammy, a "smart little yid," with a quick intelligence which he was able to use exclusively for the good-and-welfare of Sammy Glick. His ability to absorb insults and embarrassments like a sponge helped him to get a start. Dishonesty, officiousness, bullying helped him to rise ever higher and higher. Cradled in hate, hunger, and prejudice, he was fit to survive in the amoral, dog-eat-dog world of Hollywood because he could run faster than others, and he ultimately ended as the movie producer Sammy the Great.

Schulberg ended the story of his Hollywood Jewish hero with the comment: "It was a terrifying and wonderful document, the record of where Sammy ran, and if you looked behind the picture and between the lines you might even discover what made him run. And some day I would like to see it published as a blueprint of a way of life that was paying dividends in America in the first half of the twentieth century." [6] The story certainly paid dividends to the author and two decades later it was still a box-office attraction in a dramatized version when produced on the legitimate stage in 1962.

Jerome Weidman was much more merciful in his judgment of the Jewish go-getter than was Budd Schulberg. The story of the rise of the unscrupulous Harry Bogen in the dress business was told by Weidman in his first novel *I Can Get It for You Wholesale*, 1937. It was continued in the supplementary volume *What's In It for Me?*, 1938. But it was not until 1958, in his novel *The Enemy Camp*, that Weidman best analyzed the relation between Jews and non-Jews, as he experienced it in his young days. His short stories, collected in 1961 under the title *My Father Sits in the Dark*, also contained nostalgic glimpses of East Side Jews. Despite his restless, excitable style, his satiric overtones, and some unpleasant Jewish portraits, Weidman did not deal as unkindly with the ghetto world of his childhood as did his contemporaries. But his basic philosophy remained hedonistic and he was far removed from the grand enthusiasm and the desperate struggles of his embattled Jewish kinsmen of his generation.

Leo Calvin Rosten, who wrote under the pseudonym of

[6] Budd Schulberg, *What Makes Sammy Run?*, New York, 1941, p. 303.

Leonard Q. Ross, also depicted Jewish life on New York's East Side in a humorous and satiric, rather than serious vein. The stories included in his book *The Education of Hyman Kaplan*, 1938, centered about a beginners' English class in a night school for adults. There the Jewish immigrant Hyman Kaplan wrestled with the English language. He subjected it to logical analysis and found it wanting. His Anglo-American teacher, infinitely patient and kind, tried to get him to accept English usage but the stubborn Kaplan refused to yield. Though all others might compromise with linguistic absurdities, he would hold out, to the delight and chagrin of his classmates. In 1959, Rosten, sociologist, political scientist and screen writer, was again attracted to this lovable, ungrammatical rationalist and recreated him in *The Return of Hyman Kaplan*. But by 1962, in his psychiatric novel *Captain Newman, M.D.*, the author steered clear of Jewish characters and problems.

While Hyman Kaplan had the ability to laugh at himself and thus escaped tragic consequences that often inhered in Jewish otherness, the hero of the novel *Wasteland*, 1947, suffered keenly under the knowledge of his Jewishness, which separated him from the majority group. The authoress Ruth Seid, who wrote under the pseudonym of Jo Sinclair, portrayed the malady of her Jewish generation as a mental disease that necessitated psychoanalytic treatment. Her hero was resentful of his Jewish origin, but since he was not brutal, aggressive, callous, or egoistic, he was driven to despair by this hidden shame. "I hate being a Jew. Nobody in the office even knows I'm a Jew. My God, I used to wake up sweating because I dreamed they found out I was—" [7] Under such circumstances, life became a nightmare. Away from home, this American marrano lived in constant fear of being unmasked and his secret infamy brought to light. His coming home to

[7] Jo Sinclair, *Wasteland*, New York, 1946, p. 10.

his parents, on the other hand, was like sinking into a dark, dirty, familiar bed. The panorama about him was indeed a wasteland.

A still more desolate wasteland awaited those who were caught in the no-man's territory between Jews and non-Jews, according to Norman Katkov, the author of *Eagle At My Eyes*, 1948. This novel of intermarriage presented all Jews and most Christians as bigots. The hero, corroded by self-pity and self-hatred, moved between the Jewish world from which he had excluded himself and the Christian world into which he could not enter. His marriage was doomed from the start and not even intensest love could bridge the gulf between the two hostile camps.

A best-selling novel of 1947 was *Gentleman's Agreement* by Laura Z. Hobson, daughter of the Yiddish editor and scholar Goetzel Selikovitsch. This novel was later converted into a very popular motion picture. Its central character, a non-Jewish journalist, undertook an assignment to write a series of articles on antisemitism. In order to understand this problem thoroughly from the Jewish angle as well as from the Gentile, he decided to pose as a Jew and he was shocked to discover the amount of antisemitism rampant in a typical American community. The novel was favorably received by Jews, since its basic approach was sympathetic. Ludwig Lewisohn, however, voiced a dissenting view and pointed out that the author had merely scratched the surface of a deep social and moral wound. He felt that the tragic essence of Jewish life had eluded the probing journalist-hero: "Well, what does he discover? That eminent practitioners speak with subtle slights of their Jewish colleagues which, being pressed, they at once withdraw, and that there are hotels and residential districts that do not, as the saying goes, desire Hebrew patronage. It is no doubt handsome of Miss Hobson to become so eloquent concerning these trivialities. The dangerous restrictions in economic and educational opportunities, the six million martyrs, the monstrous theft of all Jewish property over half the world, the closed doors of America, these things, and I am speaking from *her* angle, seem not even to be within her grasp or knowledge. I ask myself how she could have read the daily papers and preserved an innocence so immaculate." [8]

Ludwig Lewisohn's strictures were not entirely unjustified, as becomes obvious if one compares *Gentleman's Agreement* with Sholom Aleichem's treatment of a similar theme in his drama *Hard to Be a Jew*. In the latter work by this friend of Laura Z. Hobson's father, a Gentile student, who had no concept of the myriad difficulties with which a Jew had to contend daily, changes names with a Jewish student and then comes to experience Jewish reality as it is lived in a Christian dominated world. The theme, a variant of the more universal Prince and the Pauper theme, was treated by Sholom Aleichem with sardonic humor and delved into deepest reaches of the Jewish and Christian soul and by Laura Z. Hobson with mild disillusionment and Hollywood sentimentalism.

Saul Bellow, a more talented novelist than Laura Z. Hobson, came to know Jewish life both during his childhood at Lachine, in Quebec, and when he moved to Chicago. In his novel *The Adventures of Augie March*, 1953, he told the story of a poor Jewish boy who grew up in Chicago during the Great Depression. Bellow had already attracted attention with an earlier novel *Dangling Man*, 1944, a title symbolic of his heroes. However, the main dangling characteristic of Augie March was his peripheral Jewishness.

Moses Herzog, the title-hero of Bellow's best seller of 1965, was also a peripheral Jew, who always skirted around the Jewishness that welled up from his subconscious but who never came to grips with it. In this novel, Bellow depicted

[8] *The New Palestine*, April 4, 1947, p. 118.

brilliantly the dissolution of the Jewish personality in contemporary America but not its reintegration. From the treasures of Yiddish language and literature with which Bellow
was quite familiar, he preferred to chose chiefly the colorful
vocabulary of the gutter and he larded the speech of the older
members of the immigrant generation with picturesque, in-
elegant Yiddish phrases. Nevertheless, these unassimilated
pioneers retained warmth, dignity, and close family ties,
while their ultramodern, oversophisticated offspring were
coldly logical, stripped of inner dignity, obsessed with sex.

Maxwell Geismar, who admired Bellow as the novelist of
the intellectuals, wondered whether Bellow was really happy
about his Jewish heritage. "Just as Bellow himself has always
stressed the narrowest part of the Orthodox Jewish religious
tradition—rather than the flowering of secular Jewish culture
and art in the New World—so, too, all his heroes continue to
be ashamed of and to repudiate their true religious heritage.
Judaism in Bellow's work is a source of nostalgia, but also of
guilt and anxiety rather than of pride and pleasure. It is a
constrictive and disturbing, rather than an enlarging or
emancipating force." [9]

According to Geismar, Bellow suffered under his heritage
—while Herman Wouk cashed in on it. He was referring to
Wouk's best seller of 1955, *Marjorie Morningstar,* which exposed to ridicule the Jewishness of New York's upper middle
class. His heroine exchanged her too Jewish sounding name
of Morgenstern for the more respected name of Morningstar,
dreamed of becoming a great American actress, fell in love
with the glamorous Noel Airman who could emancipate her
from the parental environment she felt ashamed of, but ultimately ended up as the dull, gossipy Mrs. Schwartz, wife of a
prosperous Jewish lawyer in suburbia.

Unlike most Jewish novelists of his generation who were

[9] Maxwell Geismar, *American Moderns,* New York, 1958, p. 223.

estranged from Jewishness, Wouk had his roots firmly planted in orthodoxy—he was a graduate of Yeshiva University—but could not resist the temptation to follow the literary fashion of satirizing and ridiculing his irreligious young co-religionists. When the fashion changed and books with a positive approach towards Jewishness were preferred by the reading public, Wouk too jumped on the bandwagon and wrote his fine affirmation of traditional Judaism, *This Is My God,* 1959.

This change in public taste was clearly demonstrated by the phenomenal success of *Exodus,* 1958, by Leon Uris, a novel which answered the hunger for positive, heroic Jewish types after the profusion of negative, unheroic Jews. This changed attitude on the part of readers and writers came about as a result of the rise of Israel in 1948 and its consolidation after the victorious Sinai campaign of 1956.

CHAPTER XIII

JEWISH ACCULTURATION

The dominant trend among European immigrants ever since the founding of the United States had been to burn the bridges with the past and to seek rapid integration into American reality. Despite heroic efforts of German or Norwegian or Italian intellectuals to build enclaves in the New World that retained the cultural aroma of the motherlands in the Old World, memories grew dimmer and dimmer and rarely survived beyond the third generation. Jews, because of their religious differentiation from the majority sector of the American population, were able to preserve certain aspects of their uniqueness longer than other minority groups. Besides, their motherland was not the land of their birth as individuals, Russia or Poland or Roumania, but rather the holy land that gave birth to Jewish peoplehood, a portable spiritual land that accompanied them throughout their centuries of exile and whose only physical link was the bit of earth which observant Jews preserved for their final resting place, their graves.

Next to religion, the strongest force cementing Jews to one another and differentiating them from their neighbors was language. As long as the Yiddish tongue flourished in Jewish homes, constant contact was retained with Jewish values and Jewish aspirations. The Yiddish newspaper acted as a daily link with the Jewish people beyond America's borders, bolstered pride in the Jewish heritage, and slowed down the process of acculturation.

For fully three decades after the founding of the first Yiddish daily, the *Tageblatt*, in 1885, the Yiddish press was the principal vehicle both for the Americanization of the Jewish immigrants as well as for the retention and strengthening of their Jewishness. By 1914 there were ten Yiddish dailies in the United States and by 1916 New York's Yiddish dailies alone reached 646,000 families. However, English increasingly replaced Yiddish. From the high level of the First World War, the circulation of Yiddish books, periodicals, and newspapers rapidly receded and, except for a brief flurry caused by immigration immediately after the Second World War, Yiddish continued to decline as the spoken language in Jewish homes.

The sons and daughters of Yiddish-speaking immigrants had no rich Old World memories. At best they had vestigial memories of deformed Jewish customs and traits, fragments of Hebrew phrases acquired in cellar classrooms, a debased Yiddish vocabulary with which to garnish witticisms, exotic gastronomic habits, and queer remnants of folkways. Escape from the past of the generations immediately preceding theirs was therefore their normal yearning and found expression in their literary documents.

The longing of the child of immigrant parents for an overidealized Anglo-Americanism was most movingly depicted in Alfred Kazin's autobiography of his early years in Brownsville, a Jewish district of Brooklyn. *A Walker in the City*, 1951, was an honest, brilliant dissection of the soul of a Jewish boy who grew up in this underprivileged neighborhood. Kazin's parents and teachers seemed tacitly agreed that the denizens of Brownsville were somehow to be a little ashamed of what they were, although it was always hard to say why this should be so. Americanism was everything they apparently were not and everything they wished to be wholeheartedly. English without a Yiddish accent was the ladder of advancement to higher social strata. Kazin climbed that ladder after tremendous exertion. Books supplied him with the key that let him in at last into the great world that was anything just out of Brownsville. He, who had at first thought of himself as standing outside of America, as not belonging, did succeed ultimately in acculturating, in becoming an insider, in belonging to the main stream of American literature and life. His yearning found complete fulfillment.

Only a few writers in the English tongue who were children of Eastern European immigrants opposed this yearning and not merely because of nostalgia or sentimentalism. They urged remembrance of things past as a principal base for an advance into an American-Jewish future. They included Howard Fast, Irving Fineman, Leo W. Schwarz, Harry L. Golden, Irving Howe, Abraham M. Klein, and Marie Syrkin. Their most vocal spokesman was Charles Angoff, who began his literary and editorial career in the 1920's but who only forged to the fore in the 1950's and 1960's as the talented, compassionate chronicler of American Jewry of Eastern European origin. In numerous short stories and in nine novels, he related the saga of this group that was compelled by a hostile regime to undertake the great trek from Russian townlets to American metropolises. He projected a typical family, the Polonskys, and depicted their acculturation in the course of the first half of the twentieth century.

Angoff writes of the joy and the wonder and the warmth and the magnificence of being a Jew. His Jews are a people not merely of scholars, sages, and prophets but also of singers, players, merrymakers, and a vast conglomeration of ordinary individuals, overwhelmingly optimists who always see sunshine behind the clouds, goodness dispelling evil, and compassion conquering hatred.

Angoff feels himself to be in the deepest reaches of his soul part of this people and never does he seek to weaken his ties to his historic heritage, as do far too many of his better known contemporaries, American novelists of Jewish origin and Jewish self-hatred. At the same time, having grown up in Boston, the cultural capital of New England, he does not want to dispense with the riches of the American heritage which he also claims as his own.

How to be a Jew in America?—is the problem he wrestles with, aware all the time that the very friendliness and democratic spirit of America make it difficult for a unique minority to retain its differentiating pre-American group traits.

In the opening volume of the Polonsky-series, entitled *Journey to the Dawn*, 1951, an entire civilization arises before us, a self-contained Russian-Jewish community that manages to exist generation after generation as a distinct enclave in the midst of a mighty empire. The foundation of this unique enclave consists of family units. Such a family were the Polonskys who had resided in their townlet since time immemorial. In the first decade of our century they began to stir under the impact of new ideas and revolutionary events until they were torn from their roots and transplanted across the Atlantic to the city of Boston.

The family is portrayed in its gray daily existence and in its festive moods, from the great-grandmother Yente, who remains even in her advanced age the strongest pillar of the Polonskys to little David, through whom the author speaks. In their Russian townlet, parents and children still lived in a one-room dwelling, little more than a hut. But, just as they were kept physically warm by a huge brick oven in a far-off corner, so too were they spiritually warmed by a huge mass of traditions and rituals that harked back to a far-off Holy Land, infiltrated their routine activities, and came to the fore on the Holy Sabbath and on the longed-for holidays.

Outside of the Jewish home, it was cold and dangerous. Children were warned at an early age not to stray beyond the Jewish neighborhood. They grew up in the knowledge that they were not in their own homeland but in an alien unfriendly realm where pogroms were always a possibility and where drunken non-Jews could spit on them with impunity. When such children reached adulthood, they reacted to their hostile environment either by taking refuge in religious mysticism, of which Chassidism was the extreme aspect, or else by embracing Zionist and revolutionary outlooks, dreaming of a Jewish state in Palestine and of a Utopian socialist regime in a liberated Russia.

To a young boy who grew up about the time of the abortive Revolution of 1905, independence, freedom, human dignity, socialism were intoxicating slogans even before he could pronounce them correctly. Somehow these slogans existed side by side and harmonized with the orthodox Judaism practiced in daily life. A father's wish that his little son might grow up to be a great scholar found nightly utterance in the lullabies with which the child was cradled to sleep. When such a son attained to the age of five, he was aware that only by applying himself with great zeal to his studies in Hebrew School could this wish become a reality. Nevertheless, many obstacles faced a Jewish boy, an entire arsenal of discriminations and, worst of all, frustrating years of impressment in the army of the hated Czar.

When a member of the Polonsky family was drafted into military service, the event was looked upon as a major tragedy. Even if no conflict arose which might entail his shedding the blood of others or endangering his own life, four years of youth would be thrown away for a nation that despised Jews and that killed them at the slightest provocation or no provocation at all. To prevent further attrition of the family by military impressment, serious consideration was given to emigration from the accursed Czarist realm to a more friendly soil beyond the Atlantic. A pioneering member of the family had already ventured on to America and reports that trickled back from there told of a wonderful country of limitless opportunities. There Jews were accorded equal rights with others. They were as free and as respected as any Christian ethnic group. They did not have to hide from priests and policemen. They could even go to universities. It was also true, however, that there in the democratic land beyond the vast waters Jews were gradually shedding their traditional folkways and were being forced by economic pressures to whittle down religious observances.

David Polonsky's father, Moshe, was sent ahead to prepare the way for the family's exodus. Despite his first impressions of swarms of people, constantly on the go, rushing about frantically, laboring to the point of exhaustion, Moshe liked the country, its unfinished roughness, its basically healthy growth. Freedom was in the air and self-confidence imbued even the poorest Jews in the slum-areas. Soon the rest of the family was brought over, led by Bobbe Yente, the incarnation of moral health and worldly wisdom accumulated in Jewish homes.

Most of Boston's Jews were orthodox and stemmed from Eastern Europe. They belonged to the immigrant generation, spoke Yiddish, and dwelt in dirty, crowded, noisy slums. Their neighbors were Irish, Italian, German, Spanish, and Negro. Despite an awareness of difference between the ethnic groups, there prevailed the feeling of good-natured tolerance. The public school performed successfully its task of integration and of instilling in all its pupils pride in American history and ideals and in America's national heroes. Synagogue, *cheder*, home continued to bring to Jewish boys and girls the cultural heritage of an older and richer past. This past persisted with the Polonsky family, immunizing the members against the ill effects of adversity, giving them a unity of purpose and a sense of belongingness. Bobbe Yente continued to wield enormous moral authority as the matriarch who embodied the best aspects of this past. All her children and grandchildren sought her advice and comfort and were helped to overcome disappointments and suffering during periods of economic depression and emotional let-down. Ultimately, each of her descendants found bread and relative stability.

With Bobbe Yente's death, the first of the Polonsky novels comes to an end. The transplantation to the New World had been successfully accomplished.

The second volume is entitled *In the Morning Light*, 1952, and encompasses the years of the Wilson Administration and the First World War. It continues the chronicle of Jewish adjustment to America. Business boomed and the Polonskys shared in the general prosperity. As their standard of living rose, they moved into better quarters, ever further from Boston's ghetto. Their attachment to their Jewish roots weakened, their values changed, tensions increased, bewilderment and unhappiness crept in. Only David, approaching manhood, faced the future with eagerness and undimmed hope.

Despite a lingering sadness at the fading of old glories and a glance backward now and then at discarded religious observances, David plunged into American activities and excitements. His first job as a messenger boy required him to desecrate the Sabbath. A full day devoted both to studying at school and to working necessitated his neglecting his morning prayers soon after his bar-mitzvah. Gradually more and more religious observances were disposed of through disuse. David came to admire his non-Jewish teachers and to associate with non-Jewish playmates. At High School he was introduced to the great interpreters of the American soul as he studied the works of Hawthorne, Poe, Whittier and President Wilson. The end of World War I coincided with his graduation from High School. While the War prosperity gave way to the post-War depression and the Polonskys were plunged into financial crises, David, elated, confident, determined, looked forward to college years and heard the bell of destiny ringing in his inner ear and calling him to great deeds ahead.

The third volume, *The Sun at Noon*, 1955, deals with the four hectic years between 1919 and 1923, the period of Harding, Coolidge, normalcy, the Golden Illusion, and its harsh aftermath. For the Polonskys it was a period of storm and stress, feudings and reconciliations, ecstasy and despair. David, the central character, spent these years at Harvard, discovering himself and wrestling with problems of good and evil, love and hate. The more maturity he acquired, the more somber he became. It seemed as if greater wisdom went hand in hand with greater sadness. Nevertheless, he was thrilled to be alive and young. By specializing in philosophy, even though it was a poor subject with which to make a living, he hoped to penetrate into the mystery of the universe into which he had been born. He felt closest to Spinoza, the Jewish lensgrinder with the magnificent mind. But he soon realized that too much questioning was not good and that beyond all rational explorations and logical answers, there persisted an irrational, illogical need for faith, the kind of faith that still warmed the few Polonskys who lived with Torah and rabbinical precepts. As these older members of the family passed away, the old warmth was dissipated. The world about David was getting bigger, more fascinating, more challenging, but also stranger and colder. As each Polonsky learned to shift for himself, David found ever fewer persons with whom he could talk of what troubled and excited him most. Soon he realized that even between himself and his father the distance had widened to such an extent that they no longer spoke the same language or thought common thoughts. David would remain a Jew by blood and inertia but the powerful force of the environment acting upon him since boyhood had re-molded him into an American far more than it had affected his father.

As an American, he was therefore disturbed when at Harvard he came in contact with unexpected evidences of antisemitism. While working at the Placement Bureau, he was puzzled by the fact that personnel managers and prospective employers rejected brilliant Harvard graduates solely on the ground of their Jewish background. The antisemitism that came to his attention was not the vulgar, blatant, dangerous sort that had prevailed in Russia. It never had official sanction. Still it was there. It irritated. It could not be conjured out of existence. Some professors even condoned it on the basis of pseudo-scientific principles. Every Jew had to adjust to its quiet, insidious presence. David's friend Albert adjusted by getting angry at his own origin, reviling the Jewish religion as a mass of superstitions and becoming wedded to pure reason. Whenever David tried to defend his love for Jewish reality on the basis of logic, he found himself on slippery ground. To him it was part of the poetry of life. It was feeling and memory, mystery and intuitive insight. He was drawn towards its rituals, from the blessing of the candles and the soft singing of hymns on the eve of the Sabbath to the inspiring Passover Seder and the awe-imbuing Day of Atonement. Often he obtained from simple Jews what no professors could give him, intimate knowledge of the inner struggles of individuals and peoples.

The fourth volume, *Between Day and Dark*, 1959, is set in the mid-1920's. The Polonskys diverge ever more in their interests and economic levels. Family frictions increase but can still be reconciled without too deep hostility. Illness, death, tragic events restore family unity after temporary rifts.

David, the hero, takes his first steps out into the world beyond Boston. He enters upon his career as a journalist and free-lance writer. The past still retains a hold upon him but the present reality makes ever more demands upon him and colors his dreams of the future. Though he would prefer to commune with nature and books, he has to come to terms with the troubles of the man-made world, jobs, money, bills. He finds no romance in writing gossip-columns or the kind of feature-stories that newspaper editors would buy. He wants to depict the inner turmoils of men and women, deep-seated regrets, persistent hopes, clouds of pessimism, breezes of optimism, attitudes toward eternal problems. Yet the necessity of earning a living forces him to accept the only available job, journalistic work for a small-town weekly. In the romance and grandeur of old-fashioned Americanism that was rooted in the Old Testament, he finds an affinity to the warm loveliness of the Jewishness he had known. Nevertheless, whenever any reference is made by a non-Jew to David's Jewish origin, a sharp shiver of embarrassment and vague hurt goes through him. He becomes ultra-sensitive to every breath and suspicion of dislike or criticism. He wonders if his kind neighbors could always be trusted to remain decent and civilized, or if they too, for example, might follow the lead of an antisemitic priest and join an antisemitic movement camouflaged under an innocuous name such as the Christian League for Christian Justice and Morality. David notices that his intellectual interests are exclusively in the American world and that he tends to submerge his Jewish heritage. Yet the ultra-modern Americanism of the 1920's that was eclipsing old-fashioned New England ways was vulgar, harsh, loud, false, and inhuman. Something was happening to decent, soft-spoken, modest, well-informed men and women during the Prohibition Era. Too much and too sudden prosperity was eating into the vitals of America and engulfing its healthy organs.

The fifth volume, *The Bitter Spring*, 1961, depicts America heading into the Great Depression that followed the rollicking Twenties. David leaves his New England home and comes to New York upon the invitation of a famous editor of a magazine for emancipated intellectuals. In this editor, Angoff paints an intimate portrait of H. L. Mencken, the feared and revered dictator of literary taste in liberal circles. Angoff was his assistant on *The American Mercury* and came in contact with the emerging literary elite in the great metropolis. The better he knew Mencken, George Jean Nathan, and their iconoclastic disciples, the more he yearned for the literature of former generations. Moving in smart, cynical, bewildering, aggressive circles of the great and near-great, in speakeasies and rich drawing-rooms, he felt ill-at-ease, lost and frightened, just as did Thomas Wolfe, who also exchanged Harvard for New York at this time. Now and then David escaped from his oversophisticated cynics to the anonymous little people in cafeterias, parks, streets, and rooming houses. Among them he could relax. Among them he found genuineness and simple joys. Among them he forgot the loneliness that overcame him in the best circles, where the talk was of liquor and food and women.

As the Depression deepened, a great questioning of values began, a reconsideration of all things and all popular idols. The blustering giants of industry, of politics, and of letters were shown up to be pygmies. David's boss, the spiritual catalytic agent, whom flatterers had likened to Dean Swift and Samuel Johnson, also shrunk in stature. Shame and sorrow replaced false pride, flamboyance and boisterousness. Sinking in the mire of poverty, people became bitter. They questioned the virtues of capitalism. They succumbed to the lure of philosophies ranging from socialism to Hitlerism. David's boss got angry with the turn of events, the harsh side of his mind came to the fore, his suppressed antisemitism emerged,

he ranted about the congenital inferiority of the slum ro-
dents who imagined themselves made in God's image. David
was ready to break with his mentor as the volume came to an
end.

The sixth volume, *Summer Storm,* 1963, deals with the
early years of the New Deal. Under Franklin D. Roosevelt,
despair gave way to new hope in 1933. The editor, once wor-
shiped by David and liberal intellectuals, found his followers
dwindling and his Nietzschean blustering falling on deaf
ears. Rugged individualism had lost its appeal and young
people preferred to huddle together under a common banner, Nazism, Fascism, Communism. The best of them followed the New Deal in Washington. For David, Jewishness
remained as the anchor for his thoughts and dreams. When
his editor-in-chief insisted on remaining publicly silent
about the Nazi menace and when in private conversations
this editor defended Hitler's efforts to curb the Jews of Germany, then David could no longer work with him. The
whole world seemed suddenly stranger, colder, lonelier, nar-
rower. Nevertheless, he did not share the inferiority feelings
rampant among his Jewish friends. Their estrangement from
Jewishness led to a hardening of their souls, a loss of spiritual
loveliness. They were espousing intermarriage as the answer
to their souls' malaise. This subject had rarely been touched
upon in the first four volumes. In the fifth volume, David
came across a single case of intermarriage among his many acquaintances: a Jewish girl who answered the call of her emo-
tions for a Gentile mate and who after marriage awoke to the
realization of the many complexities that rose up day after
day and that were in the main unsolvable. In *Summer Storm,*
intermarriage assumes greater importance, mirroring the reality of a more integrated generation.

David's friend Phil places a higher valuation upon Christian girls merely because of their Christian background. He

idealizes them as more ladylike, more polite, more pliable, less argumentative. David himself, however, still finds greater attraction in Jewish girls. His first love was Alice, whom he knew since immigrant, boyhood days. Her later turning away from Jewish interests and values led to a gradual cooling of their relationship. His second love was Sylvia, the personification of Jewish womanhood, fragile in body but strong in spirit. She brought luster and meaning and affection to his lonely years as a young editor in New York. To Angoff's hero, love was an affirmation of common helplessness in the great fair of life, common search for an escape from miseries, common yearning for self-forgetfulness, common consolation for the sadness of living.

In the three volumes awaiting publication and others still incomplete, Angoff leads his hero through the mazes of Jewish non-Jewish relationships since the Roosevelt Era. This hero is but a mask for the author himself, who is painfully aware of decadent phenomena on the present scene and who yet retains his optimistic faith in the regenerative power of America and of the Jewish community in America. As a novelist, Angoff holds that one cannot write without pity. He therefore bathes in compassion his many characters, the good and the bad. Only from the indifferent and the indolent of heart does he withhold the fountain of compassion.

Twentieth century American Jewry, in its indomitable self-confidence and vibrant vitality as well as in its affluence, flabbiness and confusion, is mirrored in Angoff's saga of the Polonskys, a fictional epic of vast scope and rich insight.

Irving Fineman did not paint on as broad a canvas as did Angoff but his insight into Jewish life was no less sound. Stemming from a Chassidic immigrant family, he received a good Jewish education as well as a thorough scientific training at Harvard and at the Massachusetts Institute of Technology. Not until he had passed his mid-thirties did literature wean him away from his engineering career. His first novels *This Pure Young Man*, 1930, and *Lovers Must Learn*, 1932, dealt with the American scene. But with his third novel *Hear Ye Sons*, 1933, he directed himself primarily to Jewish readers and for them he recreated the Jewish past out of which his parents had come and which he felt was an essential part of his personality. The novel was a synthesis of the tales he had heard in his childhood about the Jewish *stedtl* of Eastern Europe and he treated this Jewish heritage with great love and deep understanding. It won him a wider audience than his earlier novels or the following one *Doctor Addams*, 1939, which brought to the fore the dilemma of the scientist in the modern world, the scientist who was effective in the laboratory but completely ineffective in solving personal and social relations.

Fineman continued to explore Jewish and Biblical themes in later narratives such as *Jacob*, 1941, in which the patriarch was depicted as the typical man of sensibility, and *Ruth*, 1941, which expressed the author's insight into the nature of woman as differentiated from that of man. In 1961 appeared his biography of Henrietta Szold, founder of Hadassah. In her, Fineman discovered a kindred spirit who saw in Judaism a civilizing force still needed for the further progress of humanity. This biography, entitled *Woman of Valor*, aroused considerable controversy because the biographer painted a portrait of a real human being in all her weakness as well as strength, a portrait which, however, ran counter to the legend which had begun to envelop her and which was treasured by her hundreds of thousands of admirers in America and in Israel.

Like Fineman, Leo W. Schwarz was born in New York and educated at Harvard. Though best known for his popular anthologies such as *The Jewish Caravan*, 1935, and *Golden Treasury of Jewish Literature*, 1937, he achieved his most original work in his moving narrative *The Redeemers*, 1953. This book, which was based upon his experiences and observations in Germany during the post-War years when he was the Joint Distribution Committee's Director for Displaced Persons, dealt with the resurrection of concentration camp survivors to a life of renewed dignity and national heroism.

This saga of the years 1945 to 1952 dramatically portrayed five interacting groups: the occupation authorities—American, British, and French—who came as liberators; the German people, who were recovering from unanticipated defeat; the United Nations, engaged in earliest efforts at solving a complex political problem; the State of Israel, emerging out of semi-chaos; and the liberated Jewish victims, who were struggling to erase old scars and to move on to new freedom.

Angoff, Fineman, and Schwarz are not fashionable among the avant-garde experimenters of the 1960's but they are well grounded in Jewish learning and they are also well integrated into the American scene. They offer sound literary fare to hearts hungry for a healthy synthesis of Jewishness and Americanism.

CHAPTER XIV

IMPACT OF ISRAEL

The establishment of the State of Israel in 1948 had a tremendous impact upon the Jews of America and was mirrored in prose and verse, song and dance. This event, the culmination of a millennial dream, changed the attitude even of the estranged and uprooted Jews towards their historic heritage and compelled them to rethink their relationship to their fellow-Jews.

The philosophy of the melting-pot receded. Jewish self-hatred was replaced by Jewish pride and Jewish assertiveness. Assimilation became an obnoxious term even to its practitioners and was replaced by the sweeter word integration. Zionism, a cause espoused by a few intellectuals at the turn of the century and by an increasing minority of men-of-letters since the Balfour Declaration of 1917, won the allegiance of the overwhelming majority of Jews. Cultural pluralism, long advocated by non-Jewish thinkers such as John Dewey and Randolph S. Bourne and by Jewish leaders such as Judah L. Magnes, Louis D. Brandeis, Stephen S. Wise and Horace M. Kallen, suddenly found new, vociferous adherents among repentant Jewish writers at a time when cultural monism and cultural conformity had already been accepted by the American masses of divergent origins.

The debates of 1917 regarding the possibility of dual cultural loyalty combined with single political loyalty were resumed three decades later. However, the proportion between the adherents of cultural dualism—the living in American space and Jewish time—and the adherents of cultural monism—represented by the American Council for Judaism —shifted more and more to the detriment of the latter.

As early as 1909, Magnes had advocated cultural dualism but found little understanding or sympathy for his views among Americanized Jews. He held that, even though politically a person could be a member of only one sovereign state and owed undivided allegiance to it, nevertheless there were elements of nationality which a person could carry with him from country to country and discard only at the peril of his psychic stability. Such elements were language, history, customs, traditions, ideals. Obviously, there must be some accommodation on the part of every human being to his surroundings. The force of the environment compelled certain modifications. But this did not mean that, therefore, a person's traditional national culture must be abandoned. On the contrary, breaking the chain of tradition must lead to degeneracy. To set at naught the accumulated wisdom and beauty of ages was an irresponsible act. On the other hand, to foster a multiplicity of national cultures meant adding richness, picturesqueness and variety to the American scene. A garden of blossoms of many sizes and colors was certainly preferable to a vast field of flowers of the same size and color.

In 1916, Randolph S. Bourne published an essay on "The Jew and Trans-National America," in which he, the non-Jew, pointed out that the American people were offered two ideals of American nationalism: one was that of the traditional melting-pot in which all different cultures were molten into a single amalgam, the other was that of a cooperation of cultures in which each culture retained its separate identity. If the former program of Americanism, then being urged by ex-President Theodore Roosevelt, were adopted and if the distinctive racial and cultural qualities were obliterated, the

New World population would be transformed into a color-less, tasteless, homogeneous mass. Such a program was but a slavish imitation of the European nationalisms which were destroying each other in a fratricidal war. Why should the cultural soul of any human being be washed out of him?

Bourne saw in emergent Zionism, which he defined as Jew-ish trans-nationalism, a desirable pattern for a trans-national America. He felt that the Jews were facing the modern world with the problem of finding for them a place in its social structure which would enable them to live as human beings without demanding that they cease to be Jews. Was it possi-ble to owe cultural loyalty to a Jewish center and political loyalty to America? Yes, answered Bourne, if America would realize the splendid ideal of becoming the first international nation just as the Jews had realized their prophets' vision of becoming the first international race. In contrast to the nar-row nationalism of the melting-pot ideology, Bourne defined his cooperative Americanism as "an ideal of a freely mingling society of very different racial and cultural antecedents, with a common political allegiance and common social ends but with free and distinctive cultural allegiances which may be placed anywhere in the world." [1]

Among non-Jews, the Norwegian-American novelist O. E. Rolvaag also interpreted Jewish participation on the world scene in a manner not unlike that of Randolph S. Bourne. In his novel *Their Fathers' God*, published in 1931, Rolvaag called upon his Scandinavian kinsmen in America to follow the example of those Jews who were espousing cultural dual-ism. "If we're to accomplish anything worth while, anything at all, we must do it as Norwegians. Otherwise we may meet the same fate as corn in too strong a sun. Look at the Jews, for example: take away the contribution they have made to

[1] R. S. Bourne, "The Jew and Trans-National America," *Menorah Journal*, II (1916), 282.

the world's civilization and you'd have a tremendous gap that time will never be able to fill. Did they make their contribution by selling their birthright and turning into Germans, Russians, and Poles? Or did they achieve greatly because they stubbornly refused to be de-Jewed? See what they have done in America! Are they as citizens inferior to us? Do they love this country less? Are they trying to establish a nation of their own? Empty nonsense! But they haven't ceased being Jews simply because they live here in America, and because they have adopted this country's language and become its citizens. Do you think their children will become less worthy Americans because they are being fostered in Jewish traits and traditions? Quite the contrary! If they, as individuals or as a group, owe any debt to America, the payment can only be made by their remaining Jews, and the same holds true for all nationalities that have come here. One thing I see clearly: if this process of levelling down, of making everybody alike by blotting out all racial traits, is allowed to continue, America is doomed to become the most impoverished land spiritually on the face of the earth; out of our highly praised melting-pot will come a dull, smug complacency, barren of all creative thought and effort. Soon we will have reached the perfect democracy of barrenness. Gone will be the distinguishing traits given us by God; dead will be the hidden life of the heart which is nourished by tradition, the idiom of language, and our attitude to life. It is out of these elements that our character grows. I ask again, what will we have left? " [2]

Between 1933, when Hitler came to power in Germany, and 1948, when the Jewish state was founded, the soul of American Jewry was subjected to severe shocks and alternated between despair and elation. In the struggle of ideologies which took place during these years, Zionism emerged

[2] O. E. Rolvaag, *Their Fathers' God*, New York, 1931, p. 209.

triumphant as the answer to Jewish homelessness and won the support of most American Jews.

Zionism had been the solution of the Dreamers of Zion from the destruction of the Second Temple to the Hoveve Zion Movement of the eighteen-eighties. It was the solution of the Thinkers of Zion from Leon Pinsker, Ahad Haam, Theodor Herzl, and the First Zionist Congress of 1897 that adopted the Basel Platform until the promulgation of the Balfour Declaration in 1917. It was the solution of the Builders of Zion throughout all the *Aliyas* until the founding of Israel.

With the birth of Israel, the correctness of this ideology was demonstrated. Jews thereafter were no longer a people in exile. If a Jew remained in America or in any other country which permitted emigration of its citizens or subjects, then he did so because of choice and not under compulsion. Diaspora was no longer synonymous with Galuth or involuntary exile, since Israel granted to any Jew who did not feel at home anywhere in the world admission to its soil, a right embedded in the basic law of the Jewish state.

The first reaction of American Jews to the historic event of Israel's emergence in 1948 was unbounded enthusiasm. Every head among them was higher, every back was straighter, every brow was prouder, every mouth was filled with laughter and every tongue with singing.

Karl Shapiro's stanzas on "Israel" voiced the typical mood of 1948. The triumph of Israel, he held, had restored dignity to the Jewish name. No longer would one think of the Jew as yellow-badged or as the creature who harried Jesus. For the first time the poet could speak the once dirty word aloud unconsciously and proudly.

> "When I think of the battle for Zion I hear
> The drop of chains, the starting forth of feet,

And I remain chained in a Western chair.
My blood beats like a bird against a wall,
I feel the weight of prisons in my skull
Falling away; my forebears stare through stone." [3]

Already in 1949, however, there appeared the first book which faced up to the question: what now? It was Arthur Koestler's book *Promise and Fulfillment*, a thrilling narrative of the ups-and-downs of the struggle for a Jewish homeland, from the promise of 1917 to the fulfillment of 1948. The book culminated, however, in a projection of coming events which aroused considerable controversy on the American scene.

Koestler foresaw a change coming over the mentality of Jews in Israel which would alienate them from the Jews of the Western World. He noted that the native generation of Israeli was already showing a marked difference in physical appearance and mental outlook from Jews in Europe or America and he was certain that this difference would increase from decade to decade until the Jewish state ultimately became entirely un-Jewish in the presently accepted sense. For two thousand years Jews had been praying for and wishing each other a homecoming to Jerusalem in the following year. Now that insuperable obstacles were removed, they faced the alternative of either betaking themselves to the city of their heart's desire or else of stopping to repeat constantly prayers and wishes which they did not really intend to implement.

According to Koestler, the attitude of Jews who were unwilling to settle in Israel, yet insisted on remaining a community in some way apart from their fellow-citizens, had become an anachronism after 1948. The choice was either migrating to Israel or else giving up Jewish separatism.

[3] Karl Shapiro, *Poems of a Jew*, New York, 1958, p. 4.

Faced with such a choice, Koestler made his decision and concluded his book with a goodby to the Jews. He recommended to likeminded European and American Jews to wish the new state good luck but to merge themselves with the nations whose life and culture they shared, to merge without reservations or split loyalties. The mission of the Wandering Jew was over, he must discard the knapsack, settle down, and unite completely and unreservedly with the others, if not for his own sake, then for that of his children and his children's children.

What Koestler expressed as a wish and a hope in 1949, two American scholars, Oscar Handlin and Jacob Marcus, expressed as a probability if not as an inevitability when, a decade later, they launched their prophecies of the decline of American Jewry by the end of the century.

A year after Koestler's examination of his relationship to Israel and to the Occident, Meyer Levin undertook a similar examination and arrived at diametrically opposite conclusions. His autobiographic volume, *In Search,* 1950, asked basic questions of himself: What am I? What am I doing in America? Where do I stand in relation to Israel? "I know that Jews everywhere are asking themselves this question. In America, there are five times as many Jews as in Israel. Despite the immediate, fervent response to the creation of Israel, many Jews outside the homeland argue that its creation will eventually lead outside Jews to assimilation. As when any great new fact appears, there is confusion, before the new lines of orientation are clear. The Jew outside Palestine must define again not only his own relationship to his people—he must decide how to orient his children, whether to give them more Jewish education or, as Arthur Koestler suggests, to try to relieve them of the burden of Jewishness." [4]

In examining his way of life as a Jew born in America and

[4] Meyer Levin, *In Search,* New York, 1950, p. 11.

seeking the full realization of his potentialities, Meyer Levin became aware of the complexity of his Jewishness. His dominant childhood memory had been of fear and shame at being a Jew. From his earliest consciousness, he had absorbed tales of Jews being kicked around and browbeaten and despised in no matter what country they lived.

It was a trip to Palestine in 1925, during which he witnessed the opening of the Hebrew University on Mount Scopus, that changed his entire approach to Jewishness. Jewish self-hatred could no longer be retained. Indeed, on returning to America, he found he could no longer erase Palestine from his soul and so he left America again and joined Yagur, a new Kibbutz near Haifa. There he felt he could live as a Jew in a Jewish society, speaking a Jewish tongue, and raising wholly Jewish children. But 1929 saw him back in America. Soon he realized that there were two souls in his breast and that he could not cut either Americanism or Jewishness out of himself without destroying himself.

In 1937, Levin's significant novel, *The Old Bunch*, appeared. It presented a cross section of American Jewish life from 1921 to 1934, Levin's own generation in Chicago. Each character of the Bunch was aware of something missing in his life. These youngsters, who were to emerge as doctors, lawyers, artists, radical schoolteachers, ambitious businessmen, and good wives, sought something indefinable that would give a heightened meaning to their existence. Some went to Paris to seek sensations sharp enough to cut through the rot of their lives. One went to Palestine and was thrilled to participate in the building of a more moral civilization than he had known in Chicago. But most ended by becoming ordinary and normal, raising families and enjoying the charming trivialities and benevolent philanthropies of middle class Americans. They were, however, all the time aware of sneers and leers and derogatory appellations by their neighbors.

Though they seemed well adjusted, they could as little escape their Jewishness, try as they might, as their Americanism.

During the decade following the publication of *The Old Bunch,* the author continued his search for a meaning beyond himself. As a journalist, he accompanied the American forces that invaded Europe and that liberated the survivors of the concentration camps. He was at Buchenwald and at Teresienstadt. He was with the Illegals who were trying to make their way to the Jewish homeland and who were intercepted by British ships. He witnessed the struggle for Israel's independence.

By 1950, Levin had found himself. He accepted biculturalism as his way of life. He was equally at home in Israel and in America. He saw himself as a peculiar mixture of Chicago and Chassidism, of truth-seeking American reporter and truth-seeking son of the Torah. He recognized that some individuals like Koestler felt that they had to renounce one culture or the other. He was happiest living in both. Jewishness was not so much to him a religious identification or a social identification as it was a sense of belonging to the folk, to the Jewish people. "Godless though I may profess myself, I have responded with more than warmth to the mystical elements of Chassidism. As a writer, I have considered that I accept this material as folklore. But in my soul I knew that I take more than this from these legends. I accept them as expressions of truth, of spiritual comprehension from within the folk itself, just as I accepted the Messianic idea so long as I could embody it in the people instead of an individual Messiah. In these years the people have indeed carried out the Messianic return to Jerusalem in their exodus at night through forests, and over the snows of the Alps, and hunted across the Mediterranean, and through the Sinai of Cyprus." [5]

[5] *Ibid.,* p. 516.

According to Levin, Israel was the new beginning, and not the end of the Jewish question. It was a new foundation upon which positive values could be erected and a more wholesome relationship to non-Jews could be based. American Jews would now lose their oversensitivity, their acquired discomfort, their sense of shame, even as he had. They would remain Jews by affirmation. They would absorb cultural sustenance from Israel but they would also give to Israel a necessary counterbalance of cosmopolitanism, thus preventing the young state from sliding into chauvinism. "The example of Jewish history in the past few years can give courage to all humanity: if there was a Messianism in the Jewish folk that enabled it to rise out of death to attain Israel, then humanity as a whole must possess the fuller Messianism, and contain within itself the force to attain universal peace and justice." [6]

In 1953, three years after Levin's autobiography, Maurice Samuel in his book *Level Sunlight* also stressed the Messianic aspect of Israel's rebirth. It was a period of let-down in morale after the exuberance of the founding years. Samuel feared a relapse of aroused Jewry into apathy and again negation. He warned against the danger of a sundering of Israel from world Jewry and from the legacy of the many centuries in exile. He held that the objective of classical Zionism went beyond the mere building of a physical state. It included the rebuilding of the entire Jewish people in all lands with the help of the Jewish center in its historic homeland. This was Ahad-Haam's legacy, which Weizmann inherited and enriched. This vision inspired the early Chalutzim, who saw themselves as pioneers of a moral regeneration far more than of a physical rehabilitation. Because of the pressure of immediate practical problems, this vision was beginning to recede, a most dangerous development, for without its inspiration, without the Messianic urge, Israel would not fulfill its pur-

[6] *Ibid.*, p. 524.

pose. Only as the expression of the latent will and destiny of the entire Jewish people could Israel be a significant force on the world scene.

To this Jewish people belonged the five million American Jews. Samuel held that it would be a crime to reduce them to milchcows for Israel. They too were carriers of Jewish values in the world and they could offer to Israel more than money and good-will. The time had come for American Jewry to assert itself more vigorously as a cultural factor in the Jewish renascence.

Mordecai M. Kaplan, in his book *A New Zionism,* published in 1955, went beyond Samuel in urging a revision of Zionist ideology. He sought a change of direction from Herzlian Zionism, which had already become historic, to Ahad-Haam Zionism, which still awaited fulfillment. He saw the crisis in Zionism as a crisis in Judaism. He recognized that the limited objective of political Zionism, the acquisition of a legally assured and internationally recognized home for the Jewish people, had already been achieved more quickly and more successfully than most Jews expected. However, the larger objective of cultural Zionism or Ahad-Haamism was seemingly being postponed *sine die*. He, therefore, pleaded for a New Zionism which was to be based upon a strong sense of mutuality and interaction between the Jewish community in Israel and all the Jewish communities in the rest of the world. He maintained that Zionism existed for the Jews and not the Jews for Zionism. Hence Zionism must subordinate itself to the larger objective: Judaism as an evolving civilization. It must become a modern Messianic movement. It must involve all the Jews and it must assure a permanent place for Diaspora Judaism.

Otherwise, the unity of the Jewish people would be breached, an alienation between Israeli Jews and Diaspora Jews would set in, and Jewry's greatest victory in modern times would end in Jewry's greatest catastrophe. To avert this danger, the reclamation of the land of Israel must proceed simultaneously with the reconstitution of the Jewish people as a people and with the creative expansion of Torah. Torah, Kaplan concluded, would have to enter into Zionism before the Torah could go forth from Zion.

Waldo Frank, in his book *Bridgehead: The Drama of Israel*, which appeared in 1957, two years after Kaplan's book, also insisted on Messianism as the ultimate goal for continuing Jewish survival. Jews must embody in their individual and group structure the ethical principle enunciated by their prophet Micah: to do justly, and to love mercy, and to walk humbly before God, for, without this axiom, the Jew no longer changed but ceased. The Jew must continue to be or to become a Bridgehead for the redemption of the world through justice, mercy, and love.

While Frank's book was being readied for publication, the Suez Campaign exploded with tremendous international repercussions and brought to America an altogether different image of the Jew than emerged from the pages of the ivory-towered humanitarian, an image not of a humble, pacifistic group that was meekly offering its other cheek to hostile neighbors but rather of daring, resourceful neo-Maccabeans who were overcoming almost insuperable odds both on desert battlefields and at United Nations' forums.

American readers were becoming fed up with narratives of talented Jewish intellectuals and cosmopolites who were still depicting unpleasant Jewish money-grubbers that could get things wholesale or that could run as fast as Sammy of Hollywood. Such types were felt to be anachronisms. Readers were hungry for portraits of heroic Jews like those of the Warsaw Ghetto Uprising of whom John Hersey had so gloriously written in *The Wall*, 1950, or like the sabras of Israel whose exploits were filling the front-pages of the daily press in the closing months of 1956. Military chronicles of Jewish exploits such as Robert Henriques' *One Hundred Hours to Suez,* 1957, and restrained orations such as Abba Eban's *Voice of Israel,* 1957, were insufficient to sate this hunger.

The appearance of Leon Uris's prose epic *Exodus* in 1958 came as the answer to the long yearned for and long withheld fare for starved readers. Despite its literary failings, this over-sized novel was devoured in hundreds of thousands of copies. No adventure story of the wild and wooly West ever had the vogue of this glamorous, thrilling tale about the indomitable Jewish patriots who were always able to outwit their stupid British adversaries and their cruel Arab foes. Uris had no-ticed what other Jewish novelists had failed to see, namely, that the legend of the Jew had already changed in the popu-lar mind. The old stereotypes no longer seemed credible in view of contemporary reality. John Hersey, the non-Jew, had anticipated this change when he projected in 1950 Jews who refused to offer their throats to the slaughterer and went down fighting to the bitter end in the Warsaw revolt. John Hersey had pioneered and had produced a best seller in *The Wall.* Leon Uris rode the crest of the wave and performed a great deed of immeasurable propagandistic value for Israel and for American Jewry. In his wake there soon came other novels of Jewish affirmation, some of better literary quality, none of equal popular vogue.

Robert Nathan's novel of 1962, entitled *A Star in the Wind,* was typical of this genre. Its hero was an American correspondent who was fleeing from the unhappy Jewishness of his Cleveland childhood and was discovering gaiety and love and art in the Italian capital. On coming in contact with emergent Israel in the fateful month of May 1948, however, he underwent an inner conversion. Aboard a refugee ship packed with survivors of the extermination camps of Europe, he came to understand the meaning of being a Jew. On a hilltop in Galilee, standing shoulder to shoulder with young sabras and immigrant Jews from all lands, he made his commitment to his people. Their fate was henceforth to be his fate, dark and bitter though it might be with here and there clear golden lights breaking through the clouds and the storms. He was and would remain primarily a Jew.

Far more influential than Nathan's novel of Israel was James A. Michener's *The Source*, 1965, which had a worldwide vogue. On the basis of meticulous research, the novelist gave to recent events in Israel an historical background that reached back for twelve thousand years and that showed the unbreakable attachment of Jews to their holy soil throughout all the centuries of their repeated exiles.

In depicting the dilemma of the contemporary American Jew, torn between his admiration for the beckoning Promised Land of his ancestors and his new rootedness in the American home of the free and the brave, this non-Jewish writer displayed greater insight than most American novelists of Jewish origin.

In the concluding debate between the Israeli Jew and the American Jew, Michener presented two antithetical views with utmost fairness and objectivity. Michener's American protagonist, who was also a philanthropic supporter of Israel, saw no reason for pulling up stakes and emigrating to the tiny though hallowed land in the Middle East. He argued that he and his coreligionists were able to build in America a new way of life that was the best the Jew had ever known in this world. The Israeli, on the other hand, countered that the so-called new way of life was but a false old dream in a golden ghetto. "A religion that isn't Judaism. A synagogue that's a mere social center and a third generation that thinks it's been accepted by the majority if it names its son Bryan. It's a shallow, ugly, materialistic pattern of life, and it leads to one clear goal: assimilation." [7]

The American's reply was that perhaps being a people totally apart was not the most desirable destiny and that there was nothing wrong in Jews intermarrying and losing themselves in the main stream of America. What if the vision of a Jewish homeland were to perish once more! The Jewish contribution to mankind would still continue, since the heritage of Israel was by now universal. Michener repeatedly affirmed through the words and deeds of his characters the desirability both of a Jewish state and of a Diaspora as expressions of Jewish destiny.

A new pattern was emerging in American fiction. Judaism was being painted in such attractive colors that a tradition of many centuries was being reversed. The literary tradition that required the Jew or his beautiful daughter to discover the truth of Christianity was yielding to the opposite approach which had the non-Jew discover the deeper truth of Judaism. Bernard Malamud in *The Assistant,* 1957, a grim, realistic tale of a Jewish neighborhood grocer, let a Gentile assistant experience the Christian forbearance of the non-Christian storekeeper and the inner loveliness of the latter's daughter, and had the young man end by voluntarily converting to Judaism.

In another story, "The Lady of the Lake," included in the collection *The Magic Barrel,* 1958, Malamud's hero lost the girl he loved because he was ashamed to reveal to her that he was Jewish. This hero, Henry Levin, went abroad to seek romance. At Lake Maggiore, he met an attractive nymph who introduced herself as Isabella del Dongo. One of her first questions was: "Are you perhaps Jewish?" He parried by introducing himself as Henry R. Freeman, an American traveling abroad. After falling in love with her, he learned that she

[7] James A. Michener, *The Source,* New York, 1965, p. 881.

was only the caretaker's daughter. Nevertheless, he proposed to her. "She gazed at him with eyes moistly bright, then came the soft, inevitable thunder: 'Are you a Jew?' His answer: 'How many no's make never? Why do you persist with such foolish questions?' 'Because I hoped you were.' " And she revealed to him that she was once an inmate of the Buchenwald Concentration Camp, where her Jewishness had been tattooed into her very flesh. Her past was meaningful to her. She treasured what she had suffered for. Marriage outside of her faith was unthinkable for her. After her disappearance, Levin realized the irony of his situation: how easily he might have won her had he only been truthful about his own Jewish origin.

Malamud found in New York's Jews rich material for his short stories. Having grown up in their midst, he did not look upon them as an outsider and therefore did not have to overemphasize their virtues or underemphasize their weaknesses. Nevertheless, they emerge in his tales as basically good human beings. The German refugee, in the final story of *Idiots First,* 1963, does not adjust successfully to his new environment and ends as a suicide but, in all his pathetic helplessness, there is an innate dignity in his bearing. The Jewish storekeeper, who tries to make friends with his Harlem Negro neighbors in the narrative "Black Is My Favorite Color," is hardly an heroic figure but he is depicted honestly and sympathetically. Repeatedly rebuffed in his efforts to understand and to be understood by a colored youth, by a colored maid, by a colored sweetheart, he serves to illustrate the difficulties that beset Jewish-Negro relationship. In the end, he has to realize that the Negroes, though themselves an underprivileged minority, are already poisoned by a diabolical image of the Jew. Beyond the gulf separating Black and White, there are additional complexities that a Jew must reckon with in his confrontation with Negroes.

Malamud's novel *A New Life*, 1961, presented a Jew who fled from an unhappy existence in New York in search of fresh integrity in the Far West and who finally found it after exhausting emotional experiences by accepting heavy responsibilities brought on by his own guilt and that of others.

In "Eli the Fanatic," by Philip M. Roth, the best story included in his collection *Goodbye, Columbus*, 1959, Jewish squirming before Gentile neighbors was attacked with sardonic irony. A sensitive lawyer, who wanted to help his Jewish townfolk to retain the good will of fellow Americans, undertook to plead with a refugee, then still wearing a black ghetto outfit, to move to another community. But as Eli came to understand the Greenhorn's inner motivation based upon a tragic Jewish past, he exchanged clothes and donned the latter's costume as a symbol of his own acceptance of his Jewish fate. This act led his Americanized Jewish friends to assume that he must have suffered a nervous breakdown and he was spirited off to an insane asylum.

This tale illustrated Roth's efforts to find his way back to Jewishness, whose negative aspects he depicted far too often. Yet, this tale also illustrated his ignorance of the inner motivation and behavior of Jews, despite his keen observation of their outer trappings. What Chassid or head of a Yeshiva would exchange his traditional garb sanctified by many generations for a lawyer's newest suit in order to appease the residents of a gilded New York suburb? As the poetess Kadia Molodowsky pointed out, if Roth meant this act to be symbolic of a rapprochement between the traditional Jew and the assimilationist Jew, the foundation upon which this symbolic act rested was theatrical and not genuine, since a Chassidic leader was more likely to fast for three days to save a Jewish soul than to put on the lawyer's suit even once.

The talented, popular novelists of the post-War era, Arthur Miller, Norman Mailer, Irwin Shaw, were much more at ease

in writing about Jews than was Philip Roth, who only grudg-
ingly accepted the fact that he could not escape being
branded as a Jew. Furthermore, while the latter preferred to
dissect unpleasant Jews and to emphasize the seamy side of
Jewish life in most of his tales, they not only defended Jews
against detractors but also lashed out savagely in counterat-
tacks.

In *Focus*, 1945, Arthur Miller exposed to ridicule the
bigots who refused to employ Jews, or who would not tol-
erate Jews in Gentile neighborhoods, or who would restrict
hotels to Christian clientele only. He projected as his main
character Mr. Newman, the personnel manager of a firm
which did not hire Jews. One day the Vice-President in
charge of operations, who had originally laid down the speci-
fications for the type of persons to be employed by the company, looked into the face of Mr. Newman and arrived at the
conclusion that it was a Semitic face. Such a face could not be
tolerated in the front office. Thereupon Mr. Newman's
twenty-five years of faithful service terminated and he was
forced to look for another job. Everywhere this sympathizer
with the Christian Front found himself politely rejected because his name and certain features led to the suspicion that
he might be a Jew. When, as a result, his own enthusiasm for
antisemitic activities abated, his neighbors also became suspi-
cious. They began to steer clear of him. When their suspi-
cions increased, they tried to hound him out of the neighborhood even as they were hounding its only Jew, the storekeeper Finkelstein. Newman sought to rehabilitate himself
by attending a rally of the Christian Front. However, when
he forgot to applaud the harangue of a rabble-rousing priest,
he was beaten up as a probable Semite and thrown out of the
hall. Gradually there seeped into his consciousness an awareness of the injustice that was being perpetrated against fellow-
Americans of Jewish origin, injustices in which he himself

had until then always acquiesced. Finally, he realized that, if he had any regard for America, he would have to take a militant stand against bigotry at home no less than abroad. Shoulder to shoulder with the Jew Finkelstein, he would have to fight the antisemitic cancer that was eating into America's vitals.

Norman Mailer, in his best-selling novel of World War II, *The Naked and the Dead,* 1948, included a realistic account of the relations between Jews and non-Jews who were brought into intimate contact with each other while fighting together on a Japanese-infested Pacific island. In Roth, one of the Jewish privates, Mailer portrayed himself. Roth suffered under the burden of his Jewishness. It brought discriminations upon his head and it offered him no compensatory values. Yet Roth always flared up in its defense and bristled with anger when any derogatory reference was made to his origin. Indeed, he met his death trying to prove that he was as good as his non-Jewish mates in his patrol. The expression "Jew-bastard," hurled at him when he lay down exhausted, stirred him like an electric charge. He was shocked that he should be judged by his buddies not on the basis of his own capacities and incapacities but on the basis of an accident of birth for which he was not responsible, of a religion that he, the agnostic, did not believe in, of a race which, in his opinion, did not exist, of a nation which was not really a nation. He rebelled against the Jewish aspect of his personality. He was frustrated that he could not explain it away. He was furious that others saw in him primarily the Jew and not the American. "Nothing he could do was right, nothing would please them. He seethed, but with more than self-pity now. He understood. He was the butt because there always had to be a butt. A Jew was a punching bag because they could not do without one." [8]

[8] Norman Mailer, *The Naked and the Dead,* New York, 1948, p. 662.

Goldstein, another Jewish private in Roth's platoon, survived not because he was more rugged but because, unlike Roth, he was not a naked individual exposed to the savagery of a non-Jewish world. He accepted this savagery as part of his destiny. He was for the non-Jews in his platoon a "goddam Jewboy." He knew that it was hopeless to change their attitude and that it would do him no good to rage against their ingrained prejudices. He was bolstered up by his faith in God, a luxury which the intellectual Roth would not allow himself, and by his awareness that a Jew could always go to a fellow Jew to find understanding. This feeling of kinship took from him his loneliness. It enabled him to overcome moods of depression and to carry on.

Irwin Shaw's novel of the Second World War *The Young Lions,* 1948, appeared in the same year as Norman Mailer's *The Naked and the Dead.* It painted an equally grim, realistic picture of the horrors of the conflict and it also touched on antisemitism which Jewish privates in the American army had to contend with on the part of buddies and officers. But it also showed that this prejudice could be overcome at times, though not always, by exemplary behavior and courage. Two Jewish privates in this narrative found themselves assigned to the company of the antisemitic Captain Colclough and the antisemitic Sergeant Rickett. Fein, the older, stronger, and more practical soldier, maintained the view that the best equipment a Jew could have in the army as well as in civilian life was one deaf ear, which was to be turned in the direction of all insults. Without this equipment he would not last long. If Jews had to fight against every antisemite, they would have been wiped out long ago. Discretion had greater survival value than valor. Noah, the younger, weaker and less practical private, reacted more vigorously. He was prepared to go down fighting for his Jewish dignity. Indeed, he did fight bouts with the ten biggest men in the Company and was battered by nine of them but never gave up. At the Normandy Front, he proved himself a hero. In the final days of the German campaign, he died a hero's death, in contrast to the bullying Captain Colclough, who from the very first moment of landing at the Normandy beach failed to show any trace of bravery. Despite moments of despair, Noah did retain to the end his vision of a better tomorrow when decent human beings would be running the world.

Jewish negation and Jewish self-hatred continued to recede in the nineteen-fifties and nineteen-sixties. That these destructive psychic forces were still potent among some young Jewish intellectuals was evidenced by the *Commentary*-Symposium of 1961. However, the growing tide of Jewish affirmation was clearly reflected in the Symposium of the periodical *Judaism* during the same year. An intermediate position was taken by avant-garde intellectuals such as Delmore Schwartz, Leslie A. Fiedler and Karl Shapiro. Unable to evade concern with Jewishness, they defined the Jew as the eternal outsider who could not be contained within any nation or any established political entity. Delmore Schwartz saw the Jew as a symbol of alienation. Leslie A. Fiedler saw the Jew as everywhere the dissenter, everywhere an exile. Karl Shapiro equated the consciousness of being a Jew with the consciousness of being man essentially himself, man left over, after everything that could happen had happened. He called his own *Poems of a Jew,* 1958, documents of an obsession. While denying any special concern for Judaism, Jewry, or Israel, he conceded that, having been born a Jew, he could not escape a state of Jewish consciousness. He held that a Jew who became an atheist or a Catholic still remained a Jew, that being a Jew was the consciousness of being a Jew, and that Jewish identity, with or without religion, with or without history, was the significant fact.

The impact of Israel was slowing down ultra-assimilationist tendencies. It was buttressing resistance to the conformist American environment. The struggle within the soul of the American Jew against the dominant philosophy of monoculturalism was resulting in a greater preoccupation with Jewish problems and ideals. Ever more insistent grew the demand for an answer to questions such as: What did it mean to be a Jew in America? What were the Jewish values for whose sake it was worthwhile to continue Jewish separatism in the most liberal democracy of the free world? Would not Jewish insistence on retaining minority cultural characteristics and close links with a Jewish state in the Middle East strain America's tolerance of otherness? Would Jewish genius in the era of Israel Reborn burst forth in exuberant creativity in Israel alone or would it also blossom in the American centers of Jewish life? Would the rejuvenated Jewish people again make unique contributions of worldwide significance on the basis of their unique structure as a world people, would they again raise up priests and prophets, sages and educators, who would hammer into their consciousness what their purpose was here on earth as a distinct ethnic and cultural grouping? Or would the Jews of America, the largest and most prosperous of Jewish groups, give up their bicultural status and attempt to dissolve in the alluring rich Gentile civilization which America's basic friendliness made possible?

The nineteen-sixties, a decade of testing for American Jews, ushered in the generation of decision which was groping for answers to these questions and which was evolving new patterns for Jewish living.

BIBLIOGRAPHY

Chapter I

THE COLONIAL ERA

Bradstreet, Anne, *Works*, Charlestown, 1867.

Coleman, E. D., "Jewish Prototypes in American and English *Romans and Drames à Clef*," *American Jewish Historical Society Publications*, XXXV (1939), 227–280.

Colman, Benjamin, *A Discourse Had in the College Hall at Cambridge, March 27, 1722 Before the Baptism of Rabbi Judah Monis*, Boston, 1722.

Dexter, F. B., *Literary Diary of Ezra Stiles*, New York, 1901, 3 Vols.

Edwards, Jonathan, *Language of the Muhhekanew Indians*, New Haven, 1788.

Friedman, L. M., "Cotton Mather and the Jews," *American Jewish Historical Society Publications*, XXVI (1918), 201–210.

Friedman, L. M., "Judah Monis, First Instructor in Hebrew at Harvard University," *American Jewish Historical Society Publications*, XXII (1914), 1–24.

Hutchinson, Thomas, *History of the Colony and Province of Massachusetts Bay*, Cambridge, Mass., 1926, 2 Vols.

Jastrow, Morris, "References to Jews in the Diary of Ezra Stiles," *Jewish Historical Society Publications*, X (1902), 5–36.

Jones, J. R., *The Quaker Soldier; or The British in Philadelphia*, 1858.

Kalm, Peter, *Travels Into North America*, London, 1772, 2 Vols.

Katsh, A. I., *Hebrew Language, Literature and Culture in American Institutions of Higher Learning*, New York, 1950.

Kohut, G. A, "Ezra Stiles and His Friends," *Menorah Journal*, III (1917), 37–46.

Kohut, G. A., "Hebraic Learning in Puritan New England," *Menorah Journal*, II (1916), 206–219.

Langdon, Samuel, *The Republic of the Israelites an Example to the American States*, Exeter, 1788.

Marcus, J. R., *Early American Jewry*, Philadelphia, 1953, 2 Vols.

Mather, Cotton, *Magnalia Christi Americana*, Hartford, 1920, 2 Vols.

Mather, Cotton, *The Faith of the Fathers*, Boston, 1699.

Mather, Increase, *Dissertation Concerning Future Conversion of the Jewish Nation*, Boston, 1709.

Mather, Increase, *Mystery of Israels Salvation*, Boston, 1669.

Mersand, Joseph, *Traditions in American Literature*, New York, 1939.

Meyer, I. S., "Doctor Samuel Johnson's Grammar and Hebrew Psalter," *Essays on Jewish Life and Thought Presented in Honor of S. W. Baron*, New York, 1959, pp. 359–374.

Meyer, I. S., "Hebrew at Harvard (1636–1760)," *American Jewish Historical Society Publications*, XXV (1939), 145–170.

Morris, M. H., "Roger Williams and the Jews," *American Jewish Archives*, III (1951), 24–27.

Noah, M. M., *Discourse on the Evidences of the American Indians Being the Descendants of the Lost Tribes of Israel*, New York, 1827.

Pfeiffer, R. H., "The Teaching of Hebrew in Colonial America," *The Jewish Advocate*, Boston, January 27, 1955.

Sewall, Samuel, *Letter-Book*, Mass. Historical Society Collection, Boston, 1886, 2 Vols.

Sola-Pool, David de, "Hebrew Learning Among the Puritans of New England Prior to 1700," *American Jewish Historical Society Publications*, XX (1911), 31–83.

Stokes, A. P., *Church and State in the United States*, New York, 1950.

Thornton, J. W., *Pulpit of the American Revolution*, Boston, 1860.

Willard, Samuel, *The Fountain Opened*, Boston, 1700.

Willner W., "Ezra Stiles and the Jews," *American Jewish Historical Society Publications*, VIII (1900), 119–126.

Chapter II

THE YOUNG REPUBLIC

Brackenridge, H. M., *Speeches on the Jew Bill in the House of Delegates of Maryland by H. M. Brackenridge, Colonel J. W. D. Worthington, and John S. Tyson, Esq.*, Philadelphia, 1829.

Brownson, O. A., *Works*, Detroit, 1883.

Child, L. M., *Letters from New York*, New York, 1845.

Coleman, E. D., "Plays of Jewish Interest on the American Stage, 1752–1821," *American Jewish Historical Society Publications*, XXXIII (1934), 171–198.

Dunlap, William, *History of the American Theatre,* New York, 1832.

Emerson, R. W., *Journals (1833–1835),* New York, 1910.

Emerson, R. W., *Journals (1838–1841),* Boston, 1911.

Glanz, Rudolf, *Jews in Relation to the Cultural Milieu of the Germans in America up to the Eighteen-Eighties,* New York, 1947.

Goldberg, Isaac, *Major Noah, American Jewish Pioneer,* Philadelphia, 1936.

Goldmark, Josephine, *Pilgrims of '48,* New Haven, 1930.

Goodman, A. V., "A Jewish Peddler's Diary 1842–1843," *American Jewish Archives,* June 1951, pp. 81–111.

Graewert, Theodor, *Otto Ruppius und der Amerikaroman im neunzehnten Jahrhundert,* Diss. Jena, 1935.

Huhner, Leon, *Essays and Addresses,* New York, 1959.

Huhner, Leon, *Life of Judah Touro (1775–1854),* Philadelphia, 1946.

Kohler, M. J., "Isaac Harby, Jewish Religious Leader and Man of Letters," *American Jewish Historical Society Publications,* XXXII (1931), 35–53.

Kohut, G. A., "A Literary Autobiography of Mordecai Manuel Noah," *American Jewish Historical Society Publications,* VI (1897), 113–121.

Lippard, George, *The Quaker City; or The Monks of Monk Hall,* Philadelphia, 1845.

Moise, L. C., *Biography of Isaac Harby,* Charleston, S.C., 1931.

Quinn, A. H., *History of the American Drama From the Beginning to the Civil War,* New York, 1943.

Ruppius, Otto, *The Peddler. A Romance of American Life,* Cincinnati, 1877.

Webster, Daniel, *Private Correspondence,* Boston, 1857, 2 Vols.

Wish, Harvey, *Society and Thought in Early America,* New York, 1950.

Wittke, Carl, *Refugees of Revolution,* Philadelphia, 1952.

Wright, Richardson, *Hawkers and Walkers in Early America,* Philadelphia, 1927.

Zink, H. R., "Emerson's Use of the Bible," *University of Nebraska Studies in Language, Literature, and Criticism,* No. 14 (1935), 61–74.

Chapter III

THE NEW ENGLAND POETS

Appel, J. J., "Longfellow's Presentation of the Spanish Jews," *American Jewish Historical Society Publications,* XLV (1955), 20–34.

Edrehi, Moses, *Historical Account of the Ten Tribes*, London, 1836; Boston, 1858.

Holmes, O. W., *Complete Poetical Works*, Boston, 1895.

Kraines, Oscar, "The Holmes Family and the Jews," *Chicago Jewish Forum*, XVII (1958), 28–34.

Longfellow, H. W., *Complete Poetical Works*, Boston, 1893.

Pickard, A. T., *Life and Letters of John Greenleaf Whittier*, Boston, 1894, 2 Vols.

Whittier, J. G., *Complete Poetical Works*, Boston, 1894.

Chapter IV

THE NINETEENTH CENTURY JEWISH LYRIC

Cowen, Philip, *Memories of an American Jew*, New York, 1932.

Jacob, H. E., *World of Emma Lazarus*, New York, 1949.

Lazarus, Emma, "Epistle to the Hebrews," *American Hebrew*, November 2, 1882–February 23, 1883.

Lazarus, Emma, *Selections from Poetry and Prose*, ed. by M. U. Schappes, New York, 1944.

Lazarus, Emma, *Songs of a Semite*, New York, 1882.

Lesser, Allen, *Enchanting Rebel; The Secret of Adah Isaacs Menken*, New York, 1947.

Lesser, Allen, *Weave a Wreath of Laurel; The Lives of Four Jewish Contributors to American Civilization*, New York, 1938.

Mayne, E. C., *Enchanters of Men*, London, 1909.

Menken, A. I., *Infelicia*, Philadelphia, 1888.

Miller, Joaquin, *Adah Isaacs Menken*, Ysleta, 1934.

Moise, Penina, *Secular and Religious Works*, Charleston, S.C., 1911.

Rusk, R. L., *Letters to Emma Lazarus*, New York, 1939.

Chapter V

LEGEND AND REALITY

Adams, Henry, *Letters (1858–1891)*, Boston, 1930.

Adams, Henry, *Letters (1892–1918)*, Boston, 1930.

Anderson, Thornton, *Brooks Adams, Constructive Conservative*, Ithaca, N.Y., 1951.

Arms, George & Gibson, W. M., "Silas Lapham, Daisy Miller, and the Jews," *New England Quarterly*, XVI (1943), 118–122.

Beecher, H. W., "Jew and Gentile," *Menorah* II (1887), 193–204.

Conway, M. D., *Life of Nathaniel Hawthorne*, London, 1890.

Donnelly, Ignatius, *Caesar's Column, a Story of the Twentieth Century*, Chicago, 1891.

Friedman, L. M., "The Hilton-Seligman Affair," *Jewish Pioneers and Patriots*, Philadelphia (1948), pp. 267–278.

Garland, Hamlin, *Rose of Dutcher's Coolly*, New York, 1895.

Gould, G. M., *Concerning Lafcadio Hearn*, Philadelphia, 1908.

Handlin, Oscar, "American Views of the Jew at the Opening of the Twentieth Century," *American Jewish Historical Society Publications*, XL (1951), 323–344.

Harte, Bret, "That Ebrew Jew," *American Jewish Archives* (1954), pp. 148–150.

Hawthorne, Nathaniel, *Complete Writings*, Boston, 1900, III, 112–140: *Ethan Brand*.

Hawthorne, Nathaniel, *The Marble Faun*, New York, 1910.

Hearn, Lafcadio, *Japanese Letters*, Boston, 1910.

Hearn, Lafcadio, *Occidental Gleanings*, New York, 1925, 2 Vols.

Hellman, G. S., "Joseph Seligman, American Jew," *American Jewish Historical Society Publications*, XLI (1951), 27–40.

Ingersoll, R. G., *Letters*, New York, 1951.

Jessup, G. H., *Sam'l of Posen; or The Commercial Drummer*, 1881, in *Amerca's Lost Plays*, edited by B. H. Clark, Vol. IV, Princeton, N.J., 1910.

Kohut, G. A., *Henry Ward Beecher and the Jews*, Portland, Oregon, 1913.

McWilliams, Vera, *Lafcadio Hearn*, Cambridge, Mass., 1946.

Merwin, H. C., *Life of Bret Harte*, New York, 1911.

Norris, Frank, *McTeague*, New York, 1899.

Rideout, W. B., "The Jew as Author and Subject in the American Radical Novel," *American Jewish Archives*, 1959, pp. 157–175.

Rosenberg, Edgar, *From Shylock to Svengali*, Stanford, California, 1960.

Scudder, H. E., *James Russell Lowell*, Boston, 1901, 2 Vols.

Smith, H. & Gibson, W. M., *Mark Twain–Howells Letters*, Cambridge, Mass., 1960, 2 Vols.

Steffens, Lincoln, *Autobiography*, New York, 1931.

Tinker, E. L., *Lafcadio Hearn's American Days*, New York, 1924.

Chapter VI

PERSISTENCE OF STEREOTYPES

Eliot, Charles W., "The Potency of the Jewish Race," *Menorah Journal*, I (1915), 141–144.

Herzl, Theodor, "Mark Twain in Paris," *Mark Twain Quarterly*, VIII (1951), 16–18.

Kohler, Kaufmann, "The Yoke of the Torah," *Menorah*, III (1887), 140–148.

Luska, Sidney (Henry Harland), *As It Was Written: A Jewish Musician's Story*, New York, 1885.

Luska, Sidney, *Mrs. Peixada*, New York, 1886.

Luska, Sidney, *My Uncle Florimond*, Boston, 1888.

Luska, Sidney, *The Yoke of the Torah*, New York, 1887.

Magalaner, Marvin, "Henry Harland and the Jewish Press," *Chicago Jewish Forum*, XI (1953), 239–245.

Marberry, M. M., *Splendid Poseur: Joaquin Miller*, New York, 1953.

Miller, Joaquin, *Building of the City Beautiful*, Trenton, N.J., 1905.

Miller, Joaquin, *Poetical Works*, New York, 1923.

Paine, A. B., *Mark Twain's Notebooks*, New York, 1935.

Rieff, Susan, "Henry Harland, the Philosemite as Antisemite," *Chicago Jewish Forum*, X (1952), 199–205.

Twain, Mark, "Concerning the Jews," *Harper's Magazine*, September 1899, pp. 527–535.

Chapter VII

THE NEW IMMIGRATION

Armstrong, H. F., *The Book of New York Verse*, New York, 1917.

Bisno, Beatrice, *Tomorrow's Bread*, New York, 1938.

Cahan, Abraham, *The Rise of David Levinsky*, New York, 1917.

Cahan, Abraham, *Yekel, a Tale of the New York Ghetto*, New York, 1896.

Frederic, Harold, *The New Exodus; A Study of Israel in Russia*, London, 1892.

Friedman, I. K., *By Bread Alone*, New York, 1901.

Friedman, L. M., *Pilgrims in a New Land*, New York, 1948, Ch. XIII: Myra Kelly.

Glass, Montague, *Abe and Mawruss,* New York, 1911.

Glass, Montague, *Potash and Perlmutter,* New York, 1910.

Glass, Montague, *Potash and Perlmutter Settle Things,* New York, 1919.

Hapgood, Hutchins, *Spirit of the Ghetto,* New York, 1902.

Hapgood, Hutchins, *Types from City Streets,* New York, 1910.

Hapgood, Hutchins, *Victorian in the Modern World,* New York, 1939.

Hapgood, Norman, "The Jews and American Democracy," *Menorah Journal,* II (1916), 201–205.

Kelly, Myra, *Little Aliens,* New York, 1910.

Kelly, Myra, *Little Citizens,* New York, 1904.

Kelly, Myra, *Wards of Liberty,* New York, 1907.

Lessing, Bruno, *Children of Men,* New York, 1903.

Lewis, Sinclair, *Arrowsmith,* New York, 1925.

Mandel, A. I., "Attitude of the American Jewish Community towards East-European Immigration—As Reflected in the Anglo-Jewish Press (1880–1890)," *American Jewish Archives,* III, 1 (1950).

Maurice, A. B., *The New York of the Novelists,* New York, 1916.

Oppenheim, James, *Dr. Rast,* New York, 1909.

Oppenheim, James, *The Nine-tenths,* New York, 1911.

Ornitz, S. B., *Haunch Paunch and Jowl,* New York, 1923.

Riis, J. A., *The Battle with the Slums,* New York, 1902.

Riis, J. A., *How the Other Half Lives,* New York, 1890.

Roth, Henry, *Call It Sleep,* New York, 1934.

Steffens, Lincoln, *Autobiography,* New York, 1931.

Steffens, Lincoln, *Letters,* New York, 1938.

Tcherikower, Elias, *History of the Jewish Labor Movement in the United States,* New York, 1943, 2 Vols.

Tcherikower, Elias, *The Early Jewish Labor Movement in the United States,* New York, 1961.

Zangwill, Israel, *The Melting Pot,* New York, 1909.

Chapter VIII

THE PROMISED LAND

Antin, Mary, *From Plotzk to Boston,* Boston, 1899.

Antin, Mary, *The Promised Land,* Boston, 1912.

Brody, Alter, *A Family Album,* New York, 1918.

Brody, Alter, *Lamentations,* New York, 1928.

Cronbach, Abraham, "Autobiography," *American Jewish Archives,*
   April 1959, pp. 3–81.
Ornitz, S. B., *Haunch Paunch and Jowl,* New York, 1923.
Yezierska, Anzia, *Children of Loneliness,* New York, 1925.
Yezierska, Anzia, *Hungry Hearts,* Boston, 1920.
Yezierska, Anzia, *Red Ribbon on a White Horse,* New York, 1950.

Chapter IX

TWENTIETH CENTURY JEWISH POETS

Angoff, Charles, "Impressions of Contemporary Jewish American
   Poetry," *Jewish Book Annual,* XV (1957), 27–32.
Auslander, Joseph, *The Unconquerables,* New York, 1943.
Bodenheim, Maxwell, *Advice: a Book of Poems,* New York, 1920.
Cournos, John, *Autobiography,* New York, 1935.
Cournos, John, *An Open Letter to Jews and Christians,* New York,
   1938.
Nathan, Robert, *A Cedar Box,* Indianapolis, 1929.
Nathan, Robert, *A Winter Tide,* New York, 1940.
Nathan, Robert, *Selected Poems,* New York, 1935.
Nathan, Robert, *Youth Grows Old,* New York, 1922.
Newman, L. I., *Joyful Jeremiads,* New York, 1926.
Newman, L. I., *Songs of Jewish Rebirth,* New York, 1921.
Raskin, P. M., *Poems for Young Israel,* New York, 1924.
Raskin, P. M., *Songs and Dreams,* Boston, 1919.
Raskin, P. M., *Songs of a Jew,* London, 1914.
Raskin, P. M., *Songs of a Wanderer,* Philadelphia, 1917.
Raskin, P. M., *When a Soul Sings,* New York, 1921.
Reznikoff, Charles, *Poems,* New York, 1920.
Reznikoff, Charles, *By the Waters of Manhattan,* New York, 1929.
Rosenfeld, Morris, *Songs from the Ghetto,* Boston, 1898.
Rosenfeld, Morris, *The Teardrop Millionaire and Other Poems,* New
   York, 1955.
Sampter, J. E., *Brand Plucked from the Fire,* New York, 1937.
Untermeyer, J. S., *Later Poems,* New York, 1958.
Untermeyer, J. S., *Love and Needed; Collected Poems 1918–1940,* New
   York, 1940.
Untermeyer, J. S., *Steep Ascent,* New York, 1927.
Untermeyer, Louis, *From Another World,* New York, 1939.
Untermeyer, Louis, *Long Feud,* New York, 1962.

Untermeyer, Louis, *Roast Leviathan*, New York, 1923.

Untermeyer, Louis, "The Jewish Spirit in Modern American Poetry," *Menorah Journal*, VII (1921), 121–132.

Yoseloff, Thomas, ed., *Seven Poets in Search of an Answer*, New York, 1944.

Chapter X

THE JEW IN NON-JEWISH FICTION

Baumgardt, David, "Dorothy Canfield Fisher: Friend of Jews in Life and Work," *American Jewish Historical Society Publications*, XLVIII (1959), 245–255.

Baumgardt, David, "Dorothy Canfield Fisher on Her Seventieth Birthday," *Educational Forum*, November 1950, pp. 43–50.

Canfield, Dorothy, *Hillsboro People*, New York, 1915.

Canfield, Dorothy, *Raw Material*, New York, 1923.

Canfield, Dorothy, *The Real Motive*, New York, 1916.

Dreiser, Theodore, et al., "A Jewish Symposium," *American Spectator*, September 1933.

Dreiser, Theodore, *Letters*, Philadelphia, 1959, 3 Vols.

Fisher, D. C., *American Portraits*, New York, 1946.

Fisher, D. C., *Seasoned Timber*, New York, 1939.

Fitzgerald, F. S., *The Great Gatsby*, New York, 1925.

Fitzgerald, F. S., *The Last Tycoon*, New York, 1941.

Frank, F. K., "The Presentment of the Jew in American Fiction," *Bookman*, LXXI (1930), 270–275.

Gold, Michael, "The Gun Is Loaded, Dreiser!," *The New Masses*, May 7, 1935.

Gurko, Leon, *The Angry Decade: The Nineteen-Thirties*, New York, 1947.

Hapgood, Hutchins, *A Victorian in the Modern World*, New York, 1939.

Hapgood, Hutchins, "Is Dreiser Antisemitic?," *The Nation*, April 17, 1935.

Hemingway, Ernest, *The Sun Also Rises*, New York, 1926.

Hofmann, F. J., *The Twenties: American Writing in the Post-war Decade*, New York, 1955.

Lewis, Sinclair, *Arrowsmith*, New York, 1925.

Pollock, T. C. and Cargill, Oscar, *Thomas Wolfe at Washington Square*, New York, 1954.

Wolfe, Thomas, *Look Homeward, Angel*, New York, 1929.
Wolfe, Thomas, *Of Time and the River*, New York, 1935.
Wolfe, Thomas, *The Web and the Rock*, New York, 1938.
Wolfe, Thomas, *You Can't Go Home Again*, New York, 1940.
Wright, Richard, *Native Son*, New York, 1940.

Chapter XI

JEWISH AFFIRMATION

Lewisohn, Ludwig, *A Jew Speaks*, New York, 1931.
Lewisohn, Ludwig, *Israel*, New York, 1925.
Lewisohn, Ludwig, *Mid-Channel*, New York, 1929.
Lewisohn, Ludwig, *The American Jew*, New York, 1950.
Lewisohn, Ludwig, *The Answer*, New York, 1939.
Lewisohn, Ludwig, *The Island Within*, New York, 1928.
Lewisohn, Ludwig, *The Permanent Horizon*, New York, 1934.
Lewisohn, Ludwig, *Upstream*, New York, 1922.
Samuel, Maurice, *Harvest in the Desert*, New York, 1945.
Samuel, Maurice, *I, the Jew*, New York, 1927.
Samuel, Maurice, *Jews on Approval*, New York, 1932.
Samuel, Maurice, *Little Did I Know*, New York, 1963.
Samuel, Maurice, *The Gentleman and the Jew*, New York, 1950.
Samuel, Maurice, *The Great Hatred*, New York, 1940.
Samuel, Maurice, *You Gentiles*, New York, 1924.

Chapter XII

THE UPROOTED AND THE ESTRANGED

Bellow, Saul, *Adventures of Augie March*, New York, 1953.
Bellow, Saul, *Herzog*, New York, 1965.
Brinig, Myron, *Singermann*, New York, 1929.
Dahlberg, Edward, *Those Who Perish*, New York, 1934.
Geismar, Maxwell, *American Moderns*, New York, 1958.
Gold, Michael, *Jews Without Money*, New York, 1930.
Halper, Albert, *Sons of the Fathers*, New York, 1940.
Halper, Albert, *The Chute*, New York, 1937.
Hecht, Ben, *A Child of the Century*, New York, 1954.
Hecht, Ben, *A Guide to the Bedevilled*, New York, 1944.
Hecht, Ben, *A Jew in Love*, New York, 1931.

Hecht, Ben, *Collected Stories*, New York, 1945.
Hecht, Ben, *Perfidy*, New York, 1962.
Hobson, L. Z., *Gentleman's Agreement*, New York, 1947.
Katkov, Norman, *Eagle at My Eyes*, Garden City, N.Y., 1948.
Liptzin, Sol, "David Pinski, Nestor of Yiddish Literature," *Jewish Book Annual*, XV (1957), 84–87.
Malin, Irving, *Jews and Americans*, Carbondale, Ill., 1965.
Pinski, David, *The House of Noah Eden*, New York, 1929.
Ross, L. Q., *The Education of Hyman Kaplan*, New York, 1938.
Ross, L. Q., *The Return of Hyman Kaplan*, New York, 1959.
Schneider, Isidor, *From the Kingdom of Necessity*, New York, 1935.
Schulberg, Budd, *What Makes Sammy Run?*, New York, 1941.
Sinclair, Jo, *Wasteland*, New York, 1946.
Weidman, Jerome, *Enemy Camp*, New York, 1958.
Weidman, Jerome, *I Can Get It for You Wholesale*, New York, 1937.
Weidman, Jerome, *My Father Sits In the Dark*, New York, 1961.
Weidman, Jerome, *What's in It for Me?*, New York, 1938.
Wouk, Herman, *Marjorie Morningstar*, New York, 1955.
Wouk, Herman, *This Is My God*, Garden City, N.Y., 1959.

Chapter XIII

JEWISH ACCULTURATION

Angoff, Charles, *Between Day and Dark*, New York, 1959.
Angoff, Charles, *Bitter Spring*, New York, 1961.
Angoff, Charles, *In the Morning Light*, New York, 1952.
Angoff, Charles, *Journey to the Dawn*, New York, 1951.
Angoff, Charles, *Summer Storm*, New York, 1963.
Angoff, Charles, *Sun at Noon*, New York, 1955.
Fineman, Irving, *Hear Ye Sons*, New York, 1933.
Fineman, Irving, *Woman of Valor*, New York, 1961.
Janowsky, Oscar, *The American Jew*, Philadelphia, 1964.
Kazin, Alfred, *A Walker in the City*, New York, 1951.
Schwarz, L. W., *The Redeemers*, New York, 1953.

Chapter XIV

IMPACT OF ISRAEL

Bourne, R. S., "The Jew and Trans-National America," *Menorah Journal*, II (1916), 206–219.

Eban, Abba, *Voice of Israel*, New York, 1957.

Frank, Waldo, *Bridgehead: The Drama of Israel*, New York, 1957.

Frank, Waldo, *The Jew in Our Day*, New York, 1944.

Friedman, Theodore, ed., "My Jewish Affirmation. A Symposium," *Judaism*, X (1916), 292–352.

Henriques, Robert, *One Hundred Hours to Suez*, New York, 1957.

Kallen, H. M., *Utopians at Bay*, New York, 1958.

Kaplan, M. M., *A New Zionism*, New York, 1955.

Kaplan, M. M., *The Greater Judaism in the Making*, New York, 1960.

Koestler, Arthur, *Promise and Fulfillment*, New York, 1949.

Levin, Meyer, *Eva*, New York, 1959.

Levin, Meyer, *In Search*, New York, 1950.

Levin, Meyer, *My Father's House*, New York, 1947.

Levin, Meyer, *The Old Bunch*, New York, 1937.

Levin, Meyer, *Yehuda*, New York, 1931.

Mailer, Norman, *The Naked and the Dead*, New York, 1948.

Malamud, Bernard, *A New Life*, New York, 1961.

Malamud, Bernard, *The Assistant*, New York, 1957.

Malamud, Bernard, *Idiots First*, New York, 1963.

Malamud, Bernard, *The Magic Barrel*, New York, 1958.

Michener, James A., *The Source*, New York, 1965.

Miller, Arthur, *Focus*, New York, 1945.

Nadich, Judah, "The Writings of Mordecai M. Kaplan," *Jewish Book Annual*, XIX (1961), 90–97.

Nathan, Robert, *A Star in the Wind*, New York, 1962.

Nathan, Robert, *Road of Ages*, New York, 1935.

Popkin, Zelda, *Quiet Street*, New York, 1951.

Ribalow, H. U., *The Chosen*, New York, 1959.

Rolvaag, O. E., *Their Fathers' God*, New York, 1931.

Roth, P. M., *Goodbye, Columbus*, New York, 1959.

Samuel, Maurice, *Level Sunlight*, New York, 1953.

Shapiro, Karl, *Poems of a Jew*, New York, 1958.

Shaw, Irwin, *The Young Lions*, New York, 1948.

Stampfer, Judah, *Jerusalem Has Many Faces*, New York, 1950.

Uris, Leon, *Exodus*, New York, 1958.

INDEX

247